THE CITY LIBRARY
SPRINGFIELD (MA) CITY LIBRARY

940.5318 D37

Del fuego

Springfield City Library
Springfield, Massachusetts

In Memory of Holocaust Victims

From
The Carman Family Charitable Foundation

DEL FUEGO
Sephardim and the Holocaust

DEL FUEGO
Sephardim and the Holocaust

Edited by
HAHAM DR. SOLOMON GAON
and
DR. M. MITCHELL SERELS

SEPHER-HERMON PRESS, INC.
New York, 5755-1995

DEL FUEGO: Sephardim and the Holocaust
Copyright © 1995
Jacob E. Safra Institute of Sephardic Studies - Yeshiva University

Published by Sepher-Hermon Press, Inc.
1265 46th Street, Brooklyn, NY 11219

ISBN 0-87203-143-8

Library of Congress Cataloging-in-Publication Data

Del fuego : Sephardim and the Holocaust / edited by Solomon Gaon and
  M. Mitchell Serels.
      p.   cm.
    ISBN 0-87203-143-8
    1. Holocaust, Jewish (1939-1945) 2. Sephardim--History--20th
century. 3. World War, 1939-1945--Jews--Rescue. I. Gaon, Solomon.
II. Serels, M. Mitchell.
D804.3.D46   1995
940.53'18--dc20   95-22303
                                                                 CIP

This volume is dedicated

to the memory of

RAHELA PINTO

and

ISAAC GAON

who died at the hands of the Nazis

and their sympathizers in Yugoslavia

We wish to thank the Lucius N. Littauer Foundation for their generous support in the publication of this volume. Our appreciation is extended to Debra Rubin for her assistance in editing the manuscripts. All the more so we thank Carol Santana and Devora Albelda for the joyous fulfillment of the tedious task of typing. Special appreciation is extended to Barry Bender, Aaron Tirschwell and Shelly Rasekh for their technical assistance.

FOREWORD

The lectures in this volume were delivered during six years under the auspices of the Jacob E.Safra Institute of Sephardic Studies of Yeshiva University and the Sephardic House, in cooperation with the Sephardic Department of the World Zionist Organization. These lectures have not been initiated for any chauvinistic reasons, but because the annihilation of the great Sephardi centers has not been sufficiently researched and brought to the attention of the Jewish world. Scholars who have written on the Holocaust have hardly dealt with the almost total elimination of many Sephardi communities.

There has been more written about the destruction of the Ashkenazic communities, due to some extent to their geographical position, their sheer numbers, and the origin of the authors. The communities most often written of were situated in the cultural centers of Europe and were able to produce scholars and historians who have interpreted effectively the events of the Holocaust. The projects and achievements of these European communities as well as their destruction with all its agony and tragedy are well chronicled. The Sephardim had their intellectuals and historians but unlike those of European communities they were not university trained but mostly self-educated. Their work, therefore, did not have the same appeal, publicity and impact on the Jewish people.

The Sephardim who suffered in the pangs of the Holocaust were fewer in number but the ravishment was almost complete. The story of the suffering of the Sephardim at the hands of the Nazis and local anti-Semites needs retelling in order to maintain the awareness that the Holocaust was aimed at all Jews. No Jew was to be excluded, for all were condemned by the Nazis.

Part of the Nazi myth of world Jewry's attempt at domination was the concept of Jews assimilating into the local culture in order to take over. Yet the Sephardim maintained their own culture, even maintaining the Iberian language rather than learning local dialects. Jews in the Balkans continued to speak Judeo-Spanish and not Greek, Bulgarian, Serbian or Croatian. Jews in Moslem lands often spoke French and Spanish rather than Arabic or Berber dialects. But they were Jews and therefore condemned.

In most areas the Sephardim had never experienced organized governmental anti-Semitism. The Nazis broke that tradition as well.

Few, in any culture, came to the aid of the Jews. There was no haven and no succor. The realization of the State of Israel was not solely a product of the European Holocaust but also of pro-Nazi events in African and Asian lands. This lesson must never be lost nor forgotten. If it is, then we may be condemned to live the events over again.

Haham Dr. Solomon Gaon

Rabbi Dr. M. Mitchell Serels

The Haham Dr. Solomon Gaon passed away on December 21, 1994, as this book was being prepared for publication. May his memory be for a blessing.

TABLE OF CONTENTS

Foreword, *Haham Dr. Solomon Gaon* *Rabbi M. Mitchell Serels*	VII
Holocaust: Sephardim and Ashkenazim, *Dr. Erich Goldhagen*	1
The Sephardim of Holland and the Holocaust, *Jack Polak*	12
The Role of Spain in Protecting Sephardic Jews in France During the Holocaust, Haham Dr. Solomon Gaon	23
Bulgaria: A Difference, *Vicki Tamir*	32
The Holocaust in Janina, *Dr. Rachel Dalven*	45
The Holocaust of Yugoslavian Jews, *Haham Dr. Solomon Gaon*	69
The Holocaust in Salonica, *Prof. David F. Altabe*	80
Destruction of the Jews of Rhodes, *Rabbi Dr. Marc D. Angel*	98
Moroccan Jews on the Road to Auschwitz, *Dr. M. Mitchell Serels*	107
Holocaust in the Middle East: Iraq and the Mufti of Jerusalem, *Dr. Isaac Alteras*	113
Aspects of the Holocaust in Libya, *Dr. Maurice Roumani*	123
The Non-European Holocaust: The Fate of Tunisian Jewry, *Dr. M. Mitchell Serels*	129
Iraqi Jews in the Far East During the Holocaust, *Joseph Abraham*	153
Rescue of Boukharan and Gruzian Jews in France, *Dr. M. Mitchell Serels*	167
Sephardim in Vienna and Hamburg During the Holocaust, *Gertrude Hirschler*	177
Albanian Jews During the Holocaust, *Dr. Anna Kohen*	200
American Ladino Press and Reports of the Holocaust, *Dr. M. Mitchell Serels*	205
The Jews of Salonica and the Holocaust: A Personal Memoir, *Henry Levy*	213
Salvation In Volos, Greece, *Asher Matathias*	247
Amb. Angel Sanz-Briz, and the Salvation of Hungarian Jews, *Dr. M. Mitchell Serels*	254

HOLOCAUST: SEPHARDIM AND ASHKENAZIM
by Dr. Erich Goldhagen

I decided to compare the ways in which the Holocaust affected the Ashkenazi and Sephardi world. When I had the time to pause and reflect, I realized how difficult and complicated the subject was. In fact, I will confess to you that seldom before have I had such difficulties preparing a lecture as I had in preparing this one. The reason for the difficulties I encountered should be obvious. What is there to compare? There was a fire; there was a great conflagration set by insane people. The fire was destined and intended to engulf the whole house of Israel. Every Jewish community was marked for destruction. Of course, not all the houses and not all the communities burned in the same manner; each one had its own manner of perishing. In some places, the flames were more intense or the flames took a different course. But essentially, is it fruitful, is it constructive to compare these things? What would we learn from that? After all, everybody was doomed and not everybody perished, but all were doomed to destruction. So what can we learn?

After the first doubts which aroused in my mind, and which made me wonder as to the wisdom of my choice, I realized that there was some profit to be derived from the comparison, and that it would not be an intellectually barren exercise. Every comparison yields some

---

Editors' Note: This paper is a transcript of a paper presented by the author as the opening lecture of the Sephardim and the Holocaust Series. The transcript was not reviewed by the author.

knowledge and sharpens our perception of the objects that are being compared. I think in this case too, the comparison would not be barren, but would indeed be illuminating and enable us to gain a sharper insight into the somewhat still incredible phenomenon called the Holocaust. Now, every discussion of the Holocaust, as I keep emphasizing again and again, must begin with the discussion of the mind of the perpetrator, namely the Nazi mind. If you do not understand the Nazi mind, you do not begin to understand the Holocaust. I shall, therefore, begin with a brief excursion into the Nazi mind, especially insofar as it relates to our subject. As to the Nazi mind there is only a descriptive word for it - incredulity. Students again and again ask me: "Is it possible that they, the Nazis, believed what you say they believed? Did they indeed view the world as you described?" Now, the Nazi mind, as it looked out to the world, and especially to the world of Jewry, looked through lenses so distorting that reality appeared utterly transmogrified. Perhaps the best analogy would be to try to imagine Dali, the surrealistic painter, looking upon an object and then just painting it. It would bear scarcely any resemblance with that object. Similarly, the Nazi mind, as it looked upon the world, and especially upon the Jewish world, saw the world transmuted and deformed into an utterly surrealistic picture.

It is very hard to believe that men, intelligent men, men with doctoral degrees, professors of universities, leaders of state, could look upon the world through such distorted lenses and still function. Indeed, I maintain that one of the reasons why the Nazis were doomed to destroy themselves was because they could not function rationally in the world. Their visual reality was so distorted that they were doomed to destroy themselves.

Imagine a man setting out into the world with a map in which rivers that appear, do not exist, or where there is a river but the map does not show it. He cannot function. He is bound to stumble. The

Nazis destroyed themselves because they were incapable of functioning rationally in the world.

The Nazis, as they looked upon Jewry, saw an entity which had nothing to do with the reality of the entity. According to Nazi ideology, the Jews were a singular entity in the world. They were the bearers of evil. In fact, they were synonymous with evil. The Jews set out to conquer the world; they dispersed themselves among the nations so that they may subdue states and governments. These governments and nations did not even know that they were being ruled by Jews. The Jews produced all wars in the world in order to profit by these wars. They set nation against nation. They are the allies of communism; they are the agents of capitalism. They ruled the United States even though the people of the U.S. do not know it; they also ruled the Soviet Union. There was a contradiction in this claim which didn't bother the Nazis very much. How was it possible to rule both the Soviet Union and the U.S., and at the same time be at war with one another. Against this great evil conspiracy, the incarnation of evil, a cosmic evil, Nazism had risen to wage perpetual war and save the world. It was to be a war of to be or not to be. Either Nazism was to destroy Jewry or Jewry was to destroy Nazism.

This view of the world saw Jewry as an unending evil. The different sections among Jewry, religious Jews, non-religious Jews, Sephardi, Ashkenazi, that didn't concern them. If it did concern them, it was immediately interpreted in terms of the dominant mythology. Let me give an example: The Nazis were asked "what is Zionism?" They answered, "Zionism is not what we know from the books and propaganda, a movement of the Jews to create a State where they would find a haven from persecution. Zionism is part of the great plan. Its purpose being to create a strong base, whence to conduct the great conspiracy".

German intelligence service took no interest in the internal functioning of Jewry, because to them all Jews were a vast evil and should be treated as one entity. Although they regarded all Jewry as one entity whose tentacles spread out everywhere, from Belgrade to Athens to Salonica, they singled out East European Jewry as of particular importance as being the heart, the source, and the lair of the beast.

One had to strike at East European Jewry first. This other side has to be understood in light of the experience which the German Jews and the Germans and Hitler personally had with East Europeans in Vienna and in Germany. The East European Jew was viewed as an exotic figure. He had a beard and peot. He spoke a peculiar language which sounded ludicrous to the ears of the Germans.

Thousands of these Jews, perhaps 70,000 had come to Germany from the East. They had settled in Germany and were very successful. They became Germanized, their children spoke German and they became very prosperous in all the spheres of the economic life of Western Europe. Incidentally, one may believe that one of the causes of the Holocaust was the rapid Westernization of Eastern Jewry, another their rapid social and economic rise.

The Jews are a destructive element. They cut off their beards. They put on elegant shoes. They became bankers, doctors, engineers and they were ready to conquer the world. It is, therefore, necessary to strike at them with particularly great force. Towards the end of the war, after they have seen the loss, a prominent Nazi said: "We have lost the war, but the most important thing is that Jews have lost it also, because through the destruction of East European Jewry, we have destroyed the most vital part of Jewry. It is the loss which Jewry will never be able to regain."

They looked beyond European Jewry, and they began to spot a

SEPHARDIM AND THE HOLOCAUST

Jewry whose features were distinguished from Jews of Eastern Europe. First of all they were few. How did they interpret the small numbers? The small numbers suggested how deeply these Jews have submerged in the nations among whom they lived. That is why when you read Nazi statistics of Jewry of Southern Europe, Yugoslavia, Italy or Greece, you will find that the numbers are exaggerated. There are more Jews than there actually were, because they assumed that a large number of Jews were in hiding. They were disguised as Italians, Yugoslavians or Greeks. The Nazis, therefore, always exaggerated the extent of Jews in that area. Certainly that is very important because the Jews in that part of the world lived in a population which was not sufficiently enlightened as in regards to anti-Semitism. It is a population which is not very anti-Semitic and in some cases as in Italy, almost not anti-Semitic at all. In this lies the fundamental difference between East Europe and Southern Europe.

In Eastern Europe, the Nazis realized from the very beginning that they could carry out the process of extermination with the help of the local population. In Southern Europe where the Sephardi Jews resided, they realized that they would encounter resistance or at least indifference and many impediments from the local population. Let me give you just an example of how the Nazis acted. When the order for the Holocaust was given, three thousand men were assigned for the destruction of the whole Soviet Jewry. When asked how could this small force carry out this vast enterprise, the commanders of that force were reassured they would have much help from the local population.

In Eastern Europe, the resistance movement was either indifferent or hostile to the Jews. Virtually every major right-wing party in Eastern Europe not only did not help Jews, but aided the Nazis very often. There were the Ukrainians in Eastern Europe. There were 11 Polish political parties still underground. Out of these, 9 had a plank in their platform, providing that a Jew could not be a full fledged citizen in Poland after the war. Some (the more extreme) provided that a Jew could not even live in Poland after the war. These platforms were adopted at a time when the Jews were being systematically exterminated by the Nazis. Now, in Southern Europe, there was an entirely different situation. The resistance movement was very friendly to the Jews, and such platforms did not exist at all.

The position here, on the whole (with the exception of certain areas of Yugoslavia) was friendly with readiness to help, especially among the Southern European Yugoslavians.

The duration or shock of the Holocaust was much more intense among the Sephardic Jews than the Eastern European Jews. The Eastern European Jews had a relatively longer period of preparation. It began in 1939 in small stages. In Southern Europe, it came suddenly. It came to Yugoslavia in 1941, to Italy in 1943, and in 1941 to Greece. The shock was very intense.

The transition to Auschwitz was very traumatic and intense. Most Jews from Eastern Europe, even though they did not know what Auschwitz was, were already prepared for some catastrophe. Very often, Jews from Italy and Greece were suddenly plunged from a relatively benign environment straight into the hell that was Auschwitz. So, the trauma of the Sephardic Jews was far greater than of East European Jews who had been prepared for this after several years of tribulation.

Let me illustrate these points by turning my attention to one country which will not be a part of your present series, namely Italy, because it is a fascinating country. In fact, the history of the Holocaust there is fascinating. Let me just sketch some of the essential features of the course of events in Italy which will illustrate the points I have made. The fascist regime in Italy was, in its beginning, almost entirely devoid of anti-Semitism. Mussolini, on a visit to Germany stated that the Nazis should not be taken seriously.

In Italy, the Jews were highly respected, occupying very important positions. There were a good number of Jewish officers in the army. Mussolini often poked fun at racism. He said that racism was a swindle, that it is not to be taken seriously, that there are no "pure" races; the Nazis were just talking pure moonshine, and so on. In Italy the Jews were members of the fascist movement; the Jews were in the Italian army and did not feel any particular discrimination. Mussolini had the ambition of supporting the Zionist enterprise and perhaps even creating the Jewish State which would be under the benign protection of an imperial Italy.

He also had dreams of reconciling the Jews with the Arabs. When he met Nahum Goldman, he spoke contemptuously of Hitler. In fact as soon as Hitler came into power, Mussolini sent him a telegram and warned him that he should not translate into practice the anti-Semitic ideology of his party. "Now that you are a statesman, behave like a statesman and don't put into practice your vulgar anti-Semitism." Hitler was furious, and in the presence of an Italian he said; "Mussolini obviously doesn't understand the first thing about the Jewish question. I will pursue my policy against the Jews in an undeviating manner. I don't know whether I will be remembered after 200 years for anything I've done, but after 500 years, I will still be remembered for having eradicated a curse called Jewry from the world."

Mussolini tried to talk reason to Hitler and Hitler rejected Mussolini as a man who was blind. He could not understand the Italian attitude towards the Jews and especially the fact that they allowed the Jews to join their party.

This attitude of Mussolini came to a rather abrupt end in 1938 when he declared that Italy would follow a racial policy. In 1938 and 1939, he passed a number of laws which were direct imitations of the Nuremberg laws prohibiting marriage between Jew and non-Jew, forbidding Jewish professors to work with non-Jews and expelling the Jews from the civil service and army.

In fact, every word of this new manifestation of Mussolini was a contradiction to what he had said privately about racism. Rarely before had a political leader proclaimed an ideological doctrine which so profoundly contradicted his inner convictions. Why did he do it? For a long time it was believed that he was under pressure from Hitler. The fact is that Hitler never exerted direct pressure upon this matter.

It was simply a way for Mussolini to show that he was a close ally of Hitler, and the condition of an alliance with Hitler was anti-Semitism. Nobody could be his ally without being anti-Semitic at the same time. Mussolini was very anxious to be an ally of Hitler. Externally he had to accept anti-Semitism and therefore pass all these laws without any deep inner conviction. There was another cynical purpose in this. Mussolini had great contempt for the Italians.

The Italians he believed were a nation of sheep, unfit for fascism, unfit for the great empire building he had destined for them. There is a story that he stood one day on his famous balcony and looked down on an Italian crowd, easy going and amusing themselves. He threw out his hands in despair and said, "I don't have the material to build an empire with this flock of sheep."

He tried to infuse into the Italian people some vigor, and a martial spirit. He thought that he might achieve that by infusing into them a racist ideology, by setting them up against the Jewish people, and of course he failed. The Italians themselves tried to circumvent these new policies and to make as many exceptions as possible. The Italians simply did not become anti-Semitic at the behest of Mussolini.

Incidentally, when I ask an Italian, how many people did Mussolini kill between 1922-1939, the Italian does not know. He usually responds with a very low figure. So I say "2,000 people," and he says "but so many?" Imagine a dictator in power for 20 years and in the course of this period he kills 2,000 which is the equivalent of a few hours of gassing at Auschwitz.

We can ask the question: "Why was Italy so different?" It was different, first of all, because of the peculiar quality of the Italian people and we have to be conscious of it. There was a deep humanity in Italy, in the Italian culture, which defeated all fascist designs and which made this regime so unable to murder. Secondly, Mussolini himself and even the fascist movement in Italy, lacked that important ingredient, a racial biological doctrine, which was really deep-rooted among the Germans and which was the source of the murders in Nazism. In other words, in absence of a biological racism, ideology combined with the illusive but distinct temper of the Italian people made fascism more humane.

Certain humanity of the people that made it difficult to convert them into a murderous machine that is chiefly responsible for the great Italian "difference." It is partly responsible for the fact that only one-fifth of Italian Jews perished and four fifths survived. Of the 50,000 Jews, only 8,000 died ultimately and the rest survived, largely under the protective shelter of the Italian people. It is also significant that in the Second World War, the only military force that protected Jews from the Nazis, and that risked taking on the Germans in order to protect the Jews from the Nazis, were Italian troops and policemen.

In several parts of Europe, in Croatia and in Southern France, the Italian police and military sheltered the Jews and refused to deliver them to the Nazis, saying that they will not soil the honor of the Italian army by delivering Jews.

So it is indeed a remarkable story and the reasons for it essentially are ideological. I interviewed a large number of Nazi killers and I gave them a list of people and asked them: "Who among these people could not have done what you have done?" I gave them a list of nations: Americans, Frenchman and Italians. All of them pointed to the Italians. I asked, "Could you imagine Italian police killing children as you have done?" Upon reflection they said that they could not imagine, and even if Mussolini in a moment of madness issued an order to murder children this order would not have been carried out. It would have been sabotaged by his army and his police. So in a certain way, the German character was tailor-made for the discipline, blind obedience and bovine execution of orders which was used by the Nazis. The Italian character broke the straight jacket which the regime tried to impose upon the people.

In the end, one of the important lessons of Sephardic Jewry is that it is a refutation of the theory of some historians who said that the killings of the Jews by Hitler had a certain rational purpose. "Hitler was killing Jews" so said these historians, "because he wanted to depopulate Eastern Europe and create a lebensraum". Nobody who looks upon Southern Europe, from the lands of the Aegean to the Island of Rhodes, can argue that the systematic extermination of Salonica Jewry, the Jewry on the Island of Rhodes, had any rational purpose, that it was designed to create lebensraum. It clearly derived from the crazy vision which viewed that the Jews of Rhodes were part of the vast conspiracy which had somewhat taken root even in that lonely island and which menaced the world and especially the Aryan race. The use of ships by Hitler to convey the Jews of Rhodes and other islands to their destruction can be even less understood from the rational point of view if we realize that at that time he needed every boat in the struggle against his enemies.

It is also emblematic, not repeated in Eastern Europe, that when a German soldier came to Rhodes he saw the population trying to hand food to the Jews to help them. I don't know of any instance in Eastern Europe in which native population would, in the presence of Germans, try to give food to Jews and to help them.

In the end I feel it was not an idle exercise on my part to undertake this comparison. Nevertheless, ultimately, the Nazis did not recognize any difference. All communities would have perished had they been victorious. In that case there would not have been either Sephardic Jewry, or Ashkenazi Jewry, and there would not have been a Jewry at all. In remembering how close we came to total extinction and defeat, whether we are Sephardim or Ashkenazim, it is for us to consolidate our unity and to continue to prevent what Hitler had wanted to achieve, namely the weakening and the extinction of the Jewish people.

THE SEPHARDIM OF HOLLAND AND THE HOLOCAUST
by Jack Polak

The range of the topic is broad and not easy to cover in a limited period, but I will try to do so and first give you an insight into the importance of the Sephardic Community for Dutch Jewry in general but also for the non-Jewish community.

Many times I will substitute the word PORTUGUESE for SEPHARDIC. In fact, we Ashkenazic Jews in Amsterdam always used the word PORTUGUESE JEWS, never SEPHARDIC JEWS, and in the same way the Portuguese Jews talked about us Ashkenazi Jews as "Hoogduitse Joden," which translates itself into "High German Jews."

We have to go far back in history, as far as the year 1600. At that time a small group of refugees had come to Holland. They came from Portugal and outwardly were members of the Catholic faith. But deep within their hearts they cherished the memory of a more ancient faith, a faith they had been compelled to abjure about a hundred years before - Judaism. The ancestors of the greater number of these Portuguese refugees had resided in Spain, were driven away and found asylum in 1492 in Portugal. It was not long, however, before the virus of Spanish intolerance spread into Portugal, and its manifestations became even more violent than had been the case in Spain. They were subjected to cruel persecutions and their children forcibly baptized. A considerable number yielded and adjusted their outward lives to the conditions imposed upon them becoming successful and well-to-do members of their communities. The story of Uriel d'Acosta tells it all and I cite from his autobiography: "I was born in Portugal in the city that bears this name, generally referred to as 'Porto.' My parents belonged to the nobility (ex ordine nobilium). They traced their origin to the Jewish race, the members of which had been compelled to adopt the Christian faith in former years. My father was a believing Christian and man of rigid honor, who laid great store upon social rank and condition. In this home I was reared in keeping with the standing of the family. There was no scarcity of servitors, and in our stables there was a noble Spanish steed for equestrian practice, to which my father was much devoted, while I from my early years, followed his example." Uriel d'Acosta was destined for the priesthood. He matriculated at the University of Coimbra, and received an appointment as bursar of church. At this time he began to grow skeptical regarding some of the dogmas of Christianity, and there awoke in him a remembrance of the Jewish faith of his forebears. As many others had done before his day, he secretly left Portugal in the year 1615 and journeyed to Amsterdam, where he openly avowed his return to the Jewish fold.

We are here presented with a peculiar case: The father was a devout and observant Catholic; and the son a Catholic church official who had become disaffected with the tenets of his faith. In most cases, those who had left their Judaism never became true Christians. They were only crypto-Jews — Marranos, "swine," as they were contemptuously designated by the Christians. These Marranos lived in a continual state of danger. Despite their wealth and the high places they occupied in the community, perhaps, in fact, due to the envy provoked by the prominence they attained, they were compelled to be continually conscious of the menace of the Inquisition. It became known to these Marranos that a small country existed in Northern Europe where they would be made welcome without being required to deny adherence to their ancient faith.

In 1579 an union was formed in Holland declaring that "every citizen should be accorded freedom of worship and no one should be molested on account of his belief."

This promise of toleration made the Marranos emigrate to this new land of liberty. These new Jews were not by any means a group of poverty-stricken refugees, and the Dutch people soon realized the importance of their material position and commercial ability.

In 1639 three Portuguese communities merged into one community and built the synagogue, that is still in existence. It is world-famous and stands as it was founded in 1675. Menasseh ben Israel, born in Madeira in 1604 from Marrano parents, became one of the first Rabbis and received in 1642 Frederik Hendrik, King of the Netherlands for his first official visit to the synagogue, followed by regular royal visits. The Rabbi greeted the royal visitor in the words: "We do not consider Portugal our fatherland but Holland; We do not say our prayer anymore for the Spanish or Portuguese King."

The wealth acquired by the Sephardi Jews enabled them to construct imposing synagogues, to build stately residences, adopt a sumptuous manner of living and acquire major works of art. Rembrandt - when he moved to Amsterdam in 1631 - became close to the Portuguese community; he lived opposite Rabbi Menasseh Ben Israel and painted many of the prominent members of the Portuguese community. With the same zeal, however, with which the Sephardic Jews devoted themselves to caring for the needs of the poor and unfortunate, they opposed those among them who attacked the observances of the rituals of their faith. Woe unto the Jew who failed to comply with the dietary laws or who was found guilty of desecrating the Sabbath, or who expressed skepticism in the established tenets of their religion, or cast doubt, for example, upon belief in personal immortality and gave expression to such infidelity in speech or by the written word! Such a one would be hauled before the officials of the congregation, and, in the event of stubborn insistence in his recalcitrance, be severely disciplined. He would be subjected to the Major Ban which enjoined any Jew, even the nearest relative of the offender, from holding conversation with him or giving him shelter in his home. "In accordance with the judgment of the angels"—so read the text of this excommunication - "and in accordance with the pronouncements of the saints, with the consent of God, blessed be He, and with the consent of all the Holy Congregation, in front of the Holy Scrolls with the six-hundred-and-thirteen precepts which are written therein, we excommunicate, expel, curse, and damn...with the excommunication with which Joshua banned Jericho, with the curse with which Elisha cursed the boys, and with all the curses which are written in the Law. Cursed be he when he riseth up; cursed be he when he goeth out, and cursed be he when he cometh in. May the Lord never pardon him; may the anger and wrath of the Lord rage against this man, and bring upon him all the curses which are written in the Book of Law..."

It was unfortunate that this Major Ban should have been invoked against two foremost men: Uriel d'Acosta who was banned in 1623 and committed suicide thereafter, and the greatest Jewish thinker of Holland in the 17th Century, Baruch Spinoza. When he died in 1677 after having passed his last years among Christian friends, the Portuguese Jews of Amsterdam were little aware that they had ejected from their midst one of the immortals of their people.

I can talk for hours about the many prominent people the Portuguese Jewish community produced from 1600 to 1940, starting with Don Samuel Palache, Ambassador from Morocco, who received the honorary title of Haham and is buried in the Portuguese cemetery still in existence, in Ouderkerk, a suburb of Amsterdam, followed by numerous doctors, artists, poets, scholars, merchants and politicians. They contributed immensely to the wealth of their own Jewish Community as well as to Holland at large.

The 18th and 19th century saw major groups of German and East-European Jews filtering into Holland. They started their Ashkenazi communities, possessing a greater fund of general and religious learning, but materially a much poorer group. The Portuguese Jews regarded themselves as a nobler race and manifested this sense of superiority in their public and private lives.

Just visit the cemetery of Ouderkerk which was founded in 1614 and look at the tombstones and find a good part of the history of the Portuguese Jews of Amsterdam from 1600 to 1940.

With this I have given you a glimpse of the history of the Portuguese community in Holland.

I, myself, though being a member of the Ashkenazi community, felt closer than many others to the Portuguese community, as I was part of the Mizrahi youth group. Our services were held in the Sephardi pronunciation of Hebrew. In fact, many of us often went to the Portuguese synagogue, as we were not allowed to use the Sephardic pronunciation in the Ashkenazi synagogues. Even now, 50 years later, I do remember the wonderful celebration of Hoshana-Raba and Simhat Tora in that beautiful Portuguese synagogue.

I now come to the second part of my presentation THE HOLOCAUST and what happened to the Portuguese Jewish Community.

On October 1, 1941 every Jew had to register. Subsequently the raids started and in July 1942 the deportations followed. There were four possible courses of action: (1) hide, (2) flee the country, (3) join the underground, (4) obtain an exemption.

On March 20, 1943 the Germans made a summary of exemptions; They were:

1. Employees of the Jewish Council,
2. Jews married to a non-Jewish partner and the children of these marriages,
3. Descendants of mixed marriages - mischlinger-(half-Jews and quarter-Jews),
4. Jews working in branches of industry important for the German war economy: Furriers, Chemists, Metal industry, Clothing industry, Diamond industry,
5 Baptized Jews,
6 Persons claiming not to be Jewish,
7. Jews with special merit awards from Germany, e.g. First World War Veterans, Iron Cross recipients,
8. Jews under special Dutch protection - Frederik's list, Van Dam list, Berneveld list, Ettie Hillesum (Jaap),
9. National Socialist Bund Jews,
10. 1039 Jews of non-Dutch nationality,
11. Jews to be considered for an exchange for Germans held in enemy territory,
12. Portuguese Jews without Eastern European Jewish blood or with Eastern European Jewish marriage partners.

A list of 340 such persons had been drawn up by March 1, 1943. At that time no decision had yet been taken. The list was submitted to Himmler for consideration.

As you see, one of these exemptions gave the Portuguese Jews a chance to postpone their fate. Let me give you an insight as to what happened according to Prof. Presser in his great book "The Destruction of the Dutch Jews."

The Portuguese Jews who joined in the hazardous business of claiming Aryan descent - lost. They claimed that they had nothing to do with the Jewish race or with what went with that name, except for the trifling matter of sharing their religious faith. "I do want to stress," says Dr. Presser," that Jews from the Caucasus who lived in France and took much of the same line, found their efforts crowned with success." Although many of us may say that there is little justification for the means used by some Portuguese Jews to placate their persecutors, NO ONE WHO HAS NOT GONE THROUGH THE HOLOCAUST, can understand how hard it was to decide what to do or what not to do.

According to the census figures, 4,303 people had registered on October 1, 1941 as Portuguese Jews. We know that this was a very heterogeneous group - economically, culturally and even in matters of religion. In some places they had completely merged into the local population. They presented Calmeyer, the man in charge of these exemptions, with interesting puzzles. On one occasion, he was told that "several grandparents of an applicant had been more than one-sixteenth Jew by race." He was even told that the proportion of Jewish blood in Marranos living at the turn of the sixteenth century was very small. Until 1750, mixed marriages between Marranos and Ashkenazi Jews could be counted on the fingers of one hand. No wonder Calmeyer had his hands full. He insisted that each case should be treated on its own merits. As a result, the Germans were swamped by a further flood of applications.

It is impossible to do more than sketch all this frantic activity. In the end, the fate of the applicants was no less dreadful than that of their co-religionists.

One of the efforts to come to their aid was a report entitled "Die Herkunft der sogenanten Portuguese" (The origins of the so-called Portuguese Jews) by two professors. It spoke highly of the Portuguese Jews, while having nothing but scorn for their German co-religionists. Another document was addressed to Seyse-Inquart, the head of the German Gestapo in Holland. This document referred to a strong mixture of west Gothic blood among the Portuguese Jews. It listed a series of noble Iberian families, i.e. Portuguese Jews, including knights, counts, dukes, barons etc. who had settled in Holland in the seventeenth century. Another document emphasized the great patriots the Portuguese Jews have always been. Finally there was a document giving proof that the entire group was of non-Jewish origin. The Germans were supplied with a list of names borne by Portuguese Jews and still prevalent today among citizens of Portugal.

In July and August 1943 (at that time already 60% of the Jewish population of Holland had been deported!), Dr. de Froe prepared a document entitled "Anthropological Investigation of the Composition of the So-called Portuguese Jews in the Netherlands." It tried to answer the following questions:

a. Must Portuguese Jews in Holland be deemed Jews or are they belonging to another race or mixture of races?

b. If they are deemed Jews, must they be regarded as indistinguishable from other Jews or as a separate group?

c. In case they are not Jews, do they form a separate group of mixed race?

d. Do the findings apply to all pure Portuguese Jews?

e. In what way does it apply to those who are not pure Portuguese Jews? The answers were based on individual investigation of 203 men and 172 women.

Skull measurements showed convincingly that these so-called Portuguese Jews cannot by any stretch of the imagination be classified as Jews and that they show affinities with Western Mediterranean races.

The men responsible for this work were scholars of great renown. They really did not try to prove that these Portuguese Jews were Aryans. That word does not even appear in De Froe's work. The big question was whether the Germans would accept the conclusions. Calmeyer challenged the conclusions. He argued that these people had always followed the Jewish Faith. But he conceded that a number of these Portuguese Jews investigated, only 400 could be considered eligible for a special stamp. The rest of these so-called Portuguese Jews could not be given permanent protection or exemption. After this decision, Rauter insisted on screening even the favored 400.

Dutch advisors kept begging the Portuguese Jews to go into hiding. But many believed in this possible protection. One professor of exceptional intelligence, Prof. Palache, declared that the Germans themselves had given him in writing that he would never be sent to camp.

What happened thereafter?

On March 1, 1943 one can find a list of the 400 exemptions.
By April 16, 1943 the number had shrunk to 300.
On September 29, 1943 the first day of Rosh Hashana the final expulsion of the Jewish Community from Amsterdam took place.

Between 3-5000 Jews were rounded up. The only ones left behind were the Portuguese Jews and the Calmeyer Jews, i.e. those Jews whose descent was still being investigated, and Jews married to non-Jews.

In 1944, unbelievably late in light of all the previous measures already taken, came the final catastrophe. On Jan. 26, Aus der Funten was instructed to include Portuguese Jews in the deportation measures and to send them to Westerbork. On February 1, 1944, Portuguese Jews were rounded up all through Holland. On February 20, 1944, the long awaited inspection of Portuguese Jews finally took place - 22 families, 273 persons - were paraded before the Obersturmfuehrers in Westerbork.

The conclusion: "A sub-human race. As such they must not be sent to Spain or Portugal but treated like all other Jews." On February 25, 1944, the last transport for Theresienstadt left Westerbork with 811 people, among them the 308 Portuguese Jews. Only 94 survived, the others were gassed after being sent to Auschwitz.

In conclusion I want to make some personal remarks.

On the first Seder evening after the liberation, when I started the Seder reciting the Shehecheyanu prayer, many thoughts went through my mind. I was liberated on April 23, 1945 by the Russian Army, and exactly 50 years later I am still reciting the prayer thanking God for having allowed me to reach that day. And at that same Seder, I was saying the prayers so well known to all:

We were Pharaoh's slaves in Egypt
The Egyptians considered us evil
And we cried onto the Lord

For me, as for every survivor - but just as much for all other Jews in the world - Biblical history became reality in our time. As the Jews in Egypt were slaves, so were we slaves under the Hitler regime. The Nazis considered us evil and we did cry out mentally and physically - all through those terrible years.

Ignorance of history is a breeding ground for the next epidemic. That's why it is so important to study what had happened to the Portuguese Jews.

In my lecturing in schools, I meet young audiences, the majority of which is non-Jewish, who try hard to understand the Holocaust. Let me read to you one of those letters I received after a lecture, a letter which expresses this so well: "You really increased my knowledge of the Holocaust and helped me to realize what it must have been like, when you mentioned that lots of decisions had to be made. One can imagine what it must have been like to know that one decision would mean your life or death."

In closing, I quote to you from the diary of a young Dutch woman, Etty Hillesum, in "An Interrupted Life."

"One day we shall be building a whole new world. I wish I could live for a long time so that one day I may know how to explain it, but if I am not granted that wish, well, then somebody else will perhaps do it, carry on from where my life has been cut short. And that is why I must try to live a good and faithful life to my last breath: so that those who come after me, do not have to start all over again. Isn't that doing something for future generations?"

Etty Hillesum died in Auschwitz, but this is the mission spelled out for us by one of the 6,000,000 who did not survive the Holocaust.

ZACHOR-REMEMBER!

LO TISHKACH-DO NOT FORGET!

THE ROLE OF SPAIN IN PROTECTING JEWS IN FRANCE DURING THE HOLOCAUST

by Haham Dr. Solomon Gaon

On June 14, 1940, the Germans occupied Paris. Tens of thousands of French Jews were trapped as were several thousand refugees from Germany and Central Europe. (1) These people were threatened with annihilation which was already in full process in other parts of occupied Europe. The threat of Himmler seemed to be on the way to realization. In May, 1940, he had sent a memorandum to Hitler stating that there was every possibility that the concept of Jew will have completely disappeared from Europe. (2) Not only in German-occupied Europe were anti-Jewish laws being passed but also in states which were ostensibly independent but under German influence. On August 10, 1940, the Rumanian government promulgated racial laws, as did Vichy France in October of that year.

France, with the rise of the resistance, began to feel even more the brutal oppression by the Nazis. On April 16, 1941, Aron Beckerman was the first Jew to be shot for being part of the resistance in France. (3)

On January 20, 1942, the Wannsee Conference took place, where Heydrich presented his plan for the "final solution". The solution did not merely include those Jews who were under direct German rule at the time, but also some eleven million Jews throughout Europe. These included 700,000 Jews in unoccupied France, a figure which included the Sephardi Jews in France's North Africa possessions. (4) Heydrich listed among the Jews in the neutral countries of Europe the 10,000 Jews in Spain.

By the end of 1943, several Jewish resistance groups were active throughout France, among them the Organisation Juive de Combat and the Jewish Scout movement. The work of these units included preparing safe hiding places for Jewish women and children, smuggling Jews across the borders to Switzerland and Spain, and engaging the Germans in combat. A total of 124 members of the Scouts resistance group were killed in 1943. (5)

Serrano Luner, who later became Foreign Minister of Spain, related in his book ENTRE HENDAYA Y GILBRALTAR, the unbelievable impression that the capitulation of France in June 1940 made on Spain. "Many coaches full of French refugees, as well as Jews of many nationalities, began to arrive in San Sebastian. Many of them were political personalities, bankers, artists, aristocrats, humble people, all trying to escape from the inferno that France had become for them." Finally, the Nazi armies arrived at Hendaya, the French frontier town overlooking Spain. Spain was now almost entirely surrounded by the mighty Wermacht, before which Europe lay prostrated and against which there seemed to be no defense. (6)

France, feeble and deprived of almost all independence, had Vichy as its new capital, while Paris, where the great part of French Jewry resided, became the general headquarters of the German occupation army. Already, in 1940, the Germans published a decree prohibiting Jews to cross from occupied to "free" France. In October, the Germans began the registration of the businesses of the Jews, of whom over 65,000 were to be annihilated in the following years.

In 1940, there were in France about 35,000 Sephardim of whom only 367 were known to have Spanish passports. By 1944, there were about 2,000 registered as Spanish nationals. When the registration of the Jews began, both the military government in Paris and the Vichy authorities informed the Spanish Consul General in Paris that all the Jews, whatever nationality they might possess, will be considered as belonging to the Jewish race and will be treated according to the laws applying to their race. The Spanish Consul General, Bernard Rolland, stated that as there was no racial discrimination in Spain, he would have to ask for instructions from Madrid. The Spanish government wired an unequivocal answer. The Jews who were Spanish subjects should clearly declare, when registering their properties, that they were in possession of Spanish passports so they could be defended by the Spanish government. The telegram was the first instruction concerning Spanish Jews in France given by the new Spanish Foreign Minister, Serrano Luner. It was also suggested by the Spanish authorities that all Spanish Jews should register all their possessions with the Spanish consulates. This was done because the Spanish representatives in Vichy and in France were convinced that the intention the Germans was to confiscate the properties of all Jews, whether French or not. In time, the Spanish Consulate in Paris succeeded in forcing the occupying power to concede that the Spanish Jews should make their declarations as regarded their properties to the Spanish consulates instead of to the French authorities.(7) In view of these concessions obtained by Spain on behalf of its Jewish subjects, the Jewish authorities turned to the Spanish government for advice as to ways in which they could protect the interests of Spanish Jews in the occupied countries.

The Spanish, in their discussions with the French, often referred to the agreement of 1862, according to which the French subjects in Spain and the Spanish subjects in France were accorded the same rights as the citizens of the country in which they resided. The Spanish representatives in both Paris and Vichy insisted that they should be treated according to the agreement.

Although the intervention of the Spanish ameliorated from time to time the position of the Spanish Jews, the Germans in occupied France and the Vichy government very often continued to treat them as all other Jews. They were often interned, denied free movement, and even sent to concentration camps. The full crisis was reached in 1943 when the German embassy in Madrid notified the Spanish foreign office that military authorities in France, Belgium and Holland had decided, for security reasons, to treat the Jews of foreign nationality according to the law applying to the Jews in general and not to make any exceptions. The Spanish Jews now turned to the Spanish authorities asking to allow them to cross into Spain and to protect as far as possible their possessions. The Spanish representatives did their utmost to assist in accordance with the request of their Jewish subjects.

From 1941 to 1942, the Nazis were mainly concerned with depriving the Jews of France and the low countries of all their rights and plundering their property. In May 1942, the Jews of those countries were requested to wear the yellow star badge. In June of that year, arrangements were being made for the extermination of Jewry from occupied France. The Nazis, however, were not satisfied merely with the destruction of the Jews under their direct jurisdiction, but put pressure on Vichy France to hand over the Jews in their provinces for deportation to Auschwitz. The intervention of different Jewish societies with Marshal Petain and Laval did not bring much relief.

The government of Vichy France was, on the whole, Catholic, and in some ways, was the reflection of the anti-Dreyfus coalition of the previous century. There were different commissars dealing with

Jewish affairs. The French outdid the Germans in developing administrative specialization in matters of destruction. (8)

In 1939, the Jewish population of France numbered 270,000, more than 200,00 of them living in Paris. In 1940, after the start of the war and the flood of refugees, there were 165,000 Jews in the occupied and 145,000 in the unoccupied zones. In occupied France, the Germans made use of French collaborators in order to eliminate the Jews from all commercial enterprises. This resulted in an additional burden being put on Jewish organizations in France. In 1941, the French organization law provided for an automatic blocking of Jewish enterprises. A portion of the proceeds was to be retained for administrative purposes and the remainder was to be used for needy Jews.

A terrible dilemma now faced the Jewish institutions. Should they use the monies of blocked accounts of Jewish property for their poor? They decided against it and made their own appeal to French Jews and to the American Joint Distribution Committee.

In 1941, the Vichy regime dissolved all Jewish organizations and established Union Generale des Israelites de France, which had no Jews on its committees. The entry of America into the war cut the American aid. The government of Vichy and the Germans introduced new legislation to rob the Jewish population of all their possessions. Rabbi Kaplan sent a strong protest against these measures to Xavier Vallat, Commissar for Jewish Affairs, a position instituted in March 1941. The Rabbi pointed out the common basis of Christianity and Judaism. From Vallat's answer one can gather that he found it very difficult to answer Dr. Kaplan's argument. Petain asked his Ambassador in the Vatican for the views of the Vatican on the Jewish laws which Vichy promulgated. The Ambassador assured him that these laws were in keeping with the Laws of the Catholic Church. (9)

On April 6 1941, Xavier Vallat declared that a difference was to be introduced between the French Jews and the newcomers. The special category was to consist of veterans of the two world wars (1914-1918 and 1940). These veterans, however, refused to accept this "privilege" and stated that they were ready to renounce any exceptional benefits that they might derive from their status as ex-servicemen.

The Vichy government also acted against Jews in North Africa. It abolished the Crimieux Decree of 1870 by which Jews of Algeria became French citizens. It expelled Jews from civil service. (10)

Under the leadership of General Weygand, commissariats for the Jews were established in Algeria and Morocco. The Sultan of Morocco himself undertook to enforce these laws, as decreed by the protectorate agreements. (11)

In March 1942, over 5,000 Jews were removed from occupied France to Auschwitz. In May of that year, it was decreed that the Jewish badge was to be worn by all Jews. In connection with this order, a confusion arose. Some Frenchmen decided to wear it themselves. The Germans pressed Laval that all Jews in occupied and in Vichy France be interned. After Laval protested this order, a compromise was reached: French Jews were not to be deported; but only foreign Jews. (12)

Arrangements by the Germans demanded the deportation of 100,000 Jews, 50,000 from each zone. Pressure continued on Laval to let Jews in Vichy France be deported. Laval finally agreed that foreign Jews in the Vichy zone be deported, including women and children. (13)

This decision resulted in violent protests by the priests. Laval threatened that he would allow no interference, and some priests were arrested. (14)

When America protested to Laval, he asked why the Americans had not taken them. (15)

New difficulties for the French Jews arose when Switzerland sent back some Jewish refugees who had crossed the border. (16)

The Germans kept on insisting that French Jews should come under the same law as other Jews, but Petain objected and finally Himmler had to back down. (17)

Difficulties arose also with Hungarian, Rumanian and Italian Jews in France. Italy was determined to protect its own subjects and would not allow them to be deported. Hungarian and Rumanian governments also presented difficulties about their subjects. (18)

In Italian-occupied France, the Italian authorities protected the Jews against the Germans and even the French. (19)

Frenchmen were paid by the Germans for revealing the hiding places of the Jews. Payments for this treachery were made from confiscated Jewish property. (20) When the Germans did not succeed in entirely destroying French Jewry, they tried to compensate for this failure by initiating a hunt for Jewish art treasures, by seizure of their furniture and by seizing their liquid funds.

When France surrendered in June 1940, there were about 35,000 Sephardi Jews living in France, most of them in Paris and other cities. The intervention of the Spanish authorities on behalf of their subjects prompted the leaders of the Association Culturelle Sefaradite in Pairs, who claimed to represent the Sephardi Jews of Paris, to send a communication to General Franco requesting that, in view of their origin and their special relationship with the Iberian Peninsula, they be allowed to settle in Spain. This appeal was rejected. (21)

The impression often created was that Spain protected all Sephardi Jewry in occupied countries. A statement by the Spanish Embassy in Washington claimed that "because of Spanish protection, some 6,000 Jews were able to live, work and survive Nazi persecution in France." In fact, the protection given by Spain covered Spanish nationals, or those who could provide some evidence upon which to make a positive determination of Spanish citizenship. (22)

According to Haim Avni, Spain could have rescued more Jews during the war but the Allies did not put pressure on Franco to do so. England and the United States did not seem to have regarded the rescue of Jews as an important issue during the war. (23)

NOTES
1. Martin Gilbert. *The Holocaust.* p 121.
2. op.cit., 120.
3. op.cit., 152
4. op.cit., 281.
5. op.cit., 641.
6. Quotation from Frederico Ysart, *Espana y los Judios.* 100ff
7. Vide Ysart, op.cit., 102ff
8. Raul Hilberg. *The Destruction of European Jews.* p 389
9. op.cit., 399
10. op.cit., 401
11. op.cit., 401
12. op.cit., 407
13. op.cit., 408
14. op.cit., 409
15. op.cit., 409
16. op.cit., 410

17. op.cit., 410
18. op.cit., 411
19. op.cit., 413-416
20. op.cit., 418
21. Haim Avni. *Spain, The Jews and Franco.* 84ff
22. op.cit., 181
23. op.cit., 199

BULGARIA: A DIFFERENCE
by Vicki Tamir

In the collective mind of the West, Bulgaria is often a metaphor for the abstruse, even the obtuse, at best the obscure and the remote—or else an appendix of sorts in the body of Europe consigned to the realm of the expendable. Indeed, appendectomies have been attempted in the past, both surgically and culturally, in the form of Hellenization, Islamization, or Russification. The irony, however, is that once, a long time ago, Bulgaria was not just an empire of enviable proportions, the first organized Slavic state, before Russia, but—more important—the literary parent, the cultural and spiritual progenitor of Russia.

More important yet is that, until the fourteenth century, Bulgaria did not know what anti-Semitism was. Not only didn't anti-Semitism exist in Bulgaria, but Jews there were held in high regard. They were admired and even emulated. When in the seventh century the Bulgars—pagans of Mongolian origins, ethnically and culturally related to the Khazars (the Khazars who shortly thereafter adopted Judaism)— established the First Bulgarian Kingdom south of the Danube, after conquering and absorbing, or rather being absorbed by, the more populous Slavs of the land, the Bulgars exhibited an extraordinary affinity both for Judaism as a creed and for the flesh-and-blood Jews they found within their borders. Jewish religious practices began to creep into the Gentile ethos and the royal palace itself, and even after Bul garia's Christianization in the 9th century, the favorable atti tudes toward Jews endured and persevered.

These early Jews are referred to in rabbinical sources as Romaniots. Archeological evidence places the time of their settlement in Bulgaria in antiquity, long before there was a Bulgaria, in fact almost as early as any sort of organized Jewish life at all is indicated within the Roman Empire by various excavations; for instance, that of the Ostia Antica synagogue near Rome, or the recent spectacular find at Bova Marina in southern Italy. Indeed ancient is the Jewish presence in Bulgaria and it would continue uninterrupted for two thousand years! Parenthetically, the Romaniots as a distinct category, undiluted by either Sephardi or Ashkenazi admixtures, survived from antiquity well into the twentieth century only in the Greek city of Yanina.

For centuries the Romaniot Jews under Bulgarian kings, first pagan, then Christian kings, lived in freedom and security, admired and respected, unlike their Romaniot brothers in neighboring Byzantium, or Greece, where persecution and forced conversion were the order of the day. As late as 1355, Jews must have been so prominent in Bulgaria that the king divorced his first wife in order to marry a local Jewess and make her his queen. The son of the Jewish queen, in turn, himself a Jew under Jewish law, proved to be the last Bulgarian king of an indigenous Bulgarian dynasty before the country fell to the Ottoman Turks in 1395, which led to subjugation and abysmal deprivation down to the loss of identity for Bulgarians, nearly five hundred years. In other words, the last Bulgarian king of Bulgarian blood was actually half Jewish by blood, but under Jewish law he was a full Jew. It is truly ironic.

With the expulsion of Spanish Jewry in 1492, the physiognomy of Bulgarian Jewry was radically changed by an influx of numerically and culturally superior Iberian exiles. Both the native Romaniots and the small number of Ashkenazim who over the centuries had found refuge in Bulgaria from persecution in the West were rapidly and successfully assimilated into the Hispanic fabric of the Sephardim with a lingering nostalgia for things Iberian persisting among successive generations of Bulgarian Jews. Not only was the language, fifteenth-century Castilian, preserved, but so were the folklore, the customs, the songs and music, and the traditions of Spain. There is a fable that still in the twentieth century individual families in Sofia kept keys to homes in Toledo, Spain, which their ancestors had locked up and abandoned centuries earlier. The keys were allegedly preserved as a sentimental memento from the glorious days in Spain, though under the Ottoman sultans the amalgamated body of Bulgarian Sephardim lived well, prospered, and enjoyed liberties denied to the erstwhile host nation, now the most oppressed of the subject peoples in peninsular Turkey. Bulgarians bore their yoke in total submission, with a fatalism bordering on stupor, and unlike other subjugated nations, Bulgaria, in a sense, ceased to exist.

This is when the seeds of estrangement, to put it mildly, between Bulgarian Jews and Bulgarian Gentiles were planted. And with Bulgaria's liberation by Russia in 1878, anti-Semitism took root. Retroactively, the Jews became scapegoats for all the centuries of suffering. Of course, the Russian liberators carried with them, almost as prominently as their arms, their anti-Jewish animus. Traditional Russian anti-Semitism combined on Bulgarian soil with a homebred resentment against the affluent Jews who had managed to escape the scars of serfdom, to produce violent waves of persecution.

This persecution did not last long, however, for no sooner was Bulgaria declared free than the Western powers—England, France, and Germany—fearing excessive Russian influence in the Balkan region, convened the Berlin Congress, which first dismembered the newly established state, then imposed upon a severely curtailed Bulgaria constitutional democracy as a condition for independence so that in the end, at least on paper, the Jews, along with other minorities, were proclaimed equal and free to pursue their ethnic and cultural activities.

The period between Bulgaria's liberation and World War II—roughly half a century—was riddled with assorted absurdities such as senseless wars, now against now in alliance with Greece, Serbia, Turkey, or Rumania, because first and foremost in the priorities of Bulgarians was TERRITORY. Nothing has ever meant more to Bulgarians than territory. Never mind that for five centuries they had hibernated and stagnated! Never mind that they were underdeveloped and lagging behind all European nations culturally, socially, politically, and economically! Territory came first! In addition, the country was rocked by incessant internecine internal strife, unpolitic political assassinations, suspensions of parliament, and major or minor violations of the constitution. There were also overt or covert acts of anti-Semitism, some mildly ridiculous, some more ominous, especially since at the time of Bulgaria's dismemberment, England's Prime Minister had been Disraeli, a Jew, and the loss of precious territory could be, and was, blamed on the Jews.

Yet, against all odds, by 1939—when an adulation of all things German, especially of Germany's drive for Lebensraum, territory, began to sweep the country, the 50,000 Jews of Bulgaria presented an image of a superbly organized, cohesive, staunchly pro-Zionist body, free in spirit and conscious of its separate heritage and destiny even as it stubbornly continued to insist on its rights under a constitution which had never been properly upheld.

In 1940, the king of Bulgaria, Boris III, a German Saxe-Coburg by blood who had married the daughter of Italy's King Victor

Emmanuel, obtained a completely compliant parliament after appointing as prime minister and interior minister two avowed Fascists and virulent anti-Semites. In December, parliament began debating the introduction of radical anti-Jewish legislation even before the country was officially in alliance with Germany and before such a move could be blamed on German pressure. As Parliament debated and before any measure had been passed, a number of Bulgarian Jews who held foreign passports were ordered to sail illegally to Palestine on an unseaworthy ship, ironically named the Salvador, over forceful objections from both the captain and Turkey, through whose straits the overloaded, unseaworthy ship had to pass. Not surprisingly, the Salvador sank in the Sea of Marmara, and hundreds of Jewish lives were lost as a result of Bulgarian callousness or insensitivity.

Officially, Bulgaria joined the Tripartite Pact in March 1941, becoming Hitler's formal ally and the springboard for Germany's quick nefarious operations against Greece and Yugoslavia. In exchange, Hitler forced Rumania to cede the southern Dobrudzha to Bulgaria. A month later, with the swastika already fluttering over the Acropolis and Yugoslavia properly subdued, the Bulgarians, without firing a single shot, simply walked into what from now on would be known as the new Bulgarian territories, namely: a slice of Greek Thrace, a part of Yugoslav Macedonia, and the city of Pirot in Serbia. Now about 13,000 formerly Greek and Yugoslav Jews came under Bulgarian jurisdiction, to be sent, less than two years later, to their deaths by those same Bulgarians who today boast a humane disposition and unremitting courage in allegedly having rescued their own Jews. The annexation of territory produced such a euphoria among the population in Bulgaria proper that, as a time-honored emotional vent, a scaled-down version of Germany's Kristallnacht was enacted against Jewish institutions and stores in the streets of Sofia, with the connivance and full support of the authorities.

Meanwhile, anti-Jewish legislation, patterned after the Nuremberg laws and euphemistically dubbed THE LAW FOR THE DEFENSE OF THE NATION, had been passed, and it effected both native Jews and Jews in the new territories. The law was enthusiastically implemented, with only a few feeble voices raised against it by individual democrats, the Church, the writers' union, and the Medical and Bar Associations. It is noteworthy that none of those so-called protests to parliament contains even once the word "Jews" or "Jewish," representing as they do no more than a mild critique of the regime, expressing merely concern over public opinion abroad, and showing an egregious, spectacular lack of daring.

To enforce the multiple, intricate stipulations of the anti-Jewish law, an entire machine was set up, providing new job and employment opportunities for Bulgarians. This machine was headed by a Commissar for Jewish Affairs, Alexander Belev, who was to function for the express purpose of reaching the final solution in close cooperation with Germany's special SS agent in Sofia, Haupsturmfuehrer Theodor Dannecker. The law effectively stripped the Jews of everything: all human and civil right, all dignity, all possessions and property, fixed and liquid assets alike. Jews had to wear the yellow star. Jews could not own radio sets or telephones. Food rations for Jews were much smaller than those for non-Jews. Jews were not permitted to own or run businesses, to be employed, or in any other fashion to earn a living. Jews were repeatedly resettled and squeezed, sardine-like, in minimal quarters in ghetto areas of the various cities, barred even from the streets, except for an hour or two daily, to buy their bread. All Jewish males up to the age of fifty were drafted for compulsory, unpaid, slave labor on the highways. Bulgarians, with a certain inescapable glee, moved to fill posts previously held by Jews, to occupy homes previously owned or inhabited by Jews, to take over

Jewish businesses and to acquire much coveted Jewish property.

To be sure, acts of simple human kindness, however rare and erratic, often even self-contradictory, were not altogether absent. But on the whole, as a people, Bulgarians demonstrated neither the proverbial Slavic compassion so vaunted by communist pseudo-historians nor the relentless, cold-blooded barbarity of their war-time Teutonic mentors. As a constant, unmistakable national characteristic, most salient among Bulgarians was earthy greed, their gluttony centering less on blood than on tangible assets. And naturally, to a greedy populace, Jews alive but dispossessed, and most working on highways for the greater glory of Bulgaria, presented no threat but were perhaps even an asset. Yet Germany, Bulgaria's esteemed ally that had afforded her additional beloved territory, never ceased to pressure for the final solution, and Bulgarians did not put up a fight against, nor did they seem too averse to the idea of, deporting both their new and their old Jews.

Thus, in February 1943, Bulgarian Commissar Belev and German Plenipotentiary Dannecker signed an agreement for the deportation to the so-called German East of a first contingent of 20,000 Jews, supposedly only from the new territories. But since the number of formerly Greek and Yugoslav Jews did not exceed by much 12,000, the difference of 8,000 was to be made up of so-called undesirable native Jews from all over the country. The criteria for undesirability were, a) wealth—judged on the basis of blocked accounts, and b) leadership status in the community, or what Belev termed "the capacity to maintain the Jewish spirit alive." In two simple words: RICH ZIONISTS.

The agreement, with the qualifying phrase "from the new territories" left standing, was promptly ratified by the Council of Ministers. In profound secrecy feverish preparations were set in motion for interim camps and railroad transportation. Speed and secrecy were crucial, not even parliament was to learn of the deportation—in order to prevent a mass influx of Jews into the underground because Belev's overall plan envisaged, as a next step, the expulsion of all Sofia Jews and then of the remaining Jews in the country. But since Jewish guerrilla fighters in the mountains could not be easily rounded up to be sent to gas chambers, everything had to be hushed: Bulgarian commissariat agents, overcoming entrenched habits, worked efficiently, with exemplary speed.

The first to be hit were the formerly Greek Jews of the cities of Kavala, Drama, Seres, Xanthe, and Alexandropolis a total of about 5,000. Early in March, they were roused in the middle of the night, and in their night garments, in subfreezing temperatures, were virtually hurled into unheated, unsanitary tobacco warehouses. From there, about two weeks later, those who survived the subhuman conditions were loaded, like cattle, on freight cars to a destination on the Danube, where the Germans were to take over. On their way across the country, the trains carrying the human cargo stopped one night for refueling near a labor camp. Jewish slave laborers were awakened by what sounded to them like the wailing of caged birds. In the words of a young man who later relayed the experience: "These were anguished apparitions looking out into a godless world; barefoot and in rags, ghastly pale, the shadow of death already cast upon them. Yet one among them, an old, white-bearded man himself condemned to death, rose like a Biblical prophet to instill hope in the younger Bulgarian Jews. `Have no fear, brothers,' he addressed them in Judeo-Spanish, `la salvacion viene' (salvation is near)!" Alas, not for the caged birds, not for the skeletal creatures headed north! When the trains reached the Danube, according to an unconfirmed eyewitness report, the Germans did not even bother with further transportation to the German East. After all, thanks to Bulgarians, the Jews were already half-dead. Why not save the expense and time of transportation?! So, the wretched creatures were simply loaded on barges, the barges were overturned, and the blue waters of the Danube proved as accommodating as any crematorium. No one survived. No one returned. And there is no record of the arrival of this particular transport at any German concentration camp.

The same sinister scenario was reenacted again in March, in formerly Yugoslav Macedonia. A total of over 7,000 Jews from Bitola, Skopje, Shtip, and Pirot were, in a similar fashion, brutally thrown into tobacco warehouses. There Bulgarian commissariat agents ran the entire gamut of abomination, from rape of young girls and mothers in the presence of their children, to sadistic beatings. In the last two weeks of March, the Jews were shipped in three transports to Treblinka, where all were exterminated. This part of the deportation is well-documented by Yugoslavs, not by Bulgarians.

On March 9, the additional undesirable 8,000 native Jews from various Bulgarian cities had already been rounded up and assembled at a predetermined point of concentration, when suddenly, without any explanation, they were told to go back home. What produced this unexpected change of heart, far from consisting in concerted popular action, typifies as such the Bulgarian as the Jewish modus operandi. Late in February, the Interior Minister's own brother-in-law had unblushingly offered a Jew on the street to sell to him valuable information. The Jew managed to pay the price, only to learn very little: Some rumor had it that some Jews somewhere would some time be deported. A day or two later, the Commissar's personal secretary alerted another Jew, free of charge, that his name was on a list of 2,500 deportable Sofia Jews. Now the Jewish community knew something, but not enough. Its Zionist leaders, shocked and alarmed but determined not to remain passive in the face of impending calamity, sought connections within the Fascist establishment itself.

After failing with some, they succeeded in learning from a highly placed former university colleague of one of them that there was an order for the deportation of 20,000 Jews but that this order specified "from the new territories." Armed with this crucial new piece of information, the Zionist leaders of the Sofia comunity arranged for a private meeting with the Vice Chairman of Parliament, Dimitur Peshev, who pleaded total ignorance of the deportation plan at first and even refused to believe that such a plan existed.

The Jews convinced him that the order did exist. They even convinced him that he, Peshev, ought to confront Gabrovski, the Interior Minister, and attack deportation, not on humanitarian grounds, on this they insisted, knowing that it would be futile, a total waste of energy, but from a legal angle. They contended that since the order explicitly stated "from the new territories," there was no juridical justification for the inclusion of even one native Jew in the deportation. They knew the realists that they were, that however ludicrous it seemed, given the Bulgarians' predilection for paradox and absurdity, only this legal technicality could be used. The sloppiness of the Bulgarian bureaucracy that had left the qualifying phrase undeleted, could perhaps save the lives of native Jews if not those of the Jews of the new territories. Before the twelfth hour struck, Peshev did confront Gabrovski, threatening a public scandal because of the illegality of the undertaking. Morality, ethics, humanity were not at issue here. The next morning, stop orders were sent not to cancel the deportation, only to postpone it until a new, clear and unambiguous decree would unequivocally stipulate the expulsion of native Bulgarian Jews. Whether the postponement had royal sanction is unknown, but it is most unlikely that without a mandate from the top it could have occurred, for Boris III was not the type of monarch who could tolerate independent action by the cabinet.

At this point the same Zionists who had contacted Peshev

attempted through different channels and methods to intercede in behalf of the Jews of the new territories who were already concentrated in tobacco warehouses. Access was gained to the queen, through an intermediary. She reportedly responded to the plea for help only with tears, saying that however eager she was to help, and I believe that she was, in the matter of the Jews, she was powerless. The Papal Nuncio was approached too, and he did manage to save a very few families whose children had attended Catholic schools and could thus pass for Catholic. Then Italian and Spanish diplomats were informed that a few of their nationals were among the deportable Jews of the new territories, and those Jews too, in the last minute, were released from the tobacco warehouses and saved. That is all that could be achieved, given the absence of other legal technicalities to be used.

Even for native Jews, the danger was still very much present, and augmenting by the day. German pressure for the final solution would simply not abate, and Bulgarians felt that a move had to be made to placate Berlin, despite a burgeoning controversy within the ruling circles. Because by then the fortunes of war had begun to shift in favor of the allies, and Germany's final victory no longer seemed so certain.

Commissar Belev offered two alternative plans: The first would synchronize the expulsion of the 25,000 Jews of Sofia with that of the other 25,000 throughout the country; the second would begin with and separate the evacuation of the Jews of the capital to the provinces, as a preliminary step toward the gas chambers. King Boris sanctioned the second plan, possibly as a stalling device. In May a clear unambiguous decree was issued, stipulating the evacuation of all the Jews of Sofia within days. Again, not knowing if this was but a prelude to a death march, the same Zionists who only two months earlier had thought that they had forestalled disaster, attempted a replay of the March events. This time protests from non-Jewish quarters rose somewhat higher. Representatives of the Church had an audience with the king on the issue of the Jews. Yet the outlawed Communist Party, as if to offset the interest of the Church in the Jews, for purposes strictly its own, stirred up emotions among the Jews of Sofia and incited a demonstration in the streets, which was quickly aborted, resulting in nothing but brutal beatings and arrests—only of Jews. Not a single one of the non-Jewish Communist instigators was either beaten or arrested. In the end, total resettlement did take place within days, leaving the capital Judenrein. But according to the testimony of a controversial rabbi, a man, who on the one hand had been arrested as a participant in the communist-inspired demonstration, on the other, maintained very close relations with the Archbishop, the king had allegedly pledged, through the Archbishop, not to follow resettlement with final deportation beyond the borders of Bulgaria.

Whether or not one believes the rabbi, it is very possible that Boris III was not eager to send the Jews to their deaths and that he did make the pledge, but we have no way of knowing for certain. The rabbi's testimony remains undocumented. In any event, only three months later, in August 1943, King Boris III suddenly died upon his return from a secret visit to Berlin, where Hitler had personally summoned him. To this day, his death remains shrouded in mystery. He had never been sick before, nor was an adequate, satisfactory explanation offered at the time or later. There are Jews and non-Jews alike who believe that the King of Bulgaria paid with his life for having spared the lives of 50,000 Jews. If this is so, one must ask why his successors, the three pro-Nazi regents appointed to rule in behalf of Boris's minor son, did nothing to rectify the king's fatal error in the matter of the final solution, especially since Berlin had directly interfered in the selection of a regency, one of the three regents was the theretofore Prime Minister and especially since Bulgaria's pro-

German policies would remain unchanged until a year later, when the regime would be overthrown and the communists would seize power.

During the coup of September 1944, with the Red Army about to cross the Danube into Bulgaria, some documents were destroyed by Fascists fearing reprisals. Reprisals came anyhow, and with a vengeance. Other documents, seized by Communists, were later released only in part—the part that served and suited the new regime's anti-monarchist purposes. Thus the role of King Boris in Jewish survival remains, if not completely obscure, at least not sufficiently clear, and certainly not well-documented.

In any event, by 1944 it became evident that at some indeterminable point, for some indeterminable reason, the danger to the very survival of Bulgarian Jewry had somehow slipped away. No single rescuer can be named. Nor can the Bulgarian people collectively be credited with Jewish deliverance, for at no time had there been even a semblance of popular action in behalf of the Jews. Salvation had come in an undramatic fashion, over a period of time, as a result of a bewildering variety of factors and circumstances. Nothing was clear-cut, all-white or all-black. The villains, even the worst among them, had been stooges of a great villain, whereas the heroes, if any, had been so ineffectual, timid and flawed that one hesitates to call them heroes. In short, the miracle refuses to lend itself to canonization.

HOLOCAUST IN JANINA
by Dr. Rachel Dalven

When Greece surrendered to the Axis powers in April 1941, Janina—capital of the province of Epirus—and its 1,950 Jews came under the Italian zone of occupation. (1)

Most Jews resided inside the kastro (fortress), while those living outside of the kastro had homes in the newer sections of Janina: Megale Rouga, Leivadioti, Vakoufia and Boustania. A few had homes near the mall fronting the Janina Lake, renowned in antiquity as Lake Pambotis.

Most Jews were laborers, employees in stores or itinerant peddlers. None had any relatives living in the villages to assist them economically or to offer them refuge in time of danger. Of the 500 families living in Janina in 1940, only about 70 were storekeepers. Many older people lived on contributions sent by relatives or philanthropic organizations in America.

What made the majority of the Jewish inhabitants of Janina particularly vulnerable to outside danger was their insulated way of life, even within the community itself. Class distinctions were sharp; there was little exchange of opinions or sharing of ideas between the classes. Their social contacts with the Christian population were limited. Janina's independent elected community governing body, the Jewish

Council of Janina, was ineffective. The five-member body had little contact with other Jewish communities inside or outside Greece. Very few Janina Jews were aware of the fate of Jews in other countries occupied by the Germans.

From the 1947 report of Moissis Eliasaf, who found refuge in Athens in 1943 and was elected President of the Jewish Council of Janina after the war, I learned that soon after the Italian occupation of the city in 1941, Dr. Moses Coffina, physician and then President of the Jewish Council of Janina, together with the merchant Sabethai Cabilli, Vice President of the Council, paid the Italian officer in charge a visit to assess the attitude of the Italian invaders toward the Jews. (2)

"As long as we are in authority here," the Italian officer assured them, "you have nothing to fear. You will have cause to fear only after the German SS arrive and Greeks start to collaborate with the Germans." (3)

According to Eliasaf, the Italians took no measures against the Jews. They granted permits to any Jews who wanted to leave for Athens. However, of all who did receive permits, and many did, only about forty or fifty actually abandoned their homes and shops to hide with Greek friends in Athens when the road was still open to escape. Some of those who had left for Athens while the Italians were still in authority returned to Janina, thinking it safer for them to be in their native city while it was still occupied by the Italians.

"Athens was occupied by both the Italians and the Germans," Eliasaf explained.

Only one disturbing incident occurred in the Jewish community of Janina during the Italian occupation. Nissim Batish, one of the richest merchants in Janina, often took trips to Athens with his son-in-law. On one of these trips, Batish and his son-in-law were accused and tried for carrying gold liras hidden in a basket covered over with layers of figs. Carrying money out of the city was prohibited. However, at the end of the trial, the Italian tribunal found Batish and his son-in-law innocent, and set them free.

Some Janina Jews formed a resistance group known as EPON (4) and fought in the mountains with other partisans. Twenty-two others joined the EAM, (5), the ELAS (6) and EDES. (7) More Janina Jewish youth would have joined the resistance forces, but family life in Janina had always been tightly knit. Solicitous of their parents, they feared to leave them alone.

During my visit to the Jewish community of Salonika in 1947, I discussed the deportation of the Janina Jews with the late Joseph Nchama, eminent historian of Salonika Jewry, and one of those few Salonika Jews whose lives had been spared because they had acquired Spanish passports. As a historian, Nehama had been in close touch with the community leaders of the Jewish community of Janina. "The Jews of Janina were very pious," Nehama told me. "The Jewish leadership believed that the deportation of the Salonika Jews had been motivated by 'divine anger' because they did not observe the Sabbath. 'God loves Janina,' they said. 'God has no reason to punish Janina.' When we advised them to seek refuge, they sneered." (8)

The first tanks of the Adolph Hitler Division rolled into Janina on 20 April 1943; they remained there for twenty days and left the city once more in the charge of their Italian ally. No incident occurring during those twenty days had anything to do with the Jews. Nevertheless, after the departure of the Germans, President Coffina proposed to his Council members that they advise more of their young coreligionists to join the resistance forces while flight was still relatively easy. Vice President Cabilli was rigorously opposed to any Janina Jews joining the partisans, all of whom he regarded as communists. Cabilli ignored completely the fact that during the Axis occupation of their land, men and women of different political persuasions in Greece had joined the EAM, ELAS and other resistance groups, united in their efforts to free Greece of the invaders. Cabilli believed in the words of Exodus (14:14) adonai yilachem lachem veatem taharishoun ('the Lord will fight for you and ye shall hold your peace!')

He ignored completely the urgent messages of Jewish leaders in Athens. Rabbi Elias Barzelai, Chief Rabbi of Athens, whom I interviewed in the capital in 1947, told me that he had sent the Jewish Councils in all cities occupied by the Italians a more accurate account of the tragedy which had occurred in Salonika, and urged them to flee before the Germans would occupy their city. Victor Borbolis, a native of Janina, hazzan ('cantor') of the Janina synagogue in Athens, whom I also interviewed in 1947, told me that he had sent a telegram in code to the Jewish Council of Janina: "The child is seriously ill. Urgent that you leave for Athens at once." Sion Bacolas, leader of the EPON in Athens, risked making the trip back to his native city to urge Vice President Cabilli to help their coreligionists to escape. Cabilli sneered at Sion's warning. "Chicks are now giving advice to the rooster," he told Sion. (9)

Although Dr. Coffina was President, it was Sabethai Cabilli who exercised the greatest influence in the Council and in the community. And so, the three other members of the Council were persuaded to accept Cabilli's ultra-conservative religious credo and voted against resistance. Some few Janina Jews ignored the decision of the Council and went into hiding; a few others used their Italian permits and left for Athens. The SS Edelweiss Division, with Von Stettner in command,(10) arrived in Janina at the end of July 1943, set up their headquarters at the renowned Zosimaia School,(11) and turned the schoolrooms and halls into a jail. The Germans had traveled from Salonika after they sent 58,559 Jews from Macedonia to the concentration camps of Auschwitz and Birkenau. (12) The Germans might have stayed away longer, but the Italians, unable to hold back the partisans of EDES, who were in control of the whole province of Epirus, had summoned their Axis partner to come to their aid. (13)

The Germans immediately set out to learn from leading members of the non-Jewish population who was the most influential Jew in Janina. In every city the Germans occupied, they always selected one Jewish leader who could be easily led to cooperate with them in the "final solution" of his coreligionists. This was their strategy and their boast, that the Jews would be exterminated with the cooperation of the Jews themselves.

Cabilli was widely known in Janina by Jews and Christians who shopped in his dry goods store, and by his employees who worked at his two small factories where they manufactured textiles and kerchiefs. Although Cabilli was not an ordained rabbi, it was he who led the services on the Sabbath and on all religious Holy Days. Cabilli was well read; he knew languages; he surpassed the rabbi in his knowledge of Hebrew; he taught *halakha* ('Jewish Law') in the Society *Orah Hayyim* ('Way of Life'). He was the most sought after mohel ('circumciser') in Janina. He was actively involved in several philanthropic organizations. He had excellent relations with the Metropolitan Spiridon of Janina, as well as with the authorities in the Greek government. He was Vice-President of the Chamber of Commerce in Janina. (14) Although he was a rich man, he led a restricted and frugal life.

All the people whom the Germans questioned agreed that Cabilli wielded great authority over his coreligionists. He was the most respected and feared religious leader in the community. "Our Janina coreligionists, especially the heads of households," recalled a Jewish resistance fighter and native of Janina, "regarded Cabilli as the Law who could commit no error. They thought of him as a sage." (15) The Jews of Janina leaned heavily, almost blindly, on Cabilli to handle any situation that concerned their safety.

For the time being, the Germans did not concern themselves about the other four members of the Jewish Council; nor was there any need for them to appoint their own Judenrat ('Jewish Council') as they had done in other cities they occupied. They were confident from all that they had learned about Cabilli that he would cooperate with them.

Soon after the arrival of the Edelweiss Division, Von Stettner, accompanied by a Greek wearing a German uniform (not a native of Janina), went to see Cabilli at his store.

"You are not like the Salonika Jews," Von Stettner began. "You are different." (16)

Von Stettner assured Cabilli that the Germans were not going to molest the Janina Jews. They gave Cabilli permits to go to Athens as often as he wished. Cabilli spread the word of Von Stettner from the pulpit and among the people who sought his advice, as a word that could be trusted. He warned all heads of households in the community to urge their sons to avoid any daring acts that would provoke the Germans. The Janina Jews were mesmerized by Cabilli's words of trust. They were confident that their leader would handle the Germans with hokhma ('wisdom'). They did nothing to alter the course of their daily lives.

"Cabilli used to say to his Greek Christian compatriots, 'you give blood, we give money,'" recalled Mr. Zois, editor of the Greek Janina newspaper Proinos Logos ('Morning Word').

In an interview in Athens in 1947, Billy Gavrilides, a Jewish Athenian lawyer, whose father, a native of Janina, had long resettled in the capital with his family, recalled an event which reveals how Cabilli used his own economic wealth to "buy" the safety of his coreligionists.

"Sabethai Cabilli, who had business dealings with my father in Athens," Gavrilides told me, "sent his nephew to him, to get all the goods stored in Cabilli's warehouse in Athens, and bring it to Janina, so that he could turn it over to the Germans. His nephew did this. He piled it on a truck and drove back to Janina. He got as far as Agrinion; there the Germans seized the goods and killed the nephew."

For the first three weeks, the Germans did not trouble the Jewish community at all. Nevertheless, despite the reassuring words of Cabilli and this three week lull of deceptive tranquility, many Jews were uneasy, especially as they came to learn more of the gruesome facts of the deportation of the Salonika Jews.

The fears of the Janina Jews surfaced alarmingly when, at five p.m. on Saturday, 20 August 1943, the Germans surrounded a Jewish neighborhood for the first time.

"This was the neighborhood outside the kastro, where the Kahal Kadosh Hadash ('New Synagogue'), the buildings of the Alliance Israelite Universelle School and the finest homes were located." said Elias Lagaris, Vice-President of the Jewish Council in Janina in 1947. (17)

They arrested his sixty-seven year old father, Isaac, and Hayyim Levy, a brother-in-law, both of whom were conversing quietly in the courtyard of the Lagaris home, placed them in an automobile and drove them to the Zosimaia School. The Lagaris sons and their families were not with their parents at the time of the arrest.

After two hours of maddening agony on the part of the Lagaris sons and the whole community, the Germans freed the men. As soon as they were able, the Lagaris sons rushed back to their home.

"The Germans did not mistreat us," old man Lagaris recounted to his children, "and then they let us go free." After a pause, he added, "I'm afraid this will happen again, if we don't take action. You young people must leave for Athens at once. The Italians will give you permits, but you must get them now, while they are still in authority. We are too old to travel; we will hide in the homes of friends here in our town."

Isaac Lagaris insisted that his six children scatter separately, stay away from their family home, and hide in the homes of friends until such time as they could get permits from the Italians to leave for Athens. After much difficulty, two of the Lagaris children and three other couples received permits from the Italians and left for Athens at five p.m. on 23 August 1943. After many vicissitudes and narrow escapes from Nazi spies and Greek collaborators, and with the help of friends and the Jewish Agency, all arrived safely in Tel Aviv, where they remained for the duration of the war. None of them ever saw their parents again.

The Italians surrendered (18) to the Allied Forces on September 8, 1943. Now all of Greece was occupied by the Germans. On September 22, SS General Jurgen Stroop, (19) destroyer of the Warsaw Ghetto, was appointed by Hitler to be Chief of Police in Greece. Soon after his arrival in Athens, he announced in the German-controlled Greek Press (20) that Jews would be given five days to register; they were to leave their addresses in the synagogue and report there in a week.

"Whoever does not register," the order stated, "will be put to death. Any Christian who hides a Jew will be shot. Jews may circulate only from seven a.m. to five p.m."

In Janina, however, where it was relatively simple to round up about nineteen hundred Jews, most of whom lived in easily identifiable districts, the Germans led them to believe that this order did not apply to them.

The Germans found another way to strike at the Jewish community. They scorned the verdict of their former Italian allies who had found Nissim Batish and his son-in-law innocent; they arrested them again, accused them of helping the guerillas, and hanged them in Florina. (21)

After this tragic episode, the parnassim ('trustees') of both synagogues in Janina decided that it would be wise to gather their Torah Scrolls, the embroidered paroketh ('curtains') of the Ark, and their sacred vessels, and place them in a crypt in the Old Synagogue in the kastro. (22)

From October 4, 1943 to March 1, 1944, no other incident occurred to alert the Janina Jews that the Germans had already scheduled the date of their deportation. Some even wrote to their coreligionists who were hiding in Athens to return to Janina. "We are not being persecuted in any way," they wrote. The United States was planning to open the Second Front. The Jews of Janina lived in the hope that liberation day was close at hand.

On March 1, 1944, the Germans arrested four members of the Jewish Council of Janina: Dr. Moses Coffina, President; Dr. Errikos Levy, physician and an army lieutenant; the merchants Shemo Cohen and Leon Mordechai, and took them to the Nisi, the island across the Janina lake. Sabethai Cabilli was the only Council member not arrested.

"There we were kept for two nights in isolation at the home of a man named Lappas," Dr. Errikos Levy recalled when I interviewed him. Dr. Levy, now resettled in Athens, was the only Council member who survived Auschwitz.

"They evicted Lappas, requisitioned his house and used it as the Gestapo headquarters on the island. After two nights, we were removed to the Zosimaia School and placed in a windowless basement for two weeks; then we were placed in a large hall with about fifty other prisoners until the blockade." (23)

The arrest of four of their leaders was a shattering turn of events which worried the community. Cabilli thought that his fellow Council members may have been too outspoken or done something that had angered the Germans. A delegation of young Jews, determined to discover for themselves why the Germans had arrested their leaders, paid a visit to the Zosimaia School.

"They were sending food and medical supplies to the guerillas." the Gestapo told them.

With the arrest of the four members of the Jewish Council, Sabethai Cabilli was now the only official spokesman of the community. Again he went to the Zosimaia School, this time alone, to see what could be done for the safety of his coreligionists. The Germans assured Cabilli that the community would remain free, if they provided the Germans with money and supplies.

The following Sabbath, the Jews went to the synagogue as usual. The services were conducted without incident. At the end of the services, Cabilli addressed the congregation:

"I would like all of you young men to come to the synagogue tomorrow morning at eleven a.m."

About two hundred fifty young men obeyed the call the next morning at the scheduled hour. They filed in grimly and sat quietly in their seats, waiting to hear what it was their most respected leader wanted of them. Cabilli told them of his visit to the Zosimaia School, and what the Germans expected of them if they wanted to escape deportation.

"I am faced with a grave responsibility," he began, "and I need help from you young men, because, as you know, our President is in jail and I am taking his place."

"What is it you want of us?" asked Uriel Gerson (#182396), a survivor of Auschwitz.

"I want those among you here to form two committees. One committee is to go to the homes of our coreligionists and take objects; silver, chairs, dishes, etc. The other committee is to get donations of money which we will turn over to the Germans so they can purchase the objects that we do not have in our homes. This way, they have given me their word that we will remain free. You know the fate of our Salonika brothers."

"But this has been going on for at least four months," Uriel remarked.

"Things are difficult," replied Cabilli. "We will have to do our best to get along with the Germans."

"That week we really worked at this," Uriel recalled. (24) "We supplied the Germans with funds and objects. All the Germans had to do was ask for something and we supplied it to them immediately. The Germans were so satisfied with our services that they even moved into our homes, and we waited on them hand and foot. We kept hoping that our deeds would soften their hearts and spare us."

Cabilli next went to the parents of the twenty-two young men who had joined the EAM and ELAS and were now fighting with the partisans.

"Your sons are endangering the whole community," stormed Cabilli. "They have joined with the communists and all of us will suffer. Get those boys to come back! Do you want all of us to go to our deaths?"

"But how can we get them to return?" the mother of one of these boys asked. "Even we don't know exactly where they are."

"You find out where they are and get them to return," he ordered.

"You can imagine how those parents felt," Uriel reflected. "After all, they didn't want to endanger the rest of our lives. Well, they found ways to contact their sons, and succeeded in getting eleven of them to return to their homes. Now, Cabilli felt easier in his mind. We continued to supply the Germans with everything their hearts desired."

According to Mr. Zois, whom I interviewed in 1947, towards the beginning of 1944 it was rumored that a certain Christos Michaelides, whose real name was Daniel Cohen, an informer in the service of the Gestapo, had come to Janina to study the existing conditions of the Jews and prepare a detailed plan for their deportation. But the Jews were so mesmerized by the assurances of Cabilli, that either they regarded this as some kind of hoax, or they felt too trapped and numbed to be able to do anything about it. Mr. Zois also told me that an SS seaplane had descended on the Janina lake shortly before the deportation, to prepare the blockade of the Jewish community. Many Jews had no knowledge of the seaplane.

"Two weeks before we were blockaded," Nina Negrin (#77160), a survivor of Auschwitz, recounted to me in Janina in 1947, "A Greek Christian went to each Jewish home to take a census of the number of Jews living in each house. They wrote down the names. They even inquired whether we had relatives living in other cities. Some actually gave the names of their relatives, which the census taker recorded."

Dr. Moses Coffina, still imprisoned at the Zosimaia School, had been mulling over the cause of his arrest. He knew that neither he nor the other three Council members had offered any material assistance to the partisans. One day, he discovered that one of the guards did not approve of Hitler's anti-racial laws, and Coffina decided to ask him if he knew why he and the other three Council members had been arrested.

"You are here because you would not cooperate," the guard told him. "Your whole community will soon be blockaded."(25)

On 6 March 1944, a classified letter was sent by the GFP (Secret Military Police) 621 (Janina Branch) to the General Command XXII Area A.K. 10, concerning the deportation of the Janina Jews. The four Council members who had been arrested are listed in this classified letter. Another official note was sent to the Chief of the General Staff on the same day. A third note, all of which I found and xeroxed from microfilm at Yad Vashem in Jerusalem, was dated June 13, more than two months after the Jewish community of Janina had been deported to Auschwitz and Birkenau.

What is remarkable about these German documents is the guise of legal procedure and the euphemisms employed: "thorough interrogations" (meaning torture) to confess a "truth" which may not have been a truth at all; "total preventive elimination or special treatment requested," naturally meant deportation and extermination in the gas chambers.

On 17 March 1944, Dr. Coffina succeeded in smuggling a brief note out of prison, which he stuffed into a piece of bread he had not eaten; it had been brought to him with some home-cooked food by his wife, which the Germans permitted.

"Deliver this note to Cabilli," Dr. Coffina instructed his wife Chrissy. "Don't delay. This is urgent."

His wife delivered the note to Cabilli directly after she left the prison. Cabilli read it at once.

"We must say nothing about this note to anyone." Cabilli told her. (26)

A week later, on the Sabbath morning of March 25, 1944 (Greek Independence Day), Hopfer, the German political Stadkommandant, accompanied by German units and interpreters of the official collaborating police, awakened the Jews at two a.m. The order was given by Lieutenant Colonel Hafranek of the Police Class and the GFP (Secret Military Police) 621 (Janina Branch), and signed by Bergmayer, a non-commissioned officer. (27) According to Joseph Matsa, Father Athanasius managed to give some Janina Jews false identification cards which helped a few more to escape. (28)

"The Germans placed a cross on the doors of the Christian homes just before the blockade," Mr. Zois said, "so as not to blockade any of the Christians."

"Each of us was permitted to take forty kilos of anything we wanted," Nina Negrin told me.

Jews who lived outside the kastro were ordered to meet at Mavilis Square fronting the Janina Lake. There they separated the men; women and children were herded together. The Jews who lived inside the kastro were to assemble in the Military Hospital located there. At the Military Hospital, both men and women were packed together in the trucks lined up outside the hospital.

"The Christian people of the city were deeply moved on the day of the deportation," Matsa told me.(29)

"We had food," Nina Negrin continued, "because we took food with us. March 25, 1944 was a bitter cold day. The snow kept falling steadily. It was pitiful to hear infants and little children crying. Old women were freezing from the cold."

Sabethai Cabilli, as well as his wife, his sisters and their families, was also herded along with the rest of the Jews, holding a bible in his hands and praying silently. The eleven young men who had been forced to return from the mountains were also there. So were the four Council members who had been imprisoned in the Zosimaia School. As soon as Dr. Coffina saw Cabilli, he shouted, "You young men are here only because of one person."

"What do you mean?" Uriel asked. "What person?"

"Sabethai Cabilli," he replied, pointing an accusing finger at Cabilli. "He is responsible for your capture. I sent him a note through my wife who brought me food to jail. I wrote to him that the Germans were planning to blockade you. I urged him to help you escape."
"Why didn't you show it to us?" shouted another.

Several of them wanted to strike him.

"You will carry the responsibility for this tragedy," shouted Dr. Coffina.

"I told you that we were in a very grave situation," Cabilli replied.

Their accusing eyes were riveted on his; his own eyes could not avoid theirs. At this moment of intense anguish, he tore the words out of his heart: hatas eftexa ("I am guilty").(30)

There was no time to say anything more. Eighteen hundred and seventy Jews were counted and forced to clamber up into the ninety seven trucks waiting to drive them first to the concentration camp at Larissa, and then from there to the cattle cars waiting to transport them to Auschwitz and Birkenau.

At three a.m., the Germans awakened some Greek Christians who had collaborated with them and instructed them to distribute any goods left in the stores of the deportees. They were also told they could occupy the stores of the Jews, as well as their homes, which were left vacant.(31)

"After the Germans took what they wanted," Uriel Gerson told me, "Michael Tsimbris, Governor General of Epirus, formed committees and gave orders to distribute some of the merchandise to those who had suffered by fire and bombardment, civil service workers, hospitals and other welfare societies; but some of the goods were distributed to the collaborators."

Dr. Michael Matsas, who was hiding in Agrinion with his family and returned to Janina after the Germans left, wrote me concerning the distribution of the remainder of the Jewish merchandise in Janina:

ELAS units entered Janina after the Germans left. Jewish partisans guarded the warehouses where [leftover] Jewish merchandise and goods were kept. One of them gave my mother an old fur coat and a handmade blanket. The sixteen gold pounds of merchandise we received were in the form of a blue dye (loulaki) which we did not know what to do with. The EAM distributed thirty liras to every Jew present in Janina in October 1944, before the survivors returned from the concentration camps or those who were in Palestine or Athens at that time. My father received a portion of this because he had been working for ETA-EAM (ETA was the quartermaster section of EAM-ELAS). The EAM took the remaining 'fortune' to Albania. (32)

"It took the Germans a whole day to drive us to Trikkala," Nina Negrin recounted. "It was still snowing and the trucks stuck in the snow. We had a horrible time of it. We could sit only partly stretched. There were two windows in our truck, but they kept them shut. We spent that night sleeping in the Jewish cemetery. We used the blankets we had taken with us as mattresses. We arrived in Larissa the next day with the loss of two old people. As soon as we reached Larissa, we were packed into a large garage with a cement floor. It was a little larger than one of our large homes in Janina."

The Germans immediately ordered the captives to hand over any gold and jewels they had taken with them. They stressed that anyone who kept anything on them would be discovered and shot.

"Each of us dropped our gold and jewels at the spot where we stood," Nina continued, "so that they would not be found on us. They forced us to pass in front of the Germans who stood on one side and searched us. A large sack of gold and jewels was filled. One woman managed to keep her jewels in a handkerchief tied with a thread, and in this way she carried them to Poland."

The captives were detained in Larissa for ten days. The young men who had been forced to return from the mountains wanted to kill Cabilli. Fortunately, nine of them found ways to escape.(33)

"During those ten days in Larissa," Avram Zvolis, one of those who had escaped, told me in Janina in 1947, "the Germans who were in charge of the camp were Austrians and not strict. Every other day, they allowed a few of us to get water for the rest of the captives. In this way, we agreed among ourselves that each time we went for water, one of us would not return to the camp. We managed to erase the word Jude from our identity cards, and that helped us in our escape. In one or two instances, we bribed the guards who allowed us to escape. At another time, it occurred to us to say that we belonged to the Red Cross who used to bring us food. Nine of us escaped in this way; all nine of us joined the ELAS and fought in the People's Army for the duration of the war. Those who chose not to escape with us were married men who preferred not to leave their wives and children."

"They locked fifty of us in each freight car and shipped us to Poland," Nina concluded. "It took us nine days to reach Auschwitz. Some old people died on the way. Every couple of days they opened the doors, so we might get water. We used an empty barrel as a toilet. We threw a blanket over it."

When after nine days the Jews reached Auschwitz, Sabethai Cabilli was not selected for labor. He, his wife and his sisters were sent to the gas chambers with the rest of the elderly, women and children on the very first day of their arrival.

When one ponders the loss of ninety-one percent of the Jewish population of Janina, there is no question that the immediate cause of this tragedy was the unintentional betrayal by a strong-willed and opinionated religious leader. Cabilli believed that if his coreligionists gave the Germans everything they requested, they would be spared. There is no doubt that Cabilli's "cooperation" bordered dangerously on the area of collaboration. However, there were other causes which

SEPHARDIM AND THE HOLOCAUST

contributed to the deportation of the Janina Jews, and which explain in some measure why Cabilli was duped so easily by the Germans.

We must keep in mind that the German program for the "final solution" of the Jews was planned with fine cunning. One crafty device was their gradualism, which deluded the Jews into relaxing their vigil during periods when they were calculatedly not troubled at all. Another was stripping the Jews of their economic wealth to which, unfortunately, Cabilli himself had willingly contributed —to his great sorrow when his nephew was killed. Yet another was the attitude of many heads of household who believed that the individual Christians who urged them to flee probably did so in order to take over their shops, their property, and their homes.

"Many a time in the concentration camp, suffering from beatings and starvation," Uriel told me, "I used to think of Cabilli with a good deal of bitterness, but now I realize that it was just as much our fault. I think how many of our coreligionists in Janina would be alive today, if we hadn't bowed down to his money all our lives. And in the end all his money could not save his own life. Had he advised the Jews to leave while the Italians were still in authority, half of them would have been saved."

Then, too, although both the EAM and EDES accepted as many Jews as took refuge in their territory, and helped to save them from danger, they did not take the initiative to organize forcefully the exodus of at least part of the Jewish population of Janina, as they had done in Athens, in Volos and in Larissa. The only effort they made was to scatter leaflets advising the Jews to take their money and flee to the villages held by the partisans, but they left them to find their own way. Perhaps they were too absorbed in the disputes amongst themselves. Another cause was the general indifference of the Christian inhabitants on the days preceding the pitiful event.

Although the terrified Jews were lulled to sleep by the appeasement policy of Cabilli, the Christians of Janina could see more clearly the danger which threatened the lives of the Jews, and did little to help them.

Still another contributing factor was that some Greek Christians identified the Jews by their religion rather than by their nationality, which was the same as their own. This was probably aggravated by the fact that the Jews had chosen to live together in neighborhoods that were generally identified as Ta Evraika ('the Jewish neighborhoods'). The Germans were quick to detect this "vulnerable point" which existed between Greek Jews and certain Greek Christians. The Germans exploited this by mobilizing the local forces that were willing to lend their support to the invaders.

It was inevitable, of course, that personal friendships developed through the years between Jews and Christians, but the clear-cut distinction between them was always present in their daily lives. It lessened to an appreciable degree the additional help and protection the Jews of Greece might have had from the non-Jewish population at the grass roots level.

It cannot be denied that the Greek Church, the Police Department and some state services helped some Jews by forging Christian identity cards, and urged Christians to hide Jews in their homes, even though they were endangering their own lives by giving them assistance or refuge. It is also true that the resistance forces found Christian homes for the Jews to hide in, and helped them to escape to the mountains; but the German-approved Greek government in office at that time was opposed to national resistance. They participated passively with the German invaders which, in the final analysis, amounted to collaboration.

It is unfortunate, yet in keeping with what was happening to Jews elsewhere, that the Allies ignored what was happening to the Jews of Greece. As Dr. Michael Matsas, whom I have already mentioned, wrote in his illuminating article:

> It would have been extremely easy for Allies to advise the Jews to hide through the resistance network that reached every city of occupied Greece. Nobody ever thought of this although the Public Records of London and the National Archives in Hyde Park contain over five hundred pages of documents about all anti-Jewish measures taken, while the American Consuls of Istanbul and Cairo sent detailed reports and recommendations for saving Jews. These reports were filed away and were declassified in 1972, long after the people who so easily could have been saved were gone.(34)

And finally, the Germans could never have succeeded in their genocide program if they did not have the collaboration of some of the non-Jewish population. "The Germans could not have blockaded the Jewish community of Janina," Uriel Gerson observed, "without the aid of the Greek local police who collaborated with them."

The late Isaiah Trunk evaluated the situation accurately in all German-occupied lands when he wrote, "The Germans readily accepted help from local populations...members of the indigenous auxiliary police were assigned to participate in killing the Jews. (35) ...Without their assistance, it would have been impossible for the Germans to administer and dominate the occupied lands." (36)

NOTES:
1. I spent four summers (1936-1939) in Janina, to learn something of my roots. This is the city where both my parents and grandparents were born; I also had

a number of close relatives living in Janina. In the summer of 1947, I returned to Janina, to discover what had happened to the Jewish community during the German occupation of that city.

2. Moissis Eliasaf, President of the Jewish Council in Janina in 1947, gave me a report on all events which affected the lives of the Janina Jews from the Italian occupation of that city in 1941 to the time of the Italian surrender on September 8, 1943, when he managed to escape to Athens.

3. The name of the Italian officer was not known to Eliasaf.

4. EPON —Eniata Panelladiki Organosis Neon ('United Panhellenic Organization of Youth').

5. EAM —Ethnikon Apeleftheritikon Metopon ('National Liberation Front')

6. ELAS —Ethnikos Laikos Apeleftheritikos Stratos ('National Popular Liberation Army').

7. EDES —Ellinikos Demokratikos Ethnikos Stratos ('Greek Democratic National Army')

8. I discussed the deportation of the Janina Jews with Mr. Nehama, when I visited him at his home in Salonika in the summer of 1947.

9. Sion Bacolas, a first cousin and leader of the EPON, met with me on several occasions in Athens in the summer of 1947, during which time we discussed the deportation of the Jews of Janina. Sion, a native of Janina, settled in Athens after the war.

10. Eliasaf spoke of the German officer only as Von Stettner.

11. The Zosimaia brothers, natives of Janina and renowned philanthropists during the latter part of the seventeenth and early eighteenth centuries, had donated the money for the founding of the school.

12. Nikos Stavroulakis writes that 58,559 Jews were deported from territories in the German zone, and 4,212 from Thrace and Macedonia in the Bulgarian zone. Errikos Sevillias, *Athens-Auschwitz,* translated and introduced by Nikos Stavroulakis (Athens, 1983), 96. Michael Molho writes that 51,162 Jews were deported from Macedonia and 2,692 from Thrace. *In Memoriam* (Thessaloniki, 1973), 326.

13. EDES was eliminated in Epirus in 1944.

14. Epimelitireion Emporikon ('Chamber of Commerce')

15. Avram Calef Ezras, a native of Janina, who fought in the resistance and whom I met in Athens in 1982.
16. What Von Stettner implied was that Cabilli was a Greek- speaking Jew, while the Salonika Jews spoke Judeo-Spanish in their homes. Von Stettner wanted Cabilli to think he regarded him as a Greek and not as a Jew because he spoke the same language at home as the Greek Christians.
17. The arrest of Isaac Lagaris was recounted to me by his son, Elias Lagaris, in Janina in the summer of 1947. The Germans destroyed the Kahal Kadosh Hadash ('New Synagogue'), the Minyan Hadash ('New Small Synagogue'), as well as the buildings of the Alliance Israelite Universelle, where Jewish children received their education.
18. Except where other names are cited, the events which occurred in the Jewish community of Janina, from the Italian surrender on September 8, 1943 to the blockade and after the return of the few survivors, were recounted to me in 1947, in Janina, by Uriel Gerson (#182396), a survivor of Auschwitz.
19. In 1947, SS General Jurgen Stroop was condemned by a U.S. Military Court for his atrocities in Greece and for his crimes in the Warsaw Ghetto. He was extradited to Poland and hanged.
20. All newspapers in Athens were German-controlled, except those published in the underground. The announcement appeared in several Athenian papers.
21. This tragic event was widely known in Janina.
22. After the Janina Jews were deported, the Germans found the sacred objects and wanted to confiscate them. Fortunately, Mayor Demetrios Vlachides and the Metropolitan of the city persuaded the Germans to spare the synagogue, since they were going to use it as a library. Mayor Vlachides placed the sacred objects in the Municipal Museum of Janina, and returned them to the survivors after the war. The Janina Jews commemorated his act of mercy by inscribing his name on a tablet of gold.
23. I met Dr. Errikos Levy at the Jewish Center in Athens in 1964. He recalled the details of his arrest in 1944 and told me about it then. Dr. Levy resumed his medical practice in Athens after the war.
24. From what Uriel Gerson told me, the Jews of Janina had been providing the Germans with money and supplies for four months before the arrest of the four Council members on March 1, 1944.

25. Dr. Coffina wrote this in a note which he gave his wife Chrissy to deliver to Cabilli.
26. This was revealed by Dr. Coffina's wife at Mavilis Square, where they were herded on the day of the blockade.
27. I found no first names in any German records.
28. Joseph Matsa, Secretary of the Jewish Council of Janina in 1947, is the local historian of the Jewish community of Janina.
29. Matsa informed me of this on one of my later trips to Janina.
30. Hatas Eftexa ('Hatas" —sin: from the Hebrew hatati; eftexa (Greek: I am guilty). These two words were spoken in the Beth Din, the Jewish Court of Justice in Greece, when a culprit admitted his guilt.
31. In 1947, I interviewed Anastasios Vlachopoulos, a Greek Christian in Janina, who admitted to me that he was one of those who was awakened at three a.m. When I asked him why the Germans had awakened him in particular, he replied, "Well, you see, I was President of the Chamber of Commerce when Janina was occupied by the Germans."
32. Dr. Michael Matsas, now living in Washington, D.C., wrote this in a letter to me on January 15, 1979.
33. Those who escaped from Larissa are: Samuel Meir, Menachem Hadjopoulos, Moisis Myonas, Solomon Matsas, Solomon Cohen, Avram Zvolis, Jacob Gerson, Yeshua Massa, Avram Mihael Matathia.
34. Dr. Michael Matsas, "How the West Helped Destruction of Greek Jewry," in Jewish Week (April, 1978), 13-19.
35. Isaiah Trunk, *Judenrat* (New York, 1972), 27. 36. Ibid., 572.

THE HOLOCAUST OF YUGOSLAVIAN JEWS
by Haham Dr. Solomon Gaon

In Yugoslavia, the Sephardim and Ashkenazim lived united in one community, each of them preserving their religious and social traditions and their particular outlook. They lived united, and united they were murdered and burned.

Yugoslavia, before the Second World War, was a federated kingdom. The Sephardim were mainly found in Serbia, Macedonia, Bosnia and Herzegovina, as well as Dalmatia. A great change in the number of Jews living in this part of the kingdom took place in the 16th century with the arrival of the refugees from Spain.

In Bosnia and Herzegovina, the Jewish exiles from Spain began to settle in the 15th and 16th centuries. This province was then part of the Ottoman Empire. In 1878 Bosnia and Herzegovina was occupied by the Austria-Hungarian Empire. This change brought the immigration of the Ashkenazim. Before then, these communities were entirely Sephardic.

The settlement of Sephardim on the Dalmatian coast, especially in Split (Spolato) and Dubrovnik (Ragusa) pre-dates the expulsion from Spain in 1492.

The Yugoslav Jews were organized in a Federation of Jewish Communities which came into existence in 1919, and whose statutes were ratified by the Ministry of Religious Affairs in 1921. In this Federation, the Sephardim and Ashkenazim, who were the majority, cooperated in a most friendly manner. This cooperation found expression in the fact that the Chief Rabbi of Yugoslavia was a Sephardi, Dr. Isaac Alcalay. The first Jewish Seminary to be established in Yugoslavia was founded in 1928 by the Federation and was situated in Sarajevo, the great center of Sephardic life in Yugoslavia.

There were 75,000 Jews in Yugoslavia in 1941, of which only 20 - 22 thousand were Sephardim. On April 6th of that year, the Germans attacked the country and immediately began to murder the Jews. The invaders and their quislings killed 60,000 of the Jewish population of Yugoslavia.(1) Yugoslavia, after the Nazi-conquest, was divided into different districts, some under direct German occupation. Bosnia and Herzegovina became part of the so-called Free Croatian State with Pavelic at its head. Dalmatia was occupied by the Italians. The most cruel rulers were the Croats; according to different reports even worse than the Germans. The Croats never reconciled themselves to the inferior position they believed they held in old Yugoslavia in comparison to the Serbs. On April 16 1941, the Germans entered Sarajevo and immediately encouraged the mob, consisting mostly of Moslems, to fall upon the great Sephardi synagogue and to rob its beautiful furniture. The parts that they could not steal, they destroyed. In addition, they entered the offices of the community and its library, with many precious books of great antiquity and with irreplaceable archives and wrought destruction upon this ancient Jewish heritage. The Pinkas of Sarajevo going back to the 17th century were taken away and never found. The Sarajevo Hagada of the 13th or 14th century in Spain was saved by the ingenuity and courage of the curator of the Sarajevo museum.

On August 1, 8 Jews were shot by the Ustasi (the name of the army of the Croats). When the family of the murdered made inquiries, they were given a cynical reply by Bozidar Bralo, a priest who was the representative of the Croatian government in Sarajevo: "Do not worry about them, I saved their soul." The fact was that he baptized them making them believe that thereby they would save their lives. He added, "I did not guarantee that they would be left alive."(2) This contemptuous deceit was often used by Catholic priests. In my own town, Travnik, I was told by a survivor that some Jews went to the Jesuits, in whose secondary school many Jews, including myself, received their education and asked them to help save their lives. All that these "humanitarian" teachers could offer them was baptism, which would at least save their souls. The most cruel murderers in the concentration camps were the priests. My cousin, Yerko Gaon, who saved himself from the concentration camp of Jasenovac, relates in the book "Memoirs of Jasenovac" (1972; p.149) how he saw his eldest brother Solomon being cruelly murdered in 1942. This crime, he told me personally, was committed by a Catholic priest, who was, after the liberation of Yugoslavia, apprehended and condemned to death. In the palace of Stepinac, the Bishop of Zagreb (Croatia), the golden teeth of the murdered Jews were found. When after the liberation, the Yugoslavian authorities restricted the freedom of movement of this Bishop, there were protests not only from the Vatican, but also from the Archbishop of Canterbury, Dr. Fisher. In my interview with him I told him that this Bishop was a war criminal and offered him proof of this fact, then did he withdraw his protest. I have no doubt that Pope Pius XII was aware of the part that the Catholic priests and bishops were playing in the elimination of the Jews of Yugoslavia, but he did not make any move even to warn them against these crimes. When he was attacked for this after the war, not only the Vatican, but the Catholic world as a whole, found every possible excuse for his lack of action and for his cooperation with the Nazis.

Before the war there lived in the territories of Bosnia and Herzegovina about 14,000 Jews. Over 11,000 perished; 9,000 from Sarajevo alone.(3)

It has to be admitted that the Communist Party was the most active in trying to help save the Jews. Already, on July 4th, this party issued its historic appeal calling upon the people to start an uprising. In 1941 five hundred Jews from Bosnia joined Tito's liberation army.(4) Even in those difficult days, when the Jews in Bosnia were taken by surprise by the ferocity and cruelty of the occupying forces, they did not become entirely disorganized. Relatively small communities like Travnik, Mostar and larger ones like Sarajevo and Split, were without financial means because their property had been robbed by the Ustasi and the Germans. They, however, did not think of themselves, but invested great efforts in order to help those of their brethren, who tried to find temporary refuge in their town. Moreover, the enemy commissars supervised the activities of the Jewish communities, which made it almost impossible for them to be of help to those, who, in their agony, turned to them for support and guidance.(5)

In addition to Bosnia, many Sephardi communities were to be found in Serbia and Macedonia. There is evidence that the Jews lived in those provinces in the third century C.E. The Jewish population was considerably enlarged by the arrival of the Jews from Spain in the 16th century. The largest community was in Belgrade.

On April 12, 1941, the German army entered Belgrade which was almost entirely destroyed by the Nazi air force. The German soldiers immediately began to enter Jewish shops and homes, pillaging their contents. In this, they were guided by the local quislings. In Belgrade at that time, there lived 12,000 Jews. After the registration, most of them were sent to forced labor. When the older people were taken to the concentration camps, children of ages 12 to 15 had to take their place to do hard and very often dangerous manual work.(6)

Executions of Jews were frequent in Belgrade and its surroundings as the Germans and Serbian quislings were very nervous about possible uprisings and sabotage. On July 29 1941, 122 Jews were killed by a firing squad. During the first two and a half months of occupation, the Germans interned and killed over 5,000 Jews.(7)

In December 1941, women and children were taken to a special concentration camp in Sajmiste. Many of these internees, over 6,000 of them, were cruelly murdered in this camp.(8)

Not only the Germans, but also the soldiers of quisling Mihaylovic' added to the sufferings of the Jews in Serbia.

Draza Mihaylovic', who was supposed to have raised the banner of revolt against the Nazi occupation, soon began to collaborate with the Germans on the pretext that he wanted to fight against the communists and protect the monarchy. His soldiers, the "Chetniks," also took an active part in the persecution of the Jews. They were responsible for numerous murders.

Before the war, there were 837 Jewish-owned business institutions in Belgrade. All were pillaged and destroyed by the Germans and their quislings. By August, 1942, Serbia was for all intents and purposes "Judenrein."(9)

We have details on the activities of the Nazis based on the memoirs of Emilio Tolentino, the late president of the Jewish community of Dubrovnik.

The Jewish community of Dubrovnik numbered, on the eve of World War II, 148 members, 87 residing in Dubrovnik and the rest in the surrounding smaller localities. In the course of the first two years of Nazi occupation (1941-1942) about 1,600 Jewish refugees arrived in Dubrovnik. They were trying to escape from the regions occupied by the German troops and the Ustasi. Dubrovnik was occupied by the Italians. The Gestapo insisted, through the Italian government and with Mussolini's consent, that in the regions occupied by the Italian army, all anti-Jewish measures should be carried out as in the rest of Europe under German occupation. Finally, all the Jews were to be extradited to the Germans in order to be deported to the concentration camps in the East.

During the first months of occupation, when the civil authority was held by Ustasi, the Jews were subject to all measures that applied to occupied territories: they had to wear the yellow badge, their property was confiscated, they were prohibited to circulate freely through the town, many Jews were arrested and some of them deported to the concentration camps. E. Tolentino gives a description of how the Germans, in July 1941, aided by Ustasi, confiscated the archives of the Jewish community, together with the most important "Pinkas" dating from the 17th century. They could not find the Sifre Torah and other valuable objects from the synagogue museum, because they were hidden by the Tolentino family at the very beginning of the occupation. The Tolentino family was cruelly tortured but would not divulge the hiding place of these valuables which are now again to be found in the old synagogue dating from the 15th century.

When the Italian military command assumed the civil administration in September 1941, the arrests and deportations ceased, but the Jews lived in great distress. The greatest problem of the Jewish community was how to lodge and feed a large number of refugees, as well as how to collect funds, sending food and clothes to concentration camps in the territory of the "Independent State of

Croatia" in which the Germans and Ustasi had already imprisoned tens of thousands of Jews. When, in November 1942, the Gestapo continued to exert increasing pressure, in order to obtain the extradition of all Jews, the Command of the VI Italian Army Corps managed to elude the order, itself establishing three concentration camps for those Jews who were at that time in Dubrovnik. These camps were situated in Gruz, Kupari and on the island of Lopud. The Gestapo, however, was not satisfied with this measure. The Italian command, therefore, transported the Jews from its occupation zones to a new concentration camp on the island of Rab, where they remained until the Italian capitulation, on September 9, 1943. Several hundreds of young men and girls joined the armed struggle against the German invaders. The older people took part in various activities of the people's authority in the liberated partisan territory.

Of 87 autochthonous Jews of Dubrovnik - not including the refugees who sojourned temporarily in the town - 24 took part in the struggle for people's liberation and 6 of them fell in battle; 27 individuals lost their lives as victims of Fascism.

THE JEWS OF MACEDONIA

The main towns where the Jews lived in this province were Skoplje, Bitolj (Monastir) and Nish. Members of these communities were nearly all Sephardim. The community of Monastir was the oldest and its Jewish life was very active. Many of the people of Monastir already at the beginning of this century had began to emigrate to Palestine and America. It was one of the economically poorest communities of Yugoslavia, yet the most advanced in Sephardi tradition, Jewish education and loyalty to Zion.

After the Nazi invasion, the Jews of Macedonia came under the nominal rule of Bulgaria, who always claimed Macedonia as its own province as the Italians did Dalmatia. Many of the Jews of Serbia came to Skoplje and Monastir after the invasion, hoping to escape the cruel persecution of the Nazis and the Chetniks. The Bulgarians, however, were not like the Italians who tried to protect the Jews. The Bulgarians eventually gave in to Nazi pressure and arranged with the Germans to deport the Jews of Macedonia to German concentration camps. In March 1943, 8,000 Jews from Bitolj and Skoplje and other towns were shipped to the notorious camp of Treblinka.(10) None of them came back.(11)

The Bulgarian government at the same time confiscated all the property of the Jews who had been deported.

Today there are few Jews in Skoplje, but none in Monastir and Nish.

What is the future of the Jews of Yugoslavia? As in Greece, the community still lives remembering the past. Owing to the small number of Jews left it is not sure of its future. The Jews are free to leave the country and maintain their contacts with Israel and other Jewish communities. In spite of all the difficulties, the Federation of the Jewish Communities provides, as much as possible, the remnant of 6,000 people with a spiritual and cultural Jewish life. It publishes monthly booklets keeping the Jews informed about events in different communities in Yugoslavia and abroad. This Federation, in keeping with the traditions of Yugoslav Jewry, is bravely facing the challenges of the time.

With the end of the Sephardi communities in the Balkans, especially in Greece and Yugoslavia, not only had the traditions from Spain prevalent in these countries came to an end, but also the Judeo-Spanish, the Ladino language spoken by the majority of those communities and used, also, in their prayers. These communities, especially Salonica, Monastir and Sarajevo, had their communal organization, as well as their educational institutions modeled on the pattern of ancient Spanish Jewry. Turkey is the only country where these traditions still survive to some extent. The pressures of successive Turkish governments, however, on the Jews to comply with Turkish national requirements are bringing to an end the Judeo-Spanish tradition in these communities, too.

While in Athens for the commemoration of the 40th anniversary of the deportation of the Greek Jews to the concentration camps, I met the representative of the Jewish communities of Yugoslavia. Only when he gave me his name did I realized that as a young man he had been one of my students. We had not seen each other for over 50 years, therefore, it was not surprising that at first we did not recognize each other. He said to me, "It is not the 50 years of absence that makes recognition difficult, but we are now different people while we were the same when I knew you. The Nazis have not merely destroyed our parents and families, but also our way of life. We are living in cemeteries and memories".

The way of life of the Sephardim has been entirely annihilated, even more than it was the case with our Ashkenazi brethren. The Yeshivot in Poland, the academies in Germany, the great Rashe Yeshiva and the famous scholars in these lands have been destroyed. But the Ashkenazim had, even before the war, built Yeshivot and centers of learning in America and in Israel. Consequently, they were not entirely deprived of their cultural and spiritual resources as in the case of the Sephardim.

Another problem that faces the Sephardim is that the historical documents on which no scholarly research has been done, have been destroyed or stolen and not found, e.g. the Pinkasim of Sarajevo, Dubrovnik, Salonica and many others. These cannot be replaced. The Yeshivot of Salonica, Amsterdam and Constantinople, that provided

Rabbinic scholars even for Israel and were guided by the traditions of Spanish Jewry, are no longer. Their place of a broader Rabbinic and secular education has not been taken by any other institutions in Israel. The proof can be found in the personalities of Rishonim le Zion. After Yaacov Meir and Ben Zion Uziel, the bearers of the Spanish rabbinic traditions, there followed Rishonim le Zion of the Middle Eastern school. They are great scholars and halachists, but in outlook they are different from their predecessors.

The Judeo-Spanish (Ladino) language and literature have also been the tragic victims. While Yiddish is being in many ways revived by scholars who lived outside Europe or who escaped from Europe, the same effort is not being made as far as Ladino and its literature are concerned. The Ladino Theater that flourished in Sarajevo and Salonica is entirely dead, without any hope of resurrection. The great libraries such as those of Sarajevo and Salonica, with the exception of Amsterdam, have disappeared and not been found, as well as manuscripts of scholars and Rabbis.

NOTES

1. Spomenica, (written in Serbian) The memorial volume commemorating the four-hundredth anniversary of the coming of Jews to Bosnia and Herzegovina; published in Sarajevo in 1966.
2. *The Crimes of the Fascists against the Jews of Yugoslavia* (written in Serbian) published by the Federation of the Jewish Communities in Belgrade, 1952; p. 67.
3. *Zbornik* 4; p.241; (a publication of the Federation of Jewish Communities in Yugoslavia, written in Serbian).
4. *The Jews of Yugoslavia;* Friedenreich, Harriet Pass; p. 195 Eleven Jews among them 4 from Sarajevo were designated National Heroes.
5. *Zbornik* 4; p. 242
6. *The Crimes of the Fascists,* p.3
7. Op.cit., p.15

8. Many of them were women and children
9. Friedenreich, op.cit., p. 191
10. Friedenreich, op.cit., p.192
11. *The Crimes of the Fascists,* p. 195

THE HOLOCAUST IN SALONICA
by Prof. David F. Altabe

One might ask, "What is the significance of the history of the slaughter of 45,000 Jews in yet another city of Europe?" Why should 45,000 souls have any relevance when we ponder the fate of the six million Jews who were exterminated?" Of course, to those whose relatives were among the Salonican Jews who perished, the question may come as a callous insult to the memory of the departed. But for the answer to have any meaning, it must speak to the hearts of Jew and gentile alike, and to the generations that will follow us on earth. The Torah enjoins us to remember Amalek, and what the Amalekites did to the old and weak exiles who straggled behind the main body of Israel when crossing the Sinai upon their deliverance from Egyptian bondage. It is a lesson for all persecuted minorities. To paraphrase the Passover service, it was not alone our forefathers who were humiliated and annihilated in the Holocaust, but we too, we who identify with them as Jews, and we, Jew or non-Jew, who identify with them as fellow human beings. The crimes committed in Salonica, as in other parts of Europe, are a disgrace to all mankind; the atrocities perpetrated by the Nazis and their followers, a discredit to the entire human race.

The question that is often asked with regard to the Holocaust is: How did the victims allow themselves to be led like sheep to the slaughter?: With reference to communities like Salonica, one asks:

How was it possible for approximately 97% of the Jewish population to be exterminated?

We shall try to give some explanation by examining the chronology of the events that took place there. The source of the information I am about to give is a book published by the Jewish Community of Salonica, edited and written mostly by the noted scholar, Michael Molho, Chief Rabbi of the community, who lived through the horrors described in it. Its title is IN MEMORIAM; HOMMAGE AUX VICTIMES JUIVES DES NAZIS EN GRECE.

October 28, 1940, The Italian army attacked Greece after occupying Albania. Greek resistance proved successful in repelling the attack. Four thousand Jewish men from Salonica served with exemplary valor in the Greek army, motivated, no doubt, by the knowledge that Fascism meant no good for the Jews.

April 6, 1941, The Germans came to the aid of their Italian ally, and subdued the Greeks. The western part of the country, including Athens, was occupied by the Italians; the center, which included Salonica, by the Germans; and the eastern provinces of Thrace and Macedonia were given to the Bulgarians, who were non-combatant allies of the Axis powers.

April 9, 1941, German motorized columns entered Salonica. Stores remained closed. The Germans ordered them reopened, and the Jews slowly returned to their accustomed occupations. All newspapers ceased publication. Only a pro-German Greek newspaper continued to publish. Also, a new one was begun under the auspices of the invading Germans. As might be expected, it was fiercely anti-Semitic.

April 12, 1941, the German army requisitioned Jewish homes and apartments; also, the Jewish hospital, one of the finest in the city.

The offices of the Jewish Community Council remained closed.

It should be mentioned before we go on that, according to the census taken in 1940, there were close to 50,000 Jews in Salonica, and they comprised roughly one-third of the total population of the city. The Jewish community was a tightly organized one, a heritage dating back to Ottoman rule, when the Jews of the Empire were almost autonomous, maintaining their own police, fire and sanitation departments, as well as schools, hospitals and philanthropic organizations. Prior to the war, the religious, cultural and philanthropic activities of the Jewish community were still in the hands of the Community Council, which collected taxes on rents and the sale of kosher products in order to meet the expense of running schools, hospitals, orphanages, old age homes and the cemetery. There were political parties of every stamp; the socialists and the Zionists were strong factions. The delegates to the Council were elected by the community. There was a separate Rabbinical Council in charge of religious affairs.

Two delegates from the Community Council were sent to the German commandant in order to make official contact with the occupying forces. They were denied admittance, and told that they would be called when needed.

April 15, 1941, eight of the leading officers and members of the Council were arrested. Community records, typewriters, mimeograph equipment, etc. were taken from the offices of the Council, as well as a number of books from the rabbinical library.

April 17, 1941, other leaders were arrested: the president of the Bnai Brith, and dealers in typewriters and duplicating equipment. The offices of the Zionist organizations were ransacked in search of cornpromising documents.

April 20, 1941, the Sunday edition of the newspaper founded by the Germans (it was called the Nea Evropi —New Europe) came out with an editorial blaming the Jews for ruining Germany after World War I, and affirming that after the war there would be no more wars because Jews would be eliminated from the political life of Europe. That same day, the Germans visited all the synagogues to take inventory of all the precious objects.

April 29, 1941, the Jews were informed through the Nea Evropi to turn in their radios.

May 1, 1941, the newspapers announced that all Jewish stores that still remained shut would be requisitioned by the Germans.

May 4, 1941, bookstores owned by Jews were requisitioned, their owners arrested.

May 12, 1941, the editors of Nea Evropi expressed encouragement to the reorganization of an anti-Semitic Greek organization that had been banned by the Greek government under Metaxas in the 30's.

May 17, 1941, the Chief Rabbi of Salonica, Rabbi Koretz, who had been in Athens when the Germans entered Salonica, was taken into custody. He was sent to an internment camp in Vienna because of a sermon he had delivered against the Axis powers.

May 22, 1941, the Gestapo again visited the synagogues, and removed from one of them a Torah scroll dating from the 16th century.

During these early days, the Jewish community was disorganized, its leaders still in prison. Finally, the Germans named one of the Council members that had been arrested as the new leader. They selected perhaps the weakest, least intelligent and most vain of the lot, one they knew they could manipulate. Nevertheless, the community was grateful that there was someone back in charge to look after their interests, or so they believed.

The Chief Rabbi, Koretz, was also released from his internment in Vienna, and returned to his post.

The Greek Prime Minister, General Tsolaoglou, declared in a press interview that there was no "Jewish question" in Greece, and that Jews, whose patriotism in the defense of their nation was appreciated, would be treated no differently than their fellow Greek citizens. This statement, made in public by the chief of state, with the backing of the German au- thorities, was a source of comfort for the Jews and gave them hope.

For a few weeks, things were quiet. No new measures were taken. Then, on June 29, 1941, Germany declared war on Russia. Any Jew suspected of communist leanings was arrested. The Gestapo requisitioned more apartments, and brutally ousted the Jewish occupants. A Jew was executed for beating up a German soldier.

The Germans sent to Salonica a scholar to inspect the rare books and manuscripts stored in the extensive libraries and synagogues of the city. He was the director of the Hebrew section of the Institute for Jewish Studies in Frankfurt. According to Rabbi Molho, he understood quite well the value of the material he was looking for. The result was that tens of thousands of books were expropriated and sent to Germany. What happened to this prized collection, we do not know.

From the onset of the German invasion, food supplies became scarce, and the cost of basic necessities rose sharply. Salonica is a port at the mouth of a river, normally, a very active one. The products of the interior are shipped down the river to the city, and from there transshipped to all parts of the Mediterranean and the world. The city depends on this trade in much the same manner as New York, for its food. Under German occupation, trade came to a halt; the economy was at a standstill.

This particularly hurt the Jewish population. They did not have, like their Greek neighbors, relatives who owned farms in the surrounding villages to whom they could turn for vegetables, eggs, or the occasional chicken.

The Jewish Community Council, with the consent of the Gestapo, began to sell land it owned in order to feed the people. Soup kitchens were set up for the needy so they could be assured of at least one hot meal a day.

To make matters worse, a group of about forty German, Polish, Hungarian and Rumanian Jews were for some reason settled in Salonica by the Germans and pampered by them. Choice apartments were requisitioned for them, and, as Jews, they claimed a right to make all sorts of exorbitant demands on the Council, which put a further drain on the community budget.

The winter of 1941-42 was extremely cold. The undernourished and poorly clad Jews became susceptible to all sort of illnesses. The death rate rose to 60 a day. Before the war, it had been only 15 per week. Without fuel, adequate living space or soap, disease was rampant. Typhus broke out in epidemic proportions. The German health inspector ordered all the Jewish women in one of the poorer quarters of the city to shave their heads. The Greek women did not have to do so, even though their quarter was equally infested with vermin.

Though conditions were as I have described above, no racial laws had yet been applied. From April 1941 to July 1942, the abuses inflicted by the Nazis were of an individual and capricious nature. Agents of the Gestapo abused the Jews, but their acts were sporadic. One day, they seized a rabbi and shaved off half his beard. They entered the office of the representative of the Haham Bashi, the Chief Sephardic Rabbi of Istanbul, and slapped him around. Then they asked him to elaborate on the law of retaliation (an eye for an eye, a tooth for a tooth).

Still, there was not yet any systematic persecution of the Jews. People were lulled into a false sense of security, and were unprepared for the debacle that awaited them.

Suddenly, the order was given on July 11, 1942 that all Jewish males from the ages of 18 to 45 were to appear in the public square to be drafted into forced labor. Nine thousand men were assembled there and forced to stand erect in the hot Mediterranean sun of July from eight to fourteen hours. Any attempt to shield one's eyes from the sun by adjusting a cap or holding up a newspaper, or even putting on sunglasses, was severely punished. There were some who were beaten to death or died as a result of the ordeal. The newspaper founded by the Germans reported that the citizenry was highly entertained by the spectacle. No doubt some individuals might have been, but despite the revulsion the deeds of the day brought to many, there were no mass protests. Neither the Greek Governor General, nor the University faculty, nor its students, nor the unions made any formal declaration of complaint.

The order was given for the men to assemble again on July 13th. This time, they were treated almost with solicitude. Was it the contractors to the military who feared for the condition of their prospective slaves, or the Greek Red Cross who had brought this about? We don't know.

The first group of about 2,000 workers was sent to various work camps to improve the roads, drain swamps, build fortifications, etc. Their daily ration consisted of 300 grams (approximately 10 ounces) of bread, a watery soup, and no meat, or even salt. Whipped to work at hard labor for twelve to fourteen hours a day in the heat of summer in mosquito infested areas, housed in barracks with hardly any room between them, the men died by the hundreds. The Jewish community tried to send food and clothing, but seldom did it reach them. Mortality after two and a half months of work reached twelve percent of those drafted into forced labor.

Many attempts were made by the Jewish community to improve the lot of these men. The communal leaders named by the Germans were pressured by relatives of the men to intercede in their behalf. A joint commission comprised of members of the Council, the Germans and the contractors was set up. Exemptions from this levy were granted to married men, disabled war veterans, and others. Guarantees were given by the German authorities that sanitary conditions would improve. Financial assistance was given to the families of the men pressed into servitude. But the levies continued, and the men were still being literally worked to death.

The Jewish community attempted to ransom these captives. After negotiations, the price was first set by the Germans for their release at two billion drachmas, then raised to three and a half billion —an impossible sum, many times more than the community could raise. The Germans offered a solution. They offered one billion drachmas for the right to expropriate the Jewish cemetery, whose stones would be used for military purposes. On October 16, 1942, the Rabbinical Council met to consider this offer. The question: "Was it permissible to allow such a sacrilege to be committed in order to save the living?"

Their decision was Solomon-like. Under no circumstances could the community make the cemetery the object of a monetary transaction. The maximum amount the community could hope to raise was two billion drachmas. If the Germans insisted upon expropriating the cemetery, the community had no alternative but to submit to their demands. The total of two billion Drachmas was, thus, made payable by December 15, 1942 by a tax imposed on the community and from Salonican Jews living in Athens.

Despite the worthiness of the cause, the people were torn between paying what was asked of them and the need to conserve their last pennies in view of their precarious economic situation. Money could mean life or death. One could buy false identity papers with it, perhaps even safe passage to a secure hiding place. In spite of this, only three recalcitrants had to be turned over to the German authorities in order to be forced to pay. Approximately 1,400,000,000 drachmas were collected. Another two hundred million would be forthcoming from Athens within a couple of months, but the entire debt was eliminated in short order by the events that took place within the three months that followed.

December 6, 1942, the cemetery was expropriated and turned into a vast marble quarry. The Germans used the marble to line a swimming pool for the troops. The Greeks took stones for their houses. The bones of the dead lay exposed in open graves.

February 6, 1943 Shabbat. A commission of the S.S. arrived in Salonica to proceed with the application of the racial laws promulgated in Nurenburg in 1935. The first act was to order the wearing of the Jew badge, the star of David on a yellow patch identifying the wearer as a Jew. Jewish homes and businesses were likewise to be identified as such.

February 13, 1943. The further application of racial laws prohibited the Jews from:

1. changing their residence
2. using trolleys or other means of public transportation
3. appearing on the street or in public places after dark
4. using public telephones.

Private telephones were to be turned in, except for those belonging to doctors or members of the Community Council. It is obvious that the Germans wished to cut off all communication between the Jews and the outside world, and even between the Jews themselves. Radios had already been confiscated, the press closed, duplicating equipment seized.

Two zones of the city were designated as ghettos. By March 25, 1943, all Jews had to be quartered within them. Christians living in the areas designated for the Jews were to be moved to quarters abandoned by Jews. The explanation given by the Germans was that these centers would be autonomous municipal and commercial entities. A Jewish militia was organized to act as a police force with the responsibility of seeing to it that everyone behaved as ordered, and that the move to the ghettos went smoothly. There were many who saw the act of creating a Jewish police force as proof that the Jews would be allowed to govern their own affairs.

The Chief Rabbi, Rabbi Koretz, zealously went about exhorting the community to comply with the orders given. He feared that if the German orders were not scrupulously carried out, worse measures might be taken by them. Rabbi Koretz organized a group that worked around the clock to manufacture sufficient Jew badges for all. Each Magen David bore a number, which was carefully recorded and assigned to each Jew. A list was kept of the names and numbers.

Every Jew over the age of five was given two yellow badges, one to be worn on a shirt or dress, and another for a jacket or coat.

It is to the credit of their Greek Orthodox neighbors that the Jews were not humiliated any further by them for wearing this opprobrious symbol. Indeed, the priests and teachers preached to their flocks against these measures, and ordered the children to refrain from any temptation to ridicule the wearers of the yellow badge. Even the Germans seemed not to take undue notice of Jews wearing the star.

February 25, 1943. General Simeonides, Governor General of Salonica, was informed by the Gestapo that labor unions and professional organizations were to exclude Jewish membership. They were also banned from making any protest in defense of the Jews.

March 1, 1943, the Jews were ordered to declare all their possessions, from real estate and bank accounts to the most insignificant article of clothing. This was said to be merely for statistical purposes. Anyone attempting to hide anything was subject to severe penalty.

It must be said in passing that this measure, as well as some of those previously mentioned, gave rise to blackmail and extortion by Jew against Jew, as well as by the Greeks.

Although everything was done by the Germans to allay the suspicions of the Jews, many had a premonition of what was to happen. They tried to evade the orders, to hide, to escape to the Italian sector, to reach Athens, where they would be comparatively safe. Some were caught in the attempt and were summarily shot by the Germans. The executions took place in the ghetto to serve as a warning to other Jews who might have such ideas. Rabbi Koretz pleaded with the people not to endanger the community by acts of disobedience.

The Jews were, of course, forbidden to leave the ghetto. It was walled in, and machine guns and searchlights were placed on surrounding buildings. The High Command of the S.S. headquartered itself in the midst of the ghetto to ensure compliance with its orders.

Bank clerks worked night and day in the office of Rabbi Koretz to prepare the inventory of possessions the Jews were ordered to produce. The pressure put upon them by the German authorities and by Rabbi Koretz was constant. The records had to be turned in as soon as possible.

March 13, 1943. All personal possessions and bank accounts were to be turned over to the Jewish Community Council by the 15th. One hundred and four hostages were taken by the Nazis to make sure this was done. Rabbi Koretz gave them his personal guarantee that no harm would come to them.

Suddenly, three hundred and thirty freight cars pulled into the railroad station in the heart of the ghetto. The news came that all the Jews were to be deported to Krakow, Poland.

March 14, 1943 Sunday. The S.S. ordered Rabbi Koretz to assemble all the Jews in the largest synagogue in the ghetto in order to announce their forthcoming departure. Rabbi Koretz was still confident that no harm would come to them. He was reassuring.

"The great Jewish community of Krakow will welcome you and oversee that you establish yourselves properly," he told them. "You will each be given work according to your ability and liking. What else is there to do but to resign ourselves?"

In the vain belief that what Rabbi Koretz told them was true, people sold or exchanged what they had for warm clothing, boots —anything they thought they might need to live in the colder climate of Poland. The first convoy left on March 16th, the second, the next day. We are all too familiar with the scene: Jews herded into cattle cars, the doors locked and sealed, the people with hardly any room to breathe. Many died of asphyxiation before they ever reached Auschwitz. Jews from the second ghetto were moved to the embarkation point as the first convoys left.

March 17, 1943. A delegation from the community appeared before Rabbi Koretz to demand an explanation. He told them that he would address the entire congregation in the synagogue at 4:00 p.m. that day. There he exhorted them to have courage —to make sacrifices for the less fortunate so they would arrive in a presentable condition in Krakow, "for the good of the name of the Jews of Salonica," he said. He spoke glowingly of the many marriages that had taken place among those who were about to depart. The patience of the congregants was by now exhausted by the continual deterioration of the state of affairs. Some made an attempt to seize the rabbi. They would have lynched him if it had not been for the intervention of the Jewish police.

People prayed that a miracle might save them. It was the month of Adar, the month of the miraculous deliverance of the Jews of Persia at the time of Queen Esther who, like them, had faced death. Their hopes soared when, suddenly, the convoys ceased. It was rumored that Turkey had entered the war on the side of the Allies.

What had happened, however, was that the Todt Commission, charged with the installation of fortifications in Greece, needed three thousand more workers. Activities ceased while Eichmann was consulted. About one thousand men were recruited, later, others. These were exempted from the deportations for the moment.

Some Jews managed to escape, but a good number were turned

in to the Gestapo by those whom they had paid to arrange safe passage for them to Athens, to the mountains or to Turkey by sea.

Rabbi Koretz himself was arrested by the S.S. and removed from office as President of the community. He had assumed these temporal powers in addition to his rabbinical office. He and his family were confined to the ghetto and eventually deported, as were members of the Jewish police, and almost all who had collaborated with the Germans. I say almost, because one of the most infamous of the lot, one who was given command of the police and used his office to extort vast sums of money from his fellow Jews, was allowed safe passage to Albania. Other members of the Jewish police were sent by the Gestapo as agents to Athens, to ferret out Salonican Jews hiding there.

Between March 15 and May 9, 1943, sixteen convoys carried away 42,830 Jews from Salonica. The last group of Jews to be deported were 1,800 men who had survived the forced labor they had been conscripted to. They were already half dead when they boarded the transport on August 7, 1943. In all, 45,659 Jews had been deported to Birkenau (Auschwitz) and 441 to Bergen Belsen. The latter included 367 who held Spanish passports, who were subsequently sent to Morocco and from there to Palestine.

Only about 450 who were Italian subjects, and over 100 more saved by the Italians, were able to escape. The chivalry and kindness of the Italians is praised by Molho, and all they did to save as many Jews as they could remains to their credit in the annals of history.

In answer to the question, "How was it possible for such a high percentage (almost ninety seven percent) of the Jewish population of Salonica to be completely obliterated?", the following reasons have been set forth by Rabbi Molho, the editor of the study I mentioned.

1. The encouragement and the reassurances given by the Chief Rabbi, Koretz. Thousands of victims renounced any attempt to evade German orders in the face of the assertions that came from a man of such importance, one who spoke German, and had daily contact with the Germans, and who, himself, had been interned by them.

2. The lack of liquid assets. One had to have enough money to buy a false passport, and to hire guides to freedom, and still have money to live on while in hiding.

3. The difficulty in masking one's Jewish identity. Only the young who had received their education after Salonica had been turned over to the Greeks in the aftermath of World War I spoke Greek fluently or without accent. Another factor was the number of Jews involved. In Athens, for example, where there were only three thousand Jews living among one million Greeks, and where Greek police helped Jews by issuing false identity cards and the Church by issuing fake baptismal certificates, and where the Italian authorities went out of their way to defy German orders, the Jews were able to fuse with the general population and escape detection. In Salonica, the situation was quite different. The Jews accounted for about one third the population, too large a number to be swallowed.

4. The frequency of the denunciations and betrayals by the Greeks exaggerated the fears of those Jews who might have attempted to escape. They felt they could not expect much help from the Greek populace in the event that they succeeded in evading the Germans.

5. The terror inspired by the Germans. The apparent efficiency of the German army and the Gestapo made one think that it would

be impossible to get away undetected. It must be added that the Germans in Salonica had followed the same planned and pre-programmed method which they had employed in many of the other areas they had occupied. Everything was done to allay the fears of the people and to hide from them the fate that the Nazis had decreed long before the war had begun. The consistently planned deception lasted right into the gas chambers, where the victims were given bars of soap and told they were to take showers. The tightly guarded people who witnessed the capricious cruelty of their guards, and the summary executions of those who attempted to resist or escape, had little alternative but to hope that the Germans were telling them the truth.

6. The distance between Salonica and the centers of Greek partisan resistance was too great to travel easily without detection. In Salonica, there was a lack of contact between the Greek people, and even a general lack of organized resistance among the Greeks. If a young Jew did want to escape and join the partisans, to whom could he or she turn? Members of the resistance did not openly advertise their identities, or seek recruits.

7. Family solidarity. The young would not leave their aged parents to the mercy of the Germans. The elders were reluctant to allow the young to expose themselves to the dangers of flight and resistance. There were even Jews who had intermarried, and were thus exempt from the more extreme measures, who easily could have escaped but who abandoned their Christian spouses to look after their Jewish parents and suffer with their brethren.

8. The rapidity with which the Germans acted when they forced the Jews to move into the ghettos and then deported them from there within a month.

9. The zeal with which the Jewish administrators complied with German orders and helped the Gestapo establish its goals. According to Molho, Rabbi Koretz, in his efficiency, was one of the best collaborators the Germans had. In all fairness to Rabbi Koretz, it must be mentioned that the Jewish communal leaders in other cities and countries acted in much the same manner. We must assume that he was motivated by a sincere desire to save as many of his flock as he could, and that he sincerely believed that the best way of doing so was to cooperate with the German authorities. That he, like so many others, was duped by them, is a great tragedy. The German deception had been carefully planned long in advance. As Hitler's Minister of Propaganda, Herr Goebbels had put it, "A lie told often enough becomes the truth." It was a dictum the Germans followed in all their dealings. They used it with Lord Chamberlain when they marched into Czechoslovakia claiming that all they wanted was the German-speaking area, the Sudetenland. They used lies when they allied themselves with the Russians to carve up Poland. It was the keystone of their policy, and uppermost in their plans was the complete elimination of Jews from Europe. This was one of their primary objectives. There can be no doubt about it. In the last days of the war, when German defeat was imminent, trains carrying Jews to Auschwitz had priority over those that might have been used by the German army to bring reinforcements to the front lines. The Gestapo was kept busy to the very end hunting and killing Jews.

Hitler's war was a war against the Jews. What he planned to do he had written in *Mein Kampf,* in 1925. The efforts and expenditures of time and money, men and material to achieve this aim are clear evidence of this. The drain on German resources that this entailed created, of the six million Jewish martyrs, a vital force that helped defeat Germany. Their sacrifice saved the lives of many Allied fighting men.

Today in Salonica, there remains hardly a trace of Jewish existence in that city. Official guidebooks make no mention of the fact that Jews settled in Salonica soon after its founding by Alexander the Great in 316 B.C.E. The city that was known as "Ir v'em b'Israel," famous as a center of Jewish learning after the settlement of the Sephardim there upon their expulsion from Spain, is practically "Judenrein." At the turn of the twentieth century, half of the inhabitants of the city were Jewish, if not two thirds. The gentile had to have some rudimentary knowledge of Judeo-Spanish to get by. The port was closed on Shabbat. There were fourteen newspapers in Judeo-Spanish, and political parties of all persuasions. Plays were performed in that language, and novels published. True, many changes took place once the city was lost to the Greeks after World War I. Yet, before the outbreak of World War II, the Jews still counted for one third of the inhabitants, and contributed mightily to the culture and economy of the city.

The Nazis destroyed all this, but as long as there shall remain the printed word, the evidence of their infamous destruction of Jewish Salonica will stand as an indictment to their eternal condemnation.

DESTRUCTION OF THE JEWS OF RHODES*
by Dr. Marc D. Angel

The migration to and from Rhodes made a strong impact on the nature of the community. Moreover, the effects of Italianization tended to move the community away from its old traditions and patterns of thought. It was a community in process: it was changing rapidly and in many ways.

But before the Rhodeslies had time to understand or feel comfortable with the changes of the 20th century, events beyond their control caused the community's development to cease. The Nazis had taken power in Germany. Their program of world domination and destruction of Jews began to be felt in Rhodes.

When Italy aligned itself with Germany in June, 1936, the Italian government began to reflect subtle changes in its attitude towards Jews. Some marks of honor which were to have gone to Jews were rescinded.(1)

In the first half of December, 1936, Mario de Vecchi de Val Cismon was appointed governor of the Dodecanese Islands. An archfascist, his arrival marked the beginning of severe anti-Jewish measures in Rhodes. The Rabbinical College was closed. Jews were required to keep their stores open on the Sabbath and Jewish festivals.

*Reprinted from *The Jews of Rhodes* by Marc D. Angel, N.Y., Sepher-Hermon Press, 1978.

De Vecchi even demanded one hundred tombstones from the Jewish cemetery for use as building material for his new house. De Vecchi's predecessors used to visit the Jewish synagogues on Rosh Hashanah. De Vecchi, however, demanded that the Jewish Community Council visit him on that holy day.(2)

On September 1, 1938, the Italian newspapers announced the establishment of anti-Jewish laws. The local officials in Rhodes upheld this legislation strictly. Ritual slaughter of animals was prohibited. Jews could not buy property, employ non-Jewish servants, send their children to government schools. Non-Jews were not allowed to patronize Jewish doctors or pharmacists.(3)

Jewish children expelled from non-Jewish schools became estranged from their gentile friends. They studiously avoided meeting eyes when passing each other in the street.(4) For a short time, de Vecchi converted the Jewish schools into government schools where the Jewish children were given rudimentary instruction, fascist-oriented. However, the schools were soon returned to the community, albeit in a disorganized state.(5)

An anti-Jewish law published in September, 1938, ordered Jews who had come to Rhodes after January, 1919, to leave the island. Affecting about five hundred people, most of whom had come to Rhodes from Asian Turkey, Greece and Bulgaria due to the consequences of the first World War, the deadline for departure was March 12, 1939. Hizkiah Franco, a leader of the Jewish community, went to Paris to solicit aid from the Alliance Israelite Universelle, hoping to activate the large Jewish organizations in France and England to use their political influence on behalf of the Jews of Rhodes.(6)

While these political efforts were under way, a delegation of Jews from Jerusalem came to the island in an attempt to alter the government's decree and improve Jewish morale. The three-man committee —Abraham Elmaleh, David Aboulafia and Abraham Franco— met de Vecchi and argued that it was illegal to expel the Jews who had come to Rhodes after 1919, since they were granted Italian citizenship through the Treaty of Lausanne. De Vecchi, however, remained firm. But he did grant a one month reprieve, extending the expulsion date to April 15, 1939.(7) This extra month was little consolation to the victims and deep despair prevailed. One member of the community committed suicide.(8)

Following these events, Hizkiah Franco received word from the Alliance Israelite Universelle that their intervention with the Italian government had succeeded. Mussolini admitted that Jews who gained Italian citizenship through the Treaty of Lausanne could not be expelled. De Vecchi then made an ambiguous statement implying that the decree of expulsion would be suspended, but not indicating how long the suspension would be. Fearful and uncertain, the majority of the Jews in question left Rhodes. They were assisted by the officers of the Jewish community of Rhodes who provided the necessary passports and identification. Many of these exiles went to Naples, then to Tangier. Some went to Palestine.(9)

In May, 1939, an old ship docked in Rhodes to pick up several hundred Jews who were susceptible to expulsion. Approximately six hundred Eastern European Jewish refugees were already aboard. The ship was one of the "secret" ships of "illegal" emigration to Palestine. But before the vessel had traveled far from Rhodes, a fire broke out on board. The passengers safely reached the Island of Samos, but they had lost nearly all their baggage. The unhappy victims were transported back to Rhodes after midnight. The Rhodes Jews returned to their homes. The East European Jews were allowed to sleep in the stadium of the city. The next morning, the Jews of Rhodes brought food and clothing to the Jews in the stadium and even organized a kitchen on the premises.

In a short time, the community managed to procure another old ship and the refugees sailed to Palestine. The community also arranged for the transport of about three hundred Jews to Tangier. Jews of Rhodes origin from throughout the world sent money to help in these relief efforts.(10)

Admiral I. Campione became governor of Rhodes in July, 1942, and openly manifested his sympathy for the Jews by rectifying various anti-Jewish measures. For example, under previous administrators, the Jews were given less food rations than other residents of Rhodes. Campione demanded an equal division of provisions to all citizens, including Jews.(11)

Though the Jews' status improved somewhat, the community still suffered severe hardships. On February 2, 1944, eight Jews were killed by bombs dropped by British planes and many Jewish homes were destroyed. On the first day of Passover, 1944, twenty-six Jews were killed by bombs when they left the synagogue after morning prayers.(12) Thus, even the enemies of the Nazi-fascist alliance inadvertently killed Jews.

Military developments led to new uncertainties. On July 24, 1943, Mussolini was removed from power. His successor struck an armistice with the Allies on September 8, 1943, and the Jews of Rhodes thought their troubles were over. But contrary to their expectations, the Germans occupied Rhodes, overcoming the far more numerous Italian forces on the island. On July 19, 1944, the Germans ordered all Jews to appear the next morning at the aeronautic command at Tchemenlik.

A German officer told Jacob Shalem Franco, President of the Jewish community, to tell all the Jews to bring enough baggage and provisions for a ten day period. He was also told to ask them to bring all their valuables within twelve hours. The Jews were told that they would be temporarily installed in a small island near Rhodes. When the Jews appeared on July 20, their valuables were confiscated.

On July 23, 1944, the Jews were crowded into three small freight ships. At the port of Leros, the ships from Rhodes met one from Cos, which held one hundred Jewish victims from that island. After four days in Leros, they went to Samos, finally landing in Piraeus on July 31, 1944. Five Jews died due to the hardships of the voyage. The Jews were then placed in the concentration camp at Haydar, near Athens, where ten more died. On August 3, the survivors were crowded into trains and shipped to Auschwitz. Of the Jews who were deported from Rhodes, only 151 survived. Twenty-two had died on the voyage, 1145 at Auschwitz, and 437 in the labor camps.(13) The Sephardi community in Rhodes was born as the result of the expulsion of the Jews from Spain. It died in the ashes of the German concentration camps.

Thirty-nine Rhodes Jews escaped deportation because they or their spouses had Turkish nationality, and were protected by the Turkish consul in Rhodes.(14) But they too suffered greatly. They were required to appear each morning at 8 a.m. before the Gestapo, and were held for one or two hours without reason. Famine, inadequate medical care, and constant British bombardment of the island broke their morale and threatened their lives.

On August 8, these Jews were told that they would be sent to Athens where their Turkish nationality would be contested. Then they were told that genuine Turkish subjects could remain in Rhodes, but their spouses and children were to be deported the next morning. These threats were not carried out, but they served to frighten the hopeless victims.(15)

When the Nazis were finally defeated, a double emotion filled the survivors. They were relieved that the unspeakable horrors had ended; they were grief-stricken when they realized the extent of the tragedy which had occurred. April 16, 1945 brought liberation. On May 8, 1945, the armistice was signed, officially bringing the war to an end. The primary problem of the Rhodian Jewish survivors was not to reconstruct the Rhodes Jewish community: that was almost an impossibility. Their main concern was to reconstruct their own shattered lives. They had to free those Jews still in bondage, to settle them in new homes, to start new lives. From the ashes, new life was to emerge.(16)

Following the war, Rhodes was under English military occupation. It went to Greece on March 31, 1947. During this short period, some of the survivors of the war had made their way back to Rhodes. In April 1946, there were about fifty Jews in Rhodes.

In order to help the Holocaust survivors, Jews of Rhodes descent throughout the world raised funds. In Rhodesia, the Sephardic Benevolent and Cultural Youth Society collected money for the survivors.(17) In New York, a very active organization was established to help resettle the survivors of war.(18) All other communities of Rhodeslies also assisted in the reconstruction effort.

In April, 1946, the remaining Jews of Rhodes tried to reorganize the community, but the attempt could not succeed.(19) Gradually, Jews left Rhodes to join communities of Rhodeslies in the United States and Africa. Some went to the Holy Land. Only a handful of Jews live in Rhodes at present.

A number of memorials rose to honor the victims of the war. In 1933, the family of Salomon Alhadeff had donated a large park to the city of Rhodes. The head of the municipal council at the time, Alfred

Biloti, had the main street of the park named Salomon Alhadeff Avenue. In 1941, the street name was crossed out by anti-Jewish fascists, and de Vecchi renamed the street after a fascist hero.(20) Following the war, the street was again given the name of Alhadeff. The main avenue through the Jewish quarter was renamed "Martyron Evreon," street of the Jewish martyrs.

A marble plaque was erected in the Jewish cemetery. Inscribed in Greek, French and Hebrew, it says:

> In memory of the 2,000 martyrs of the Jewish community of Rhodes and the Island of Cos, brutally butchered by the barbaric Nazis in the concentration camps of Germany, 1944-45. May their souls rest in peace.

On another portion of the memorial is an alphabetical list of family names of those who were destroyed in the crematoria. Memorials stand where Jewish life once was.

EPILOGUE

The armistice between Israel and her Arab enemies following Israel's War of Independence in 1948 was signed in Rhodes. The presence of Israeli officials and soldiers profoundly affected the few Jews who still lived in the city. The Rhodian survivors of Nazism, the remnants of an ancient and vibrant community, could not help but be moved by the presence of representatives of the new Jewish state, symbol of the rebirth of the Jewish people. A number of Rhodian Jews who lived in Rhodes at the time, or whose relatives lived there, proudly display photographs of the Israelis in Rhodes.

That the State of Israel signed its first armistice in a place where Jewish life had been almost totally wiped out is perhaps symbolic of the experiences of Jewish history. Out of the ashes new life arose. From the pits of despair, dreams and hopes for the future came forth.

In general, Jewish communities in the Diaspora were like flowers without roots. They blossomed, grew and developed; but they were ultimately destroyed or withered away of themselves. Jewish communities in the Land of Israel were for centuries like roots without flowers. They held fast to their ancient land, but they lived in desolation, in poverty, and in small numbers. Now, in Rhodes, the root and the flower were joined together symbolically. The destruction of a large segment of Diaspora Jewry was followed by the re-establishment of Jewish government in Eretz Israel. The Guardian of Israel neither slumbers nor sleeps.

NOTES

1. Albert Franco, *History of the Rhodes League of Brothers* (New York, 1954), pp. 17-18. This is a pamphlet.
2. Ibid., pp. 19-21;79.
3. Ibid., pp. 30-4.
4. From interview with Mrs. Esther Shear of New York.
5. Franco, p. 57; Galante, Appendice, pp. 29-31.
6. Franco, pp. 60-63.
7. Ibid., pp. 63-65.
8. Ibid., pp. 66-67.
9. Ibid., pp. 70-72. Information was also drawn from an interview with Mr. Sami Notrica of New York who was an official of the community at that period.
10. Franco, p. 74; Galante, Appendice, p.33.
11. Franco, pp. 87-89.
12. Ibid., pp. 90-91.
13. Ibid., pp. 100-109; Galante, Appendice, pp. 38-40; Raul Hilberg, *Destruction of European Jews* (Chicago, 1961), pp. 452-3; Joseph Nehama, *In Memoriam: Hommage aux Victimes Juives des Nazis en Grece,* Vol. 2 (Salonika, 1949), pp. 74-6.
14. Franco, pp. 108-9. Information was also drawn from an interview with Mr. and

Mrs. Daniel Turiel and their son Bernard of New York City who lived in Rhodes during the war. Mrs. Turiel was of Turkish nationality.

15. Galante, Appendice, pp. 44-5.
16. Franco, p. 111.
17. Ibid.
18. Leaders of the New York organization included Mr. Acher Touriel, Mr. Victor Tarry, Mr. Hillel Franco, Mr. Marco Shemariah, Mr. Victor Capelluto and others.
19. Galante, Appendice, p. 71.
20. Ibid., pp. 74, 85-7.

MOROCCAN JEWS ON THE ROAD TO AUSCHWITZ
by Dr. M. Mitchell Serels

With the collapse of the French Republic, the Vichy government was installed in a small segment of unoccupied France. The Protectorate government of Morocco, as well as that of Tunisia, became subject to Vichy regulations. While fortunately, Jews in Morocco suffered minimal discomfort, Moroccan Jews elsewhere were declared stateless. The Vichy government refused to accept them as protected persons while the Moroccan government was not independent and could not act independently. This same vague legal status applied to Jews from the Spanish zone, as well as from the international zone. The international zone was occupied by Spain, supposedly to protect the neutral presence in the area. While the Spanish government extended passports to the Sephardic Jews in the Balkan, the Moroccan Jews of the Spanish zone did not receive the same treatment.

The Vichy government assembled the stateless Jews, and those from other parts of France, and kept them with the help of the Germans in the concentration camp at Drancy, France. All the tens of thousands of Jews of Drancy were transported to Auschwitz, with only tens returning.

The Germans kept meticulous lists of the internees, including name, last known address, date of birth, place of birth, convoy to

Auschwitz number. Included in these lists are many Moroccan Jews who were trapped in France as the war began, who, with other stateless Jews, were isolated, deprived of family and foreign intervention. For many, their formerly presumed citizenship derived from a spouse or a part of their family being born in a European county. Some families were separated cruelly in the course of the deportations. In the case of the Dray family of Casablanca, the parents were transported in convoy 57 on July 18, 1943. The children were deported on a later convoy on January 20, 1944. For six months the children remained without parental love. The convoys transported the Jews in three days to Auschwitz, a journey made without food and with little water. The majority upon arrival passed directly to the gas chambers. Only ten percent were selected out. One convoy, number 73, went to Kovno- Reval in occupied Lithuania. Convoy 78 went from Lyon, France directly to Auschwitz. All children, upon arrival, were marched directly to the gas chambers. Most convoys consisted of young men and women in their twenties. All told, 153 Moroccan Jews grouped in Drancy lost their lives in the gas chambers of Auschwitz, Poland. They represent cities throughout Morocco: Casablanca, Fez, Tetuan, Ouezan, Tangier, Marrakesh, Sale, Larache, Rabat, Melilla, Mogador, and Tiaret. The oldest was Messaoud Aknine of Tangiers, age 73. The youngest was Michael Dray of Casablanca, who was but one year old. We, as Sephardim, must realize that the Holocaust is part of our history. We cannot pretend that the Holocaust was a European problem experienced only by Ashkenazi Jews in Eastern Europe.

The following table includes names and birthdates of victims, place of birth or relation, convoy numbers, date of departure of convoy from Drancy to Auschwitz (add three days generally to determine date of gassing), and age at departure.

DEL FUEGO

Name	Date of Birth	Place of Birth	Convoy Number	Date of Convoy	Age or Status
Abecassis, Mordechai			78 Lyon	8/11/44	Survived
Abergel, Maklouf		Marrakesh	34	9/18/42	57
Aknine, Messaoud	6/10/70	Tangiers	52	3/23/43	73
Amar, Charles	30/12/24		57	7/18/43	19
Amar, Juliette	2/5/04		57	7/18/43	39
Amar, Robert			78, Lyon	8/11/44	Survived
Aziza, Dora	8/6/11		74	5/20/44	32
Barmocha, Esther		Casablanca	66	1/20/44	45
Barmocha, Mardochee	10/93	Mogador	66	1/20/44	50
Benabou(?), Meyer	15/12/91	Mogador	63	12/17/43	52
Benaich(e), Sarah	15/5/08	Tetouan	52	3/23/43	34
Benaich, Maurice	27/1/06	husband	52	3/23/43	37
Benaich, Fernand	3/6/10	brother	52	3/23/43	33
Benaich, Joseph	13/10/12	brother	52	3/23/43	31
Benaich, Sarah(?)	1/1/22	niece	52	3/23/43	21
Benaich, Isaac	4/7/08	Telanet	2	6/2/42	34
Benaioun, Falvien	6/8/18		57	7/18/43	25
Ben(a)haim, Albert	12/2/82	Tangiers	52	3/23/43	61
Benarrosch, Maurice	5/2/99	Casablanca	67	2/3/44	45
Benarrosch, Rosalie	18/8/09	wife	67	2/3/44	34
Benarrosch, Roger	31/7/36	son	67	2/3/44	7
Benarrosch, Micheline	23/7/41	daughter	67	2/3/44	2
Benassayag, Edmond	2/24	died in Drancy		7/44	20
Benbounan, Moise	11/12/09		60	3/7/44	34
Bendayan, Sultana	10/4/07	Quezzan	61	10/28/43	36
Bendayan, Simone	31/1/31	daughter	61	10/28/43	12
Bendayan, Albert	21/11/32	son	61	10/28/43	10
Bendayan, Georges	17/1/35	son	61	10/28/43	8
Bendayan, Clarisse	30/8/26	daughter	61	10/28/43	17
Benguigui, Fortunee	30/4/04		58	7/31/43	39
Benguigui, Joseph	7/11/97		81	5/31/44	46
Benguigui, Yahya	1899	Fez	53	6/25/43	44
Benguigui, Djoher	30/1/01	wife	53	6/25/43	43
Benguigui, Marie	5/3/25	daughter	53	6/25/43	18
Benguigui, Helene	5/5/27	daughter	53	6/25/43	15
Benguigui, Adolphe	28/9/30	son	53	6/25/43	12
Benguigui, Yvonne	3/3/33	daughter	53	6/25/43	10
Benguigui, Andre	2/5/35	son	53	6/25/43	7
Benguigui, Huguettel	16/8/38	daughter	53	6/25/43	4

SEPHARDIM AND THE HOLOCAUST

Name	Date of Birth	Place of Birth	Convoy Number	Date of Convoy	Age or Status
Benguigui, Jacqueline	8/4/40	daughter	53	6/25/43	3
Benhaim, Haim	1883	Mogador	76	6/30/44	61
Benhaim, Isaac	8/2/96	died in Drancy		8/17/44	47
Benhaim, Sadia	18/12/82	Benu Bougar	34	9/18/42	61
Benhamou, Fortunee	3/7/01	Larache	71	4/13/44	42
Benhamou, Marie		sister	77	5/31/44	Survived
Benhamou, Rachel		sister	77	5/31/44	Survived
Benhamou, Simone		sister	77	5/31/44	Survived
Benhamou, Rene			78, Lyon	8/11/44	Survived
Benloulou, Joseph			41	2/23/43	21
Benloulou, Maurice	5/7/17	Casablanca	52	3/23/43	25
Bensadoun, Georges	5/7/17	Casablanca	executed	8/23/44	BduPlus
Bensoussan, Edmond	2/22	Marrakesh	52	3/23/43	27
Bensoussan, Nisan			78, Lyon	8/11/44	Survived
Benzaquen, Maurice	28/8/08	Casablanca	53	6/25/43	34
Benzaquen, Yahya	22/2/04	Casablanca	53	6/25/43	39
Bitton, Barouch	1889	Marrakesh	76	6/30/44	55
Bitton, Jacqueline	6/10/23		74	5/20/44	20
Bouhanan(e), Messodie	15/1/13	Mogador	59	9/2/43	30
Bounan, David	28/8/15	Tangiers	64	12/7/43	27
Bouzaglo, Messoud			78, Lyon	8/11/44	Survived
Cazes, Jacques	45	11/11/42	47		2
Cohen, Elie	1893	Mazagan	75	5/30/44	51
Cohen, Isadore	12/1/18	Melilla	73, Kovno	5/15/44	26
Cohen, Jean	16/6/07	Casablanca	53	6/25/43	35
Cohen, Mayer	25/6/01	Mogador	36	9/23/42	39
Cohen, Messod	15/10/96	Fez	3	6/22/42	45
Cohen-Azancott, Maurice	28/12/91	Tangiers	53	3/25/43	54
Conqui, Leonie			76	6/30/44	
Dahan, Adolphe			78, Lyon	8/11/44	Survived
Dahan, David	19/9/83	Mogador	74	5/20/44	60
Dahan, Clarisse	3/7/24	daughter	74	5/20/44	19
Dahan, Rosine	2/4/27	daughter	74	5/20/44	17
Dayan, Miriam	1914	Casablanca	66	1/20/44	
Dray, Marius	19/2/01	Casablanca	57	7/18/43	42
Dray, Marguerite	7/3/07		57	7/18/43	35
Dray, Simone	3/10/41	daughter	74	5/20/44	2
Dray, David	5/2/32	Casablanca	66	1/20/44	11
Dray, Leon	12/2/35	brother	66	1/20/44	8

DEL FUEGO

Name	Date of Birth	Place of Birth	Convoy Number	Date of Convoy	Age or Status
Dray, Jacqueline	7/2/39	sister	66	1/20/44	4
Dray, Michel	5/4/42	brother	66	1/20/44	1
Drai, Paulette			77	5/31/44	Survived
Drai, Marcel		brother	77	5/31/44	1
Elbaz, Albert		Tangier	40		
Elbaz, Georges			76	6/30/44	
Elbaz, Hanania (Herman)	15/1/09	Casablanca	52	3/23/43	34
Elbaz, Jacob	9/12/20	Tangier	62	11/20/43	42
Elbaz, Mazaltov			76	6/30/44	
Elkerab, Mesoda	8/8/23	Casablanca	59	9/2/43	20
Elkoubi, Rachel	28/9/95		58	7/31/43	47
Elkouby, Abraham	1895	Marrakesh	66	1/20/44	49
Eskenazi, Raphael	14/5/07	Larache	73, Kovno	5/15/44	37
Ezzaoui, Sultana	24/1/92		57	7/18/43	51
Ezzaoui, Simone	9/8/31	daughter	57	7/18/43	11
Halphon, Alphonse			45	11/11/42	
Hamon, Moise	4/5/95	Fez	36	9/23/42	47
Hazan, Marie	20/2/03	wife of POW	80	7/21/44	40
Ittah, Perla			78, Lyon	8/11/44	Survived
Kadosh, Simon	8/3/24	Rabat	73, Kovno	5/15/44	20
Kadouch, Miriam	1904	Casablanca	66	1/20/44	40
Kassis, Mahlouf	26/4/03		71	4/13/44	41
Kassis, Clementine	21/11/02	wife	71	4/13/44	42
Kassis, Louise	26/12/24	daughter	71	4/13/44	19
Kassis, Huguette	3/5/26	daughter	71	4/13/44	17
Kessu(s), Albert	9/2/22	Tangier	61	10/28/43	21
Lachkar, Esther	19/12/99	Casablanca	63	12/17/43	44
Lascar, Albert	11/10	Belgium	25	2/19/44	34
Lasri, Rosette	19/7/26	Sale	52	3/23/43	16
Levi, Sol					
Levy, Esther	15/6/04	Casablanca	74	5/20/44	39
Malka, Ovadia	1/7/08	57	7/18/43	35	
Medrach, Rachel	7/12/09	Casablanca	52	3/23/43	33
Mouyal, Isaac	78	Lyon	8/11/44	47	
Mouyal, Maklouf	26/4/96	Casablanca	66	1/20/44	47
Mouyal, Rachel	28/11/00	Larache	59	9/2/43	42
Nahon, Isaac	78	Lyon	8/11/44	Survived	
Nahon, Maurice	executed in Miremont		2/6/44		
Nahon, Robert	21/12/19	executed in Bron.	12/8/44	24	3

SEPHARDIM AND THE HOLOCAUST

Name	Date of Birth	Place of Birth	Convoy Number	Date of Convoy	Age or Status
Obadia, Albert			78, Lyon	8/11/44	Survived
Ohayon, David	9/5/21	Mogador	executed in Suresnes	14/5/42	21
Ouaknin, Charles	25/12/23	Melilla	53	3/25/43	29
Orhagoun, Sol	15/12/16	Tangier	59	9/2/43	26
Ouizman, Eleazar	1898	Mogador	2	6/2/42	44
Picard, Alfred	3/2/29	Rabat	73, Kovno	5/15/44	15
Poznanski, Rachel	4/1/04	Fez	71	4/13/44	40
Poznanski, Antoinette	28/4/28	Casablanca	71	4/13/44	15
Sebag, David	28/2/93	Mogador	49	3/2/43	50
Sebag, Messaoude	28/5/12	Mogador	60	3/7/44	32
Sebag(?), Rachel	31/8/87	Larache	59	9/2/43	55
Sebbah, Isaac	14/7/96	Casablanca	62	11/20/43	47
Sebban, Simon	19/9/18	Marrakesh	36	9/23/42	24
Seboni, Samuel	17/10/14	Casablanca	52	3/23/43	28
Semtob, Salomon	1894	Casablanca	66	1/20/44	48
Semtob, Jeannette	24/4/02	wife	66	1/20/44	41
Semtob, Anna	13/10/35	daughter	66	1/20/44	8
Seraf, Makluf	1893	Mogador	35	9/21/42	49
Serels, Menahem	1888	Marrakesh	40	11/4/42	54
Serels, Rivka	1904	wife	40	11/4/42	38
Serels, Samuel	5/8/24	son	40	11/4/42	18
Serels, Leah	21/1/26	daughter	40	11/4/42	18
Serfati, G			70	3/27/44	22
Souissa, Chalom	15/2/99	Marrakesh	60	3/7/44	45
Souissa, Szandla	29/11/11	wife	60	3/7/44	31
Souissa, Salomon	17/6/30	son	60	3/7/44	13
Souissa, Aicha	3/3/32	daughter	60	3/7/44	12
Timsit, Yaich	23/4/05	Mogador	77	5/31/44	39
Timsit, Yaich			78, Lyon	8/11/44	Survived
Tordjman, Meyer	1/1/21	Casablanca	63	12/17/43	22

The Nazis had proposed and executed a war against the Jews with no regard for origin, language or customs. There was no quarter for any Jew. The final measure of the Holocaust is not merely the unimaginable number of six million; it is the tears in the eyes of any Jewish child who hears of the suffering of our people during that terrible time.

THE HOLOCAUST IN THE MIDDLE EAST:
IRAQ AND THE MUFTI OF JERUSALEM
by Dr. Isaac Alteras

In this article I would like to pay attention to what had taken place in the Middle East during the period from 1939 until 1945, and focus on two basic issues. First, the sympathy of the Arab masses to the Axis powers, that is to say to Germany and Italy, and the collaboration of the Arab leaders with Germany and Italy. The second part of the article will deal with the major events in Iraq and the pro-Nazi anti-Semitic activities of the arch hater of the Jewish people, Haj Amin El-Huseini, the ex-Mufti of Jerusalem.

It is important to understand that the unpolitical Arab masses were in full sympathy with the Axis powers. Their animosity toward Britain was well known. As far as the leaders were concerned, not only did they sympathize with the Axis powers, they actually were in close contact and collaboration with them so much so that Nazism, as an ideology, was not imitated in the Arab world, but actually paralleled. The various clubs, associations, and nationalist parties, were pro-Nazi, anti-British and anti-Semitic. It must be recorded that Egypt, Saudi Arabia, Lebanon, Syria, declared war on Nazi Germany in late February 1945 when it was clear to everyone that Germany was about to be defeated, so as to be eligible for membership in the United Nations. Iraq declared war on Nazi Germany in large part because of the failure of the revolt to oust the British from Iraq during April-May of 1941. Iraq had tried to atone for that sin and declared war on Germany in 1943. Only Transjordan, under a British mandate, declared war on Germany in September of 1939. This association, the link between the masses and the rulers of the Arab world with the Axis powers, took place in a process that began from 1934 and proceeded until 1945.

How did it all begin? First of all, by 1934 and 1935 many Arab students were invited to study and visit universities in Germany. German scientists, scholars and agents visited the Arab world. They disseminated pro-Nazi propaganda. They brought with them magazines, journals and speeches of the Fuehrer. Those speeches were broadcast throughout the Arab world. Furthermore we know that the Nazis had subsidized and helped the major Arab revolt in Palestine which took place from 1936 to 1939. The ex-Mufti of Jerusalem, Haj Amin El-Huseini was in close contact with Mussolini and from January 1941 in contact with Hitler. Haj Amin El-Huseini informed Hitler in January 1941 about the coming revolt by Iraqi officers to overthrow the pro-British government, at the time headed by Nuri Said.

In Syria and Lebanon, by 1936, there were a large number of nationalist Pan-Arab associations which were very conducive and tolerant to Nazi propaganda. Among those prewar Arab Nazi organizations in Syria and Lebanon, we found for example the Iron Shirts, the League of National Action, the Ah-Nadi al-Arabi Club of Damascus, the Councils for the Defense of Arab Palestine, headed at the time by the well known pro-Nazi leaders such as Nabich Al-Azma and Adil Arslan. There was the Syrian Popular Party which was led at the time by a well known Fascist, Anton Saade. He escaped during the war to Germany, and from there with the help of Nazi leaders Saade settled in Argentina. In addition, there was the Syrian National Block, the principal party in Syria and more particularly the Istiqlal group headed by Shukri al-Kuwatli. A Nazi sympathizer, Kuwatli became

President of Syria in the 1950's. Before the war, the Germans had a liaison who maintained contacts with all these organizations in the Arab East. His name was Baldur von Schirach. He was the leader of the Hitler youth movement and had visited Syria on a special mission to establish close contact with these circles, particularly the An-Nadi Arabic Club, and with Arab youth organizations. Iraq played a major role in the Nazi military and political strategy to destroy the British Empire and gain control of the Middle East oil. So Iraq, generally, and the Iraqi capital Baghdad, from 1935 onward was the hub of Nazi activity, the center from which Nazi propaganda was disseminated throughout the Middle East. It is no wonder therefore that the German Foreign office appointed as Ambassador to Baghdad one of the most prominent orientalists, a man who spoke Arabic very well, Dr. Fritz Grobba. Dr. Grobba with his legation in Baghdad was the center of all Nazi activities. Fritz Grobba was personally a rather charming person and made friends easily. He began to organize in Baghdad propaganda centers classified under three main headings.

First, they used commercial purposes, trade, as means of propaganda. Germany began increasing its trade with Iraq trying to prove that she was more helpful to the Iraqi economy than the British. Trade was a pretext, a means, a conduit for the export of pro-Nazi propaganda and Nazi activity. With increased trade came journals, magazines, speeches, explosives, and demolition experts. All engaging in all kind of actions detrimental to the British, and favorable to the axis powers. German businessmen, under the guise of promoting trade with Iraq, visited many Arab villages, trying to tell the peasants and the farmers that it was Germany who cared for their welfare and therefore Germany deserved their support in the coming struggle.

Secondly, there were cultural means. There was the cultural conduit for the dissemination of German propaganda. The Germans promoted the teaching of the German language and civilization in Iraqi schools. They wanted to stimulate an emotional interest in the Nazi form of government. Kindergarten schools attended by German and Iraqi children between the ages of 5 and 10 were run by the Germans. German teachers were brought to Iraq and introduced into secondary schools along with Nazi educational measures. Iraqi students were given scholarships to attend these schools. They were so popular that the German language soon ousted French as the second foreign language spoken in Iraq. There were other means of cultural activities to disseminate Nazi ideas. For example, in 1937, Dr. Fadhil al Jamali (who later became the foreign minister of Iraq during the 1950's) was the Director General of Education. He visited Germany and was accorded an official welcome. Upon his return he sent an Iraqi delegation to the Nuremberg rally of 1938. The delegation was headed by Al-Aqid al Jarabi who was personally introduced to Hitler. When he returned to Baghdad, Al-Aqid organized an Iraqi youth movement association called the Futuwa on the lines of the Hitler Jugend. Those of the medical profession were also used by the Germans as a means to disseminate propaganda. Doctors who received their training in Germany were prevailed upon to spread Nazi ideals among the medical students. The principal of the Royal Hospital and the Dean of the Iraqi Medical Faculty, Dr. Saib Shawak, a founder of the ill-famed Muthana club, became a tool in the hands of the Germans after he had visited Germany in 1937. Shawak was officially received by high officials of the Nazi party. He wore the Nazi uniform and gave the "Heil Hitler" salute.

Of course, there was also the political field for the dissemination of propaganda. The Nazis, indeed, had in a large measure their work done for them. We must understand that many Iraqi politicians had already been contaminated with pro-Nazi and anti-British views and therefore it was very easy to exploit them to do Hitler's work. In Iraq, especially after 1936, the army was involved in politics. The army became an instrument, a weapon in the political struggle for power. After 1936, General Bekr Sidqi, the Chief of the General Staff, led a coup d'etat and received moral and financial support from Germany. By September 3rd, 1939, when the war had broken out in Europe, Iraq severed diplomatic relations with Germany. But this act taken by the Prime Minister Nuri Said, was unpopular, especially with the army. The four commanders of the various branches of Iraqi army were known by the collective title of the "Golden Square." The two most prominent officers in that Golden Square were the head of the Iraqi military intelligence, Sala Hudine and Muhamed Salmin, the head of the Iraqi cavalry. They were the ones who wanted to move Iraq into the Nazi orbit. They were convinced that as a result of the British and French setbacks in Europe, and the German armies moving to the western desert, the future belonged to the Axis powers. They believed that Germany and Italy would win the war, therefore, the time had come to rid themselves of the British and especially force the British to surrender the two very important air bases in Iraq at Habbaniya and Shewaba. They would also deprive the British from the very important item they needed from Iraq, the oil of Mosul. On March 31, 1941 a coup d'etat took place. The Golden Square commanders appointed Rashid Ali El-Khailani as the Prime Minister. The revolt against the British was launched in April 1941. One of the first acts that this new government had taken was to renew de facto relations with Germany previously severed by Nuri Said. Secondly, they promised the Germans oil from Mosul and the use of Iraqi railways and airports. These acts were done with the full participation and the conspiratorial role of Haj Amin El-Huseini, the ex-Mufti of Jerusalem, whom the British expelled from Palestine in 1936. From Palestine the Mufti went to Syria and in October of 1939 he moved to Iraq. Nuri Said allowed him to come to Iraq because the Mufti promised that he would not engage in any kind of political activity. However, the ex-Mufti did not keep his word. He brought with him many Palestinians and Syrian emigres, all pro Nazis. He began infiltrating the most important cabinet posts in the Iraqi regime. He conspired with the Iraqi officers in bringing about this revolt and the removal of the British presence from Iraq. Haj Amin also cooperated with many pro-Nazi organizations in Iraq such as the Rover Society, the Palestinian Defense Council of Baghdad, the Red Crescent, the Muthana Club and others.

Obviously the situation was very critical as far as the British and the Jews of Iraq were concerned during those terrible months of April and May of 1941. Had the Iraqi revolt succeeded in defeating the British, the British would have found themselves in a most precarious military situation. One must understand that the military situation, already at that time, had been as bad as possible. The British had lost Greece. They were fighting for Crete. Rommel was advancing in the desert. If the British had lost Iraq, The Empire would have been split into two halves. The western half would have been conquered by the Germans, that would have meant loss of contact with India. The eastern half would have fallen by default. Hitler would have been able to connect his armies with the Japanese at the Indian Ocean. Iraq and Iran would have been used easily by Hitler as a means of invading Russia from the South, conquering the Caucasus and thereby Stalingrad. Had the Iraqi revolt succeeded, El-Alamein would not have taken place. Fortuitously, the British protected their air bases at Habbaniya and Shewaba by bringing in troops from India and a brigade from Palestine. Also British civilian personnel were involved in the defense of these bases. When 9,000 Iraqi soldiers surrounded the bases, the British Royal Airforce bombed the Iraqi forces. The Iraqis had received support from Germany and from Italy through Syria. Were it not for the British resistance in Crete, German support would have been far more extensive and the British may have been defeated in Iraq. Fortunately, the revolt was quelled.

In April, when the revolt took place, hundreds of Iraqi Jews were mutilated and kidnaped; women were raped; children disappeared; property was burned to the ground, losses were in the millions. In the first two days of June, during the holiday of Shabuout, the most extensive pogrom took place. It is estimated that over 900 Jews of Baghdad were slaughtered by the mob. The army that was brought into Baghdad to disperse the mob were not Iraqi troops because Iraqi troops had already been infected by the Nazis with anti-Semitism. Those troops deployed to quell the rebellion and to put an end to the pogrom, were from Kurdistan. They were soldiers who did not belong to the regular Iraqi army. They were Kurds. This was not the only pogrom that took place in the Middle East. Soon after El Alamein there were at least 30 or more pogroms against Jews in the Arab world. There was a pogrom in Alexandria and in Cairo, Egypt. There were pogroms in Tripoli and Bengasi, Libya, in Morocco and Tunisia.

How did the Arab leaders react to all these events? King Farouk of Egypt sent a telegram to Rashid Ali congratulating him for coming to power. The Mufti of Jerusalem had become the liaison between King Farouk and the Nazis. Medical students at the University of Beirut actually wanted to volunteer to fight on the side of the Iraqi army against the British. Haj Amin declared a Jihad, holy war against the British. The masses, the Shiite spiritual leaders and the Sunni spiritual leaders all backed the rebellion against the British. Now, with the failure of this rebellion, the Mufti and Rashid Ali escaped to Iran. They reached Teheran and found political asylum in the Japanese Embassy there. In October of 1941, both of them reached Rome and held their first audience with Mussolini and volunteered their services to the Axis cause. They claimed that all they wanted when Hitler won the war was a declaration of liberty and freedom for all the Arab peoples, i.e. self determination. Mussolini and Hitler found the declaration a very small price to pay for Haj Amin El-Huseini's support against the Allies. But Haj Amin noticed that the important player in this arrangement was not Mussolini, but Hitler. The Mufti therefore moved his headquarters from Rome to Berlin. We have in our possession the records of a very important conversation that Haj Amin had with Hitler on November 21, 1941. This was a two hour-audience that Hitler gave the Mufti. In that conversation, Hitler declared that the Nazis and the Arabs have a common interest. First, the extermination and the elimination of the Jewish people. Secondly, the defeat of Bolshevism in the Soviet Union, because, as Hitler stated it, Bolshevism and Judaism go hand in hand. The defeat of one will bring about the defeat of the other. Thirdly, to see to it that a Jewish national homeland in Palestine must be finished with a final blow that must come even before the end of the war. Hitler promised Haj Amin El-Huseini that German planes would start bombing the city of Tel Aviv and its surroundings in order to bring about the elimination of the Jewish presence in Palestine. Fourthly, the Fuehrer promised Haj Amin that as soon as the invasion of Russia was completed, the German army would move southwards to conquer the Caucasus. Then Hitler would issue a declaration saying that the aim of the war is to bring about self-determination to the Arab people from British imperialism.

Based on these promises and his own personal inclination, the ex-Mufti began playing several very important roles for the German war effort.

First, he disseminated propaganda on behalf of Nazi Germany. He used the radio stations in Berlin, Rome, Bari, and even in Tokyo to broadcast calls to all Arabs and all Moslems throughout the world to rise against the British oppressors and in the process kill the Jews wherever they can find them.

Secondly, Haj Amin organized an entire espionage network with offices in Geneva, Istanbul, Athens, Germany, and in other parts of Europe to train Moslems to carry out acts of espionage in the Middle East, behind the British lines. Thirdly, the ex-Mufti organized fifth column activities in the Middle East. Under his leadership, parachutists trained in Athens were dropped behind the British lines in Palestine, Transjordan, Iraq, Morocco and Tunisia. They destroyed ammunition depots, railways, and very important electrical stations. The British in return had to appoint guards in order to maintain those installations thus harming their war effort because of the drain on available fighting manpower. The Mufti also organized Moslem legions to fight on the side of the Axis powers. About 15,000 Moslems, mostly from Albania and Yugoslavia, were organized by him and under his supervision. He visited them and encouraged them to keep on the fight until the end of world Jewry and British imperialism. He began organizing about 500,000 Moslems in Morocco, Tunisia, and Algeria. In his letters and correspondence with Himmler and von Ribbentrop, the Mufti promised that he would also organize an army of Moslems within Russia itself. His aim was the formation of an Arab Brigade. He wrote to Himmler in early 1944 stating that since Churchill has accepted a Jewish Brigade to fight along the British in the Middle East, there should be an Arab Brigade to fight along the Axis powers. Arab students in Germany were organized to fight in this Arab Brigade. Their aim was to join the SS wherever they could in order to liquidate whatever Jewish remnants there were in Europe and then move towards the Middle East. In Hungary Haj Amin, met with Eichmann. He encouraged Eichmann and the Hungarian anti-Semitic authorities to proceed as soon as possible with the extermination of Hungarian Jewry and European Jewry wherever they were still left. He said the fewer Jews that are left alive, the fewer of them would be available to go to Palestine to fight against the Arabs after the war. Thus the ex-Mufti played a leading role in the process of the "final solution" of the Jewish problem and should have been brought to trial as a criminal and Nazi collaborator. Instead he slipped into France, where the French authorities kept him under house arrest. In 1946 he was allowed to go to Egypt and Farouk welcomed him with open arms.

In summation, the evidence presented above clearly demonstrates that the Holocaust was not confined to Europe only. The Jewish communities in the Middle East were not spared the Nazi barbaric acts carried out by their Arab friends and allies.

ASPECTS OF THE HOLOCAUST IN LIBYA
by Dr. Maurice M. Roumani

INTRODUCTION

The Holocaust is usually associated with European Jewry. Little is known as to whether other Jewish communities, such as those in the Middle East and North Africa, had also suffered a fate similar to that of their brethren in Europe. The extent to which these communities suffered at the hands of the Germans or their proxies, it was minimal in number compared to the suffering in Europe. Nevertheless, Germany's penetration into the Middle East and North Africa did not spare the Jewish communities with whom they came in contact from suffering the same destiny as their brethren in Europe. The fact that their success was only partially realized was due to the turn of events at the battle of El-Alamein and the eventual defeat of the German forces on North African soil. Racial Laws

Italy occupied Libya in 1911 and remained in control until 1943. During this period, the Jewish community had known ups and downs in its relations with the governing Italian authorities in the new colony. This relationship had several positive facets. It facilitated for the occupiers the promotion of their commercial and industrial interests in Libya, but above all it provided the Libyan Jewish community with the opportunity to reform its own educational system and its rabbinate.

However, from the year 1935, and especially after the self declaration of Mussolini to be the "Protector of Islam," the attitude of the Italian Authorities in Libya towards its Jews worsened. In effect, the declaration set in motion a process of delegitimization of the activities of the Jewish community in the fields of Jewish education and Zionist activities. The decree also touched on such fields as commerce and trade. This period was marked by a closer rapprochement between Mussolini's Italy and Hitler's Germany.

By 1938, the Italian Authorities began to implement the "Fascist Racial Laws" for its Italian Jewish subjects in Italy and in the colonies. These laws were due in part to the pressure brought to bare on the Mussolini regime by Hitler. In Libya, however, the implementation of these laws was slower than in Italy due to the important role that Jews played in the economy of the colony. When the Second World War began and Italy joined the Axis powers on the side of Germany, these laws were rigorous ly upheld. The Fascist Racial Laws in Libya included the following provi sions: -The expulsion of Jews holding foreign nationalities. -The expulsion of Jews from high schools and institutes of higher education. -The dismissal of Jews from government offices, banks and munici pal councils. -The dissolution of all Jewish-Italian joint ventures. -The demotion of Jewish soldiers in the Italian army. -The stamping of "Jew" in all official documents carried by Jews. Additionally, the laws prohibited foreign Jews from living in Italy, Libya and the Aegean Islands. To ingratiate himself to Germany, Mussolini issued a later decree banning Jews in Italy and in Libya from public schools.

Import-export licenses in Libya were limited to Italians, Maltese and Arabs. Jews were not allowed to participate in public bids for the needs of the army, prisons or the police force. This field was traditionally in the hands of the Jews but now they were to be excluded. The Italian daily and weekly press began to attack Jews with anti-

Semitic overtones, calling them by names such as "Porco Giuda" (Judah the Pig), "Ebreo Lurido" (Dirty Jew) and "Ebreaccio" (Jewboy).

Jews who refused to open their shops on Saturday were flogged in public squares. When this policy gave no results, two Jews were executed. Only then did Jews open their shops reluctantly on the Sabbath. However, they refused to benefit from the sales of that day. To do so they put an Arab in charge of the store with the understanding that the income of that day belonged exclusively to him.

In addition, there were frequent punishments of Jews for minor offenses which were normally overlooked, such as not standing on attention when the Italian flag was poised.

From the correspondence between Italo Balbo (governor of Libya) and Mussolini (De Felice, 1985:197), it appears that Balbo was reluctant to carry out the Fascist Racial Laws in Libya because he believed that these laws would do irreparable damage to the domestic and foreign prestige of the country. Balbo's reluctance was satisfied only in part. On June 10, 1940, Italy officially entered the war on the side of Germany by declaring war against France and Britain. Jews suffered most from this turn of events.

Tripoli and especially its Jewish quarter came under daily heavy bombardment from the Allied ships as well as from planes which took off from bases in Malta. Jews were forced to find refuge outside the city. In addition, they suffered economically not only because of the raging war, but also from the enforcement of the racial laws discriminating against them in their food and gasoline rationing.

During the war, all schools, cultural and social clubs were closed and no activity was permitted.

As the Italians began to suffer setbacks on the battlefield in September 1941, they even more strongly enforced the racial laws against the Jews. Many of the 1600 Jews of French nationality and 870 British subjects were arrested and placed in detention camps that were built for this purpose. Between January and March 1942, an agreement was reached between the Italian and the French authorities to facilitate the transfer of French subjects and those holding protected status to Tunisia. Three hundred others of British nationality were sent to Italy. There, they were interned in various places in the country including Civitella del Tronto and Bagno near Ripoli. (De Felice,1985:174) Those in Civitella were later put to work by the Germans in military camps along the Sangro frontier. In May 1944, a few of these detainees were sent to Bergen Belsen and Biberach, near Munich. Most of them managed to survive and were liberated by the Allied Forces in 1945.

On the Western frontier, the Jews of Cyrenaica were ordered by Mussolini to be sent to a detention camp in Libya. This "clearing out" process (De Felice, 1985: 179) was aimed at evacuating 591 Jews from the capital, Benghazi, and sending them to an internment camp in Giado, 235 kms. from Tripoli. When the Italians ran out of space in this camp, some Jews were sent to another camp set up for foreigners in Gharian near Tripoli.

By late June 1942, more than 2500 people were removed from Cyrenaica. Those who were interned in Giado faced many hardships and bad conditions which resulted in the breakout of typhus in the camp causing the death of young and old members of several families. About 500 people perished in the camp.

In August of that year, another camp was set up in Sidi Azaz, near Tripoli. According to De Felice, one thousand Jews were sent to this camp to work as slave laborers. Of those, 350 were employed in

Tobruk. When the Axis forces withdrew, they were abandoned in the desert. After a long march across the desert, they managed to reach Tripoli, exhausted but safe.

Jews of British nationality were removed to Italy and put in several detention camps across the country. When the Germans occupied Italy, many of these Jews were taken for forced labor and for fortification of the front lines. Between July and October 1943, about 100 Jews were deported to a concentration camp in Innsbruck, Austria where they remained until April 1944. Their liberation came at the insistence of the British forces.

Those Jews considered natives of Libya, between the ages of 18 and 45 were put to forced labor. Hundreds of these were sent to the Cyrenaican front especially to Bukbuk. There they faced hard labor, building roads and front lines under inclement desert weather conditions and undernourishment.

CONCLUSION

At the end of the war, the Jewish community of Libya was shattered, in disarray and too exhausted to embark on any serious recovery program. There was a lot to be done but they were overwhelmed by where to begin. The JDC and other Jewish organizations were instrumental in rehabilitating the community.

However, the experience of the war years left a bitter taste in the minds of Libyan Jews. They did not only suffer from the war, but also tasted some of the experience that befell their brethren in Europe. The Jews felt that their former friends, the Italians, had no choice but to cooperate in implementing the Third Reich's racial policies once they allied themselves with Germany. This alliance included the promotion of German anti Semitism in North Africa.

BIBLIOGRAPHY

De Felice, Renzo, *Jews in an Arab Land, Libya, 1835-1970,* 1985. Austin: University of Texas.

Zuaretz, F.A. Guweta Ts. Shaked, G. Arbib and F. Tayer, eds. *Libyan Jewry.* Tel-Aviv: Committee of Libyan Jewish Communities in Israel. 1960.

Roumani, Maurice M. *"Zionism and Social Change in Libya at the Turn of the Century."*

Studies in Zionism. Vol. 8, No. 1 (1987).

THE NON-EUROPEAN HOLOCAUST:
THE FATE OF TUNISIAN JEWRY
by Dr. M. Mitchell Serels

Too often, when one hears of the fate of the Jews during the Holocaust of World War II, one brings to mind the great communities of Central and Eastern Europe, and, to a lesser extent, the communities of Western Europe. The enormity of the event and the masses involved demand our attention and the attention of future generations. But one must never forget that the Third Reich waged war on Jews wherever they lived and whenever those Jews were unfortunate enough to fall under the rule of the Germans. Geographic boundaries served only as temporary obstacles to the Nazi determination to eradicate Jews wherever they were to be found. No Jew was permanently excluded and no Jew was safe.

It is most unfortunate that some of the major historians of the Holo- caust, Davidowicz (1) and Hilberg(2), ignore or overlook the effect of the Nazi extermination program on non-European Jewry. Jews around the world, under Germany and her Axis, were affected by the racial attitudes of the Nazis. The legislation and action were applied not only against European Jewry. North African Jews were also affected by the German occupation and anti-Jewish legislation. Einsatzgruppen, the Nazi murder squads, were in Africa.(3) This is fact, not fiction. The yellow star of David was amongst Arabic Jewry.

The events are not newly discovered. It is only that we have forgotten this sad chapter. It has been overshadowed by the tragedy in Europe. But the tragedy in Africa, particularly in Tunisia and Libya, is part of the history of the Jews and part of the story of the Holocaust. Never can we permit any chapter to disappear or allow any event to be lost. These events are part of the people and its history.

Tunisia had been a French Protectorate since 1881 as part of the agreements of the Congress of Berlin. The French were represented by the Resident-General who could enact legislation without the permission of the local native ruler, the Bey of Tunis. However, the Bey could not enact legislation without the permission of the Resident-General. Generally, the French were favorably disposed in their dealings with the Tunisian Jews. Many Jews had obtained French citizenship and there were close relationships between the Protectorate government and the Jewish community as a whole, and individual Jews in particular.

At the onset of World War II, the Resident-General was Admiral J. P. Esteva. With the fall of France, the Vichy government was the legitimate Protectorate government. In June, 1940, Tunisia became a Vichy Protectorate. Resident-General Admiral Esteva, along with M. Lamotte, who was responsible for Tunisian justice, resisted for several months the introduction of anti-Jewish legislation, Status des Juifs. Possibly because they were both devout Catholics and heard the mass said daily, they were reluctant to pursue the matter of the "Jewish question." However, under pressure from Vichy, anti-Jewish decrees were enacted in Tunisia on 20 November 1940, particularly, the numerus clausus. The decrees included limitations of Jewish professions. Jewish doctors were limited in their practice to Jewish patients. Jewish lawyers were prohibited from practicing. The German ambassador to Paris, Abetz, pushed for the complete aryanization of Jewish property and the institution of the yellow Star of David. He did succeed in the dissolution of Jewish organizations. In February of 1941, Jewish real estate agents and insurance brokers were barred from their professions. On August 21, 1941, Xavier Vallat,(4) the Vichy Commissioner-General for Jewish questions, visited Tunisia to insist on the uniform application of the yellow star, a more rapid removal of Jews from the economic life of Tunisia, and greater residential isolation. Esteva resisted the rapidity suggested by Vallat.(5)

On September 29, 1941, the last vestiges of Jewish communal organization, the Jewish newspapers, were dissolved. Le Petit Matin, a Jewish newspaper in Tunis, was stopped, but later permitted to reappear as "Journal Israelite de Tunisie," exclusively for Jewish readers. In December 1941, Stuttgart radio called Admiral Esteva a pro-Jew, who should be removed because of his interference in the maltreatment of Jews.(6)

Until November 1942, the Jews began to learn to adjust to the restrictions of Vichy France which were imposed upon their North African Jewry. The situation was distressing, but one found ways to live within the system. The laxity and lack of uniformity in application of the anti-Jewish legislation allowed the Jews the feeling that this, too, would pass. The Jews of one city might be forced to wear the yellow star, while the Jews elsewhere were exempt. Jews were permitted to obtain more rations than Arabs. But everything was a delusion and only a temporary respite.

On November 8, 1942, the Allies invaded North Africa, landing in southern Morocco and on the Algerian coast. The Vichy governments in Morocco and Algeria quickly fell before the invasion by the British, American and Free French forces. The Axis responded by moving their troops from Libya into Tunisia and into a small area of eastern Algeria. General von Nehring was placed in charge of the operations in Tunisia.

Not content with fighting the advancing Allied forces, the Germans turned their attention to the local Jews. In addition to signing war orders and communications, Generals von Nehring and von Arnim (7) signed anti-Jewish orders. Minister Rahn of the Nazi foreign office was sent to deal with the Jews. An Einsatzkommando group of SS and police were sent to Africa to solve the Jewish problem. The Germans began by arresting the communal leaders.(8)

Unfortunately for the Nazi plans, the older Vichy legislation had dissolved Jewish communal organizations. Von Nehring's first order then was to establish a "Conseil Juif" (Jewish Council) similar to the Judenrat of Europe. However, the former president of the Jewish Community Council, M. Moise Borgel, was under arrest. On November 23, 1942, Minister Plenipotentiary, Rudolph Rahn,(9) had arrested all the leaders at 11:00 p.m., when a platoon under the command of SS Hauptscharfuhrer Pohl came to the home of M. Moise Borgel, age 70. Also arrested were Felix Samama and M. Cittanouva, a Jew who served as the honorary Consul of Finland in Tunisia. They were taken to the Kasbah. Admiral Esteva tried to intercede on behalf of the Jewish leaders.(10)

The Wehrmacht was facing transportation difficulties. Tunisia had only one train line and a very poor network of roads. This antiquated system interfered with the type of war the Wehrmacht was accustomed to waging. The Wehrmacht needed railways and well-paved roads to bring its supplies to the front and to continue the war. General Kesselring was instructed to mobilize the population for fortification and road construction.

It was decided that the Jews should be forced into labor. Von

Nehring instituted Le Comite de Recruitment de la Main-d'oevre Juive (The Committee for the Recruitment of Jewish Manpower). Moise Borgel, the elder leader, was selected by the Nazis to head the Committee. Borgel was released on November 29, 1942 and instructed to report twice daily to the kommandantur for his orders. At Borgel's request, and with the intercession of Adm. Esteva, the other incarcerated Jews, except Cittanouva, were released.

The leaders were released in order to obtain twenty million francs to pay the fine imposed by the Nazis. The money was collected and given to the Germans, who handed the funds over to the Arab-Italian-French committee for the victims of Allied bombings. This was one of many steps taken by the Nazis to incite the other ethnic groups in Tunisia against the Jews. The Wehrmacht Propaganda Office, or the OKW, had wanted to dispatch a propaganda platoon to Tunisia in order to incite the population to rioting against the Jews and to looting Jewish homes and businesses. Minister Rahn objected to the proposed mission of the propaganda squad because of the proximity of the Allies. The platoon did not arrive. The Jews were too valuable to the war effort as potential slave labor. There would be time for riots later. Borgel was asked to submit a list of one thousand Jewish apartments for requisitioning. He never really produced the list, nor was it used. The Germans at SS headquarters at 168 Avenue de Paris had bigger plans.(11)

On December 6, 1942, Moise Borgel and Grand Rabbi Haim Bellaich visited SS headquarters to ask for additional housing space for Jews who were fleeing Bizerte and other war zones. They were accompanied by Maximilian Trenner, a French Jewish refugee living in Tunisia. Trenner was a known specialist in radio and acted as a German interpreter. SS Colonel Rauff shocked them by informing these leaders that a new Jewish Committee would be formed under the Chief Rabbi. The Committee would have nine members. They had until 6:00 p.m. that evening to produce the names of the Jews who would serve on that Committee. The Committee then had until 8:00 a.m. the following morning to produce a list of two thousand Jews, aged 15 to 50, to serve as forced laborers. If they delayed, the laborers would get no food, clothing, or tools. If the labor force was not produced, the communal leaders would be shot, and others, who would cooperate, would be appointed to replace them. Borgel and Rabbi Bellaich decided to divide their work. Borgel would begin the establishment of the Committee and the production of lists, while Bellaich, along with M. Moatti, would see Admiral Esteva in order to request his intercession. Esteva was able to obtain an eight hour delay, and to reduce the number of Jews required for the labor force to one thousand.(12)

On December 8, 1942, the Committee thus appointed presented its list to SS Colonel Rauff. The Nazi was irate that the Jews had appealed to Esteva. Rauff ordered the number of forced laborers raised to three thousand. They were to assemble at the Foch Barracks and at Route de Moghrane. Borgel called a meeting of the Committee at his office on rue Marceshau. The Allies were only fifty kilometers from Tunisia. If they could delay the implementation of the Nazi forced labor laws, and if they could keep an account of all Jews, they could perhaps protect their people until the Allies liberated the country. The Committee decided again to apply to the Resident-General, Admiral Esteva, to appeal to the native ruler, Moncef Bey, and to the Italians, who, as allies of the Germans, had occupied southern Tunisia, establishing an Italian sector.(13) Esteva could no longer help, as he was now powerless. Von Nehring was now in power. Moncef Bey told the Jews to submit to their destiny. Only the Italians assisted. On December 9, 1942, the Italian Consul General protested the inclusion of Italian Jews in the Jewish forced labor consignment. The Consulate offered protection to Jews of Italian citizenry. The

Germans exempted, at the Consul General's insistence, all Italian Jews from forced labor assignments.

The Committee was able to assemble very few Jews who would volunteer for the Jewish slave labor force. One hundred and twenty Jews reported at the New Synagogue on Avenue de Paris. Another eighty eight reported to the Foch Barracks. SS Colonel Rauff was angered. He entered the synagogue, which was being used as a temporary shelter for refugee Jews, despite the protests of Rabbi David Hagege. These Jews were attacked and beaten.(14)

Jacques Krief offered the Alliance Israelite Universelle School on rue Malta as a recruitment center and assembly area. It became known in the Jewish community that they could no longer stall and delay. The SS had obtained the civilian list of the names of all Jews from the Vichy government.

On December 10, 1942, the first assembly of one thousand Jews took place. Paul Ghez was assigned by the Committee to register the workers. Krief was assigned to calm the people, and Tenner acted as interpreter. Under the two SS officers in charge, Saewecke and Pohl, the workers were divided into twenty groups of fifty. Excluded from the registration were veterans, war victims and orphans, as well as one hundred and fifty pharmacists. Vichy Police Prefect Philip assisted in forcing the maintenance of order. The Committee agreed to three main purposes in their relationship with the Germans:

1) to eliminate all acts of disobedience;
2) to ameliorate, to the maximum possible, the conditions of the workers;
3) to preserve a dignified attitude. (15)

The Committee also reviewed three attitudes toward the situation:

1) Resist —which would have meant bloody reprisals, and, since the Germans frequently took hostages, certain executions;

2) Escape —not very feasible, since most Jews lived in the "Hara", the Jewish ghetto in urban areas;

3) Comply —stall for time, keep lists of all Jews, and utilize the Bey and Resident-General to ease the situation.

Paul Ghez assumed a major role of leadership in the Committee. M. Hayoun was charged to keep a record on each Jew forced into labor in the camps. Since the Germans required that the Tunisian Jewish community feed, clothe, and equip the laborers, the Jews needed to know the exact number of their interned brethren. The German propensity for minutiae and detail allowed the Jews to maintain an accurate record of the forced laborers.

In the first few days, 3,885 men left for the labor camps. By the middle of January, the number of workers had reached 4,500. This was far below the 15,000 figure of total mobilization.

Ghez (16) organized the Committee to best serve the needs of the laborers and their families. The services of the Committee were divided into eight parts:

1) administrative service
2) a center for betterment of the forced laborers
3) service to sick workers in their homes
4) an out-patient clinic service
5) a medical service for the camps
6) pharmaceutical services
7) laboratory services
8) special services

These services were the only aid the Jewish community was permitted. From December 15, 1942 to April 30, 1943, the doctors saw 1,666 cases, and the pharmacists filled 1,680 prescriptions.

The Committee for the camps included Rene Solal (head), Max Berdah, Edmond Slama, Jules Cohen-Solal, and M. M. Maarek, Veroli, and Cohen-Tanugi. From December 12, 1942 until February 10, 1943, the Committee delivered the following supplies:

bread and flour	70,000 kg
breakfast food	13,000 kg
dried vegetables	13,000 kg
canned goods	30,000 kg
oil	2,600 kg
sugar	1,500 kg

The Committee also supplied the following clothing to the forced laborers:

boots and shoes	5,000 pr
kachabias (a local garb) 9	30
blankets	160
socks	3,500 pr
shirts	3,000
sweaters	2,000
handkerchiefs	1,000
overalls	2,500
toiletry sets	3,000

Fifteen trucks and five half-trucks were obtained to deliver the listed supplies and 320 liters of fuel in six months.(17)

A Finance Committee, comprised of Victor Cohen-Hadria, Henry Ghez, Guy Boccara, Simon Krief and Eli Levy, raised a sum of 35,748,898 francs to defray expenses. The money was used for the supplies and to help the families of the slave laborers.

THE CAMPS

There were three basic sectors for the forced labor camps: the German sector, the Tunis area, and the Italian sector.

THE GERMAN SECTOR CAMPS—Mater and Bizerte (the air base), 1,050 workers; Massicault and Ksar-Tyr, 300; Cheyles, 420; La Mornaghia, 250.

THE AREA NEAR TUNIS CAMPS—El-Aouina, 500 workers; Sidi Ahmed, 250; the Port of Tunis, 150.

ITALIAN SECTOR CAMPS—La Goulette, 97; Enfidaville, 256; St. Mary of Zit, 250; Mohammedia, 26; Zaghouan, 345.

There was a network of information between the camps carried out by an underground called "the Termites," headed by the pharmacist Maurice Taieb. This network informed the Committee and inmates of other camps exactly what was transpiring amongst the forced laborers.

EL-AOUINA

The central camp often had a transit stop at El-Aouina. More than 500 Jews served as a permanent slave force in the camp. They were divided into work platoons of fifty, each with a head. They worked from sunrise until 6:00 p.m. with a break for lunch, which consisted of one piece of fruit. Later in the day, workers were given a one-half hour break, which was often used to say Minha and Kaddish. The work consisted of moving wood and rocks weighing 80 to 100 kilo for distances of approximately 500 meters in order to build roads in the area of Tunis. The first Jew to die in this camp was Ernest Saada, age 24.(18) Four Jews died and thirty-nine were injured when the Allies bombed the camp.

SIDI AHMED

In this smaller camp in the Tunis area, the Jews were headed by

Henry Bismut and Alex Bonan. A German soldier, Schbuttes, killed the Jew, Edmond Azria, by smashing in his head as punishment for slow labor. On April, 15 1943, the Jews here escaped in the execution of a bluff by Bonan.(19)

BIZERTE

The air base at Bizerte was also the location of the largest concentration camp in Tunisia. The Jews interned there had nicknames for their Nazi tormentors. One soldier, referred to as "Fritz," killed Gilbert Naccache. Soldiers Ruhr and Walter were said to simply enjoy beating Jews. The soldier nicknamed Petit Pere (little father) enjoyed whipping the laborers. The guard called Le Tueur (killer) murdered Victor Lellouche, 45, of Ferryville. "Grand Mere" (grandmother) killed Alfred Hababou and Elie Saadoum, age 29. "Momento" used to force the Jews into cold showers and then expose them to the elements. Lt. Elfess was responsible for killing three Jews he did not like, although, after the Allied bombardment of January 6, 1943, Elfess permitted fifty wounded workers to be evacuated. Feldwebel Thild generally tortured Jews. Others died in the Allied bombardment as the Germans tried to hold on to this last piece of Tunisia. The German guards allowed the Jews at the Bizerte concentration camp to eat only 200 grams of bread and one teaspoon of jam per day, a very limited intake, indeed.(20) The first Jew to die at the Bizerte camp was Albert Fitousi, age 22.(21)

THE PORT

Colonel Meyfer, who wore a monocle, was in charge of this labor camp at the port of Tunis. He had two Jews executed, Robert Guedj and Aldo Saadoun. Jacques Kakou-Cohen, age 20, died on 11 April 1943. His dismembered body was found in the German blockhouse. Meyfer used the Jews as protection from the Allied bombings.(22)

KSAR-TYR

This concentration camp was one of the first to be filled with Jews who had assembled in the Alliance Israelite Universelle School on December 9, 1942. The Jews were assigned to digging and maintaining anti-tank trenches. The internees were required to walk two hours each way to and from the work area.(23)

ITALIAN SECTOR

The Jews taken in forced labor to the Italian sector fared much better than did their co-religionists in the German-occupied areas. These camps were fewer in number, and the Italian guards manifested less anti-Jewish behavior. The Jewish Council in the Italian sector was headed by Henry Sfez, Jules Taieb and M. Baranes. The Italian commander was Colonel Impellizzeri, who dealt with the camps as if they were solely work camps, allowing for the replacement of sick Jewish workers. Most of the Italian camp guards were Tunisian-Italian either by birth or by residence. However, because of their desert location, the camps were subject to other problems; for example, Sbikha lacked water. The largest camps in the Italian sector were at Zaghouan and Saouaf, with smaller camps in Enfidaville, Djebibina, Djaugger, Djelloula, and Sbikha. These camps were subjected to frequent Allied bombardments. Robert Bellaiche headed the Jewish inmates of the Zaghouan camp. Little could be done to negate the effects of bombardment or disease. Elie Mettoudi, at Djelloula, and Joseph Chemouny, at Djaugger, were both wounded from Allied bombing.(24) At Djebibina, Andre Assuied died, the first victim of an epidemic which devastated the camp. On April 25, 1943, as the Allies made their final attack on the camp at Djaugger, the head of the Jewish inmates, Raymond Raccah, was told that the Jews were to be given a "vacation." Thirty workers left the camp.(25)

TUNIS

Those Jews who were not sent to camps faced other sanctions and restrictions. One example occurred on December 21, 1942, when SS Colonel Rauff declared the Jews responsible for the Allied bombing of Tunis and demanded that they pay twenty million francs by 4:00 p.m. the following day. The President of the Jewish community, Borgel, arranged to meet with Resident-General Admiral Esteva. A meeting was set up for 5:00 p.m. that day in the Kasbah of Tunis. The participants included Messrs. Binoch, the Secretary-General of the Tunisian government; Carty, Director of Finance of the Tunisian government; Reydon, Chairman of the Board of Caisse Fonciere, and their lawyer. The Jews were represented by Borgel and Nataf. An agreement was reached, whereby the Caisse Fonciere would advance the sum of 20 million francs for a period of six months, at an interest rate of 8% per annum. The loan was to be guaranteed by the individual members of the Jewish Community Council. Borgel had put his own worth on the line for the sake of the entire community.

The following day, December 22, 1942, at 4:00 p.m., exactly as prescribed, Borgel delivered to Colonel Rauff a sack weighing 15 kilo, filled with banknotes.

General von Arnim gave the money to the Comite Ouvrier de Secours Immediat (COSI). Von Arnim, proclaiming that the Allied bombardment was part of a plot by international Jewry, designated the funds for Italian, French and Arab victims of the bombings. COSI was founded and headed by Georges Guilbaud and Fernand Lefevre, both prominent anti-Jews. The money they received from the Nazis to form and fund the COSI was more of a bribe to stir the three victimized groups to anti-Jewish feeling than any real measure of concern for relief for the bombing victims. As part of their anti-Jewish propaganda, Guilbaud, who had come to Tunis in November 1942 under orders of the Vichy Ministry of Information, was instructed to edit an anti-Jewish newspaper, "Tunis-Journal." Guilbaud and

Lefevre reported directly to Rahn, the Reichminister in Tunisia, for their orders. In this way, Jewish money was used by COSI to foment public opinion against Jews. (26)

In another example, at a meeting of the Committee on February 4, 1943, SS officer Saewecke declared that the Bizerte concentration camp required an additional 300 men. The Committee replied that it could not deliver the men. Saewecke responded by threatening refugee families with internment at the barracks of the Alliance School compound, and promised worse punishment, if necessary.

On February 6, 1943, the Nazis entered the Hara (Jewish ghetto), robbing and beating individuals, and looting Jewish homes of their furniture. They left dozens of families suffering in the cold. The Nazis then requisitioned other furniture for their lodgings at the Majestic Hotel, where German officers were stationed. The Committee asked Emile Hagege to serve as liaison with the Germans to handle requisitions for furniture in order to prevent robberies and eliminate beatings. In addition to the requisitions, SS Inspector Smeets and First Lieutenant Loba also demanded Jewish property.

In response to the Committee's "defiance," Colonel Rauff called the Jewish leaders to his office on February 15, 1943. He demanded three million francs to pay the salary of workers needed to fulfil the work requirements of the three hundred Jews the Committee had failed to produce. The Committee met this 24-hour deadline. However, the appetite of the Nazis was whetted, and the impoverishment of the Jewish community continued. Colonel Rauff also demanded a list of all Jewish owned merchandise.(27)

As the Allied forces drew closer, acts of Nazi terror increased, particularly from Saewecke and his aide, Pohl. Victor Nataf, an 18 year old rabbinical student, was killed with a bullet through the heart.(28) He was posthumously accused of signaling the Allies, as was the young cripple, Gilbert Nasouz, age 19.(29) German soldiers pillaged the Hara, while the French police did nothing. The Committee protested this random violence. Saewecke responded by allowing the Feldgendarmerie (military police) to patrol the streets of the Jewish ghetto, to "protect" the Jews from random violence. The ensuing Nazi violence was not random, it was orderly and organized. After all, if looting of Jews was the order of the day, it might as well be Saewecke's troops who did the job.

Many of the Jewish leaders had outlived their usefulness. Saewecke had them deported. Lawyer Victor Cohen-Hadria, head of financial services of the Committee, Dr. Benjamin Levy, an influential member of the Radical Party, Serge Moatti, a socialist journalist, Victor Silvera, member of the finance committee, and twenty others, were arrested and deported to Auschwitz. Only Moatti and Silvera survived. Raymond Samama, of an influential family, was deported, and died in Oranienburg. Guy Boccara, who replaced Cohen-Hadria on the finance committee, was later deported and died at an unknown locale. The German-Jewish refugee, Ruhlmann, who used the alias Rousseau, was also deported to the European death camps. Madame Louise Hanon, a resistance leader, was deported and later found in the Alexanderplatz prison, in Berlin.(30) Alfred Valensi, a philanthropist and lawyer, and contributor of articles to leading European newspapers, died during the deportations.

Even in the face of advancing Allied troops, the Nazis continued their persecution of the Jews. The French anti-Jew, M. de Font Reaux, protested the laxity in the local application of racial laws and the wearing of the yellow Star of David insignia. As of March 12, 1942, all Jews over the age of 18 had to wear the yellow star. Now the law would be enforced regardless of the proximity of the Allied troops. In another instance, fifty five Jews were killed at La Marsa, but the

French police prohibited their burial. Eventually, the Jews were able to obtain a common grave for their murdered brethren.

OTHER CITIES

Jews in other cities suffered, as well. In the town of Gofsa, eighty two Jews, mostly women and children, were killed in a single action.

The city of Sfax had five thousand Jews when the Germans occupied the town on November 19, 1942. First the Italian Bersaglieri came. Then, the Germans, with their Stadtkommandantur, Jamor Kurchner, and his aide, First Lieutenant Wope, became part of the municipal administration. Finally, of course, the Gestapo arrived, headed by SS officer Volmer, and the Feldgendarmerie. Jewish affairs were in the hands of SS Obergruppenfuhrer Best, brother to the German governor of occupied Denmark.(31) Best's adjunct was SS Sturmbannfuhrer Jensen. Best and Jensen reported directly to SS Colonel Rauff. Henri Cohen was appointed president of the Jewish Community Council. Best demanded of him ten slave workers. A curfew was established. By February 1943, all Jews had to wear the yellow star. The Jewish Council complied with every directive. Isidor Sperber, a Polish-Jewish physician, headed both the translation and the sanitary services. All Jewish-owned bicycles were confiscated. On March 26, 1943, the Nazis demanded fifteen million francs for the COSI, and an additional five million francs to pay for supplies for the Jewish slave laborers. The Jewish community was able to borrow the funds. As the Allied troops advanced in April, the Nazis demanded an additional twenty million francs, which were obtained by bor- rowing against Jewish possessions. With the Allies practically at their doorstep, the Nazis took fifty hostages, including five members of the Jewish Community Council. These Jews were later deported to Europe. The fleeing Nazis also robbed the Jews of an additional five million francs.

Some three hundred slave laborers were liberated by the Allies from nearby camps. At Wadi Akarit, bodies of eighty five Jews were found and brought for burial in a common grave in the Sfax Jewish cemetery.(32)

In Sousse, the Jews were under the control of Colonel Eyraud, a French anti-Jew. Eyraud was noted both for his mistreatment of slave laborers and for the appropriation of hundreds of thousands of francs. The President of the Jewish Community Council here was Georges Binhas. When Saewecke visited Sousse, he was disappointed with Eyraud's work there, and had the city placed under the control of Best. Best ordered all male Jews between the ages of eighteen and fifty to report for forced labor. They were assembled at the barracks Ardent du Picq. The laborers were used to repair the damage to the docks caused by Allied bombings. They were used as slave labor in target areas and offered no protection or shelter from bombings. At night, they were returned to the concentration camp. Best ordered all Jews over the age of six, regardless of sex, to wear the yellow star. This law was enforced. Binhas was ordered to appear twice daily to Gestapo headquarters for his instructions. Binhas complied. On one of his visits, Saewecke demanded fifteen million francs, which the community had to borrow in order to pay. On March 17, 1943, Captain Crebs of the Gestapo and Captain Fehling of the Kommandantur demanded ten million francs, payable in sixty hours. It was to be the final ransom to the Germans, before the invaders fled.(33)

The town of Gabes faced smaller demands from the retreating Nazis. Three hundred and ninety thousand francs were removed from Jewish bank accounts. The Germans demanded and received twenty kilo of gold. Homes and businesses were robbed and ransacked. Women were raped during Nazi-inspired Arab attacks on the Jews, used to cover the German retreat. The Italians tried unsuccessfully to protect the Jews. When the Nazis finally withdrew, the Jews regrouped sufficiently to help repair a bridge in order to assist the advancing British troops.

When Kairouan was liberated on April 10, 1943, the Jews tore off the hated yellow stars they had been forced to wear and replaced them with a "V", for the anticipated Allied victory.(34)

The isolated island of Djerba saw its Jewish community pay a ten million franc ransom on February 13, 1943. Just prior to the German withdrawal of troops that spring, the Nazis demanded fifty kilo of gold, stating the two Luftwaffe airplanes circling overhead would bomb the Jewish community if they did not comply. The Chief Rabbi was given two days to deliver the ransom. And so the rabbi of this ultra-orthodox community had to ride on the holy Sabbath to collect the gold, obtaining only 43 kilo by the deadline. He appealed for more time to assemble the remaining seven kilo, and was granted an extension of 24 hours. Before the rabbi finished collecting the gold, the Allies landed and the Germans fled, leaving behind an impoverished community.(35)

RESISTANCE

The Jews actively participated in the resistance movement, fighting the Axis and aiding the Allies. Alfred Rossi, a brilliant lawyer, militant Zionist and reserve officer, headed the Jewish resistance. He was later taken prisoner in Sicily. He was awarded the Croix de Guerre for his efforts. Victor Attias served on many missions out of Malta, and ended the war serving in the R.A.F. He was awarded the Legion of Honor and the Croix de Guerre. Sylvain Lumbroso, Andre

Nataf, Raoul Sitruk, and Jules Cohen-Solal also fought and spied for the Allies. At Cap Bon, Dr. Albert Benattar, Lucien Lumbroso and Raymond Uzan led the Allies to destroy seventeen transport planes. Lumbroso was also awarded the Croix de Guerre. Other spies included Samuel Benattar and Henry Smadja, who were active in the port area and train stations.(36)

Some of the Jewish spies exhibited unusual courage. Sylvain Karoubi was parachuted into southern Tunisia. He was arrested and imprisoned as a political detainee on the "Le Lassigny", moored at the fishing docks near Bizerte. Despite his imprisonment, he continued to smuggle messages to the Allies. When again caught, he was tortured, and was finally released through the efforts of M. Laffont, a member of the entourage of Admiral Esteva.(37)

Women played their role, as well. Mme. Francoise Grumbach continued to transmit clandestine messages to the Allies despite the arrest and detention of her gentile spouse. At the end of the war, she, too, was awarded the Croix de Guerre. Mentioned previously was Mme. Louise Hanon, second in command of espionage near Bizerte-Ferryville. She was arrested, deported to Germany, and later awarded the Croix de Guerre and the rank of Captain upon her release from Alexanderplatz prison in Berlin.

Some Jews demonstrated their bravery by protecting Allied soldiers. Raoul Benattar hid two English escapees from the prisoner of war camp near Kef. The two remained with Benattar throughout the German occupation. Henry Sfez, who headed the communications network of the Jewish inmates in the camps, also helped stray parachutists.

Other resistance fighters did not fare so well. Maurice Taieb, who headed the underground network called "Termites," M. Tibi from Sousse, and M. Assous of Jodjeb El-Ayoun were caught and deported to the European death camps. Only Taieb survived Buchenwald to receive the Croix de Guerre. Joseph Chemia and his two sons, Gilbert and Jean, were arrested and deported as agents of the resistance. First sent to Buchenwald, they were later transferred to Torgau. There, they were beheaded by axe, the youngest first, then the other son. After watching his children die, the elder Chemia was beheaded.

The Germans were finally withdrawing in the face of the advancing Allied troops. Some Jews rejoined the French army of liberation, while others joined the British troops under the Jewish Brigade. As the Axis troops withdrew, a Jewish doctor serving on the coast near the Beach of Kram discovered the body of SS Kommandant Saewecke. He had died without enjoying the fortune he had robbed from the Jews .

On August 8, 1943, three months after the Allies entered Tunis, and at the instigation of Jewish lawyers, including Rene Cohen-Hadria of the Court of Appeals in Tunis and Elie Nataf, both members of the Bar, the Comite Francais de la Liberation Nationale removed all anti-Jewish regulations. The war against the Tunisian Jews was over.(38)

The military requirements of the German army ironically helped create the framework for the salvation of the majority of Tunisian Jewry. The Wehrmacht did not stop the killing, pillaging and raping of the Jewish community, they merely deferred it by harnessing it for slave labor. Lacking proper railways, the Germans could not institute mass deportations. The well organized and often defiant Jewish community, by manipulating the German love for detail, maintained lists of camp inmates and provided for their needs as much as possible.

Mutual responsibility, however, was the main key to this Jewish community's survival, although not all individual Jews did survive. Some died through acts of violence by German camp guards, some by disease. Some were killed during the Allied bombardments; others were deported to European death camps after experiencing their first air travel.

A total of 2,575 Tunisian Jews died. The Holocaust had spread to the Sephardic communities of North Africa. It is most unfortunate that most people, including noted scholars of the Holocaust, do not note the fate of these maltreated Jews. It was not a lack of desire to perpetrate the "final solution of the Jewish problem" on Tunisian Jewry and their co-religionists in Libya that prevented the extermination of these Jews, but merely the lack of time, the needs of warfare, and the lack of railways and proper roads that caused the timely delay. Had the Allies not been so close at hand and had transportation routes been generally sound, the efficient German application of the "final solution" might have been realized in these countries as well.

Yet this knowledge will not lessen the scars of death and suffering borne by Tunisian Jewry at the hands of the Nazis, who noted very well that they, too, were part of the Jewish people.

NOTES
1. Lucy S. Davidowicz. *The War Against the Jews.* (New York, Bantam, 1976). Davidowicz totally ignores the fate of the Jews of North Africa, despite the title of her work.
2. Raul Hilberg. *The Destruction of European Jews.* (Chicago, Quadrangel, 1967). Hilberg very briefly and somewhat inaccurately describes some German activity in Tunisia. It is a very small monument to those deprived Jews. However, since the title of the work clearly defines geographic area, Hilberg cannot be herewith faulted.

3. `Ibid., 412-413.

4. Xavier Vallat was the anti-Jewish Commissioner in France. After the war, Vallat was sentenced in France to a ten year imprisonment. He was released by Justice Minister Rene Mayer in 1950.

5. Jacques Sabille. *Les Juifs de Tunisie Sous Vichy et L'Occupation* (Paris: Edition du Centre, 1954), p 24-28.

6. Gaston Ghez. *Nos Martyrs.* (Tunis, 1946) unnumbered.

7. General von Arnim replaced Rommel on March 8, 1943. Von Arnim had been Rommel's deputy.

8. Jacques Sabille. op.cit., p 29-34.

9. Rudolph Rahn was attached to the German foreign office and served in North Africa. Later he became ambassador to Italy. Rahn was denazified in 1950 and was never bothered by the authorities.

10. The native ruler, Moncef Bey, was already powerless under the French, and became just a figurehead.

11. Jacques Sabille. op.cit., p 34-38.

12. Ibid., p 38-42

13. Raul Hilberg, op.cit., p 411. The Italian Jews were exempted from forced labor even in the German zone because of the influence of the Italian Consul General in Tunis. This spared nearly five thousand Italian Jews from enslavement despite German attempts to have them included in the camps' labor force.

14. Jacques Sabille, op.cit., p 45-47.

15. Ibid., p 48-52

16. Paul Ghez has been frequently cited as one of the most able men on the Committee. His administrative ability along with Borgel's strength are credited with assisting in the salvation of Tunisian Jewry.

17. Jacques Sabille, op.cit., p 65-82.

18. Gaston Ghez, op.cit., unnumbered.

19. Gaston Ghez, *Tadkarat el-Khaddama el-Yehud, Tahat jil Almania fi Tunis* (Tunis, Matba'at Uzan, 1946), unnumbered.

20. Jacques Sabille. op.cit., p 110-113.

21. Gaston Ghez. op. cit., unnumbered.
22. Jacques Sabille. op. cit., p. 114.
23. Ghez, Gaston. op. cit. unnumbered.
24. Jacques Sabille. op. cit., p 115.
25. Gaston Ghez. op. cit., unnumbered.
26. Jacques Sabille. op. cit., p 117-118.
27. Ibid., p 119-121.
28. Ghez, Gaston. op.cit. unnumbered. Victor (Haim) Nataf was killed by the Germans near Ariana.
29. Ibid. Gilbert Nazous was killed on the road to Bir M'Cherfa.
30. It is clear from these actions that the Nazis had every intention of eliminating Tunisian Jewry. These deportations to the European death camps would only have been the beginning, had the Germans won.
31. Werner Best, the Nazi governor of occupied Denmark, was condemned to death in Denmark after the war. His sentence was commuted to five years and he was released in 1951.
32. *American Jewish Year Book,* vol. 45 (1943-44), p 258-259.
33. Jacques Sabille. op.cit., p 148-149.
34. Ibid., p 150-151.
35. Based on an article in Aufbau, an American German-Jewish publication, Hilberg reports that the Germans gave the Jewish community only two hours to raise the gold, and that the community raised 47 kilo. Both Sabille and Ghez report the same story, in which the Nazis gave a two day ultimatum and received 43 kilo. Robert Attal, in the Jewish Journal of Sociology, vol. 2, no.1 (1960), reports that the Germans extracted all 50 kilo of gold from the Djerban Jewish community. It almost seems as if, the tragic events having occurred in such a small community, it has become less important that facts be documented carefully.
36. Jacques Sabille, op.cit., p 136-141.
37. Ibid., p 134-135
38. Ibid., p 156-158

IRAQI JEWS IN THE FAR EAST
DURING THE HOLOCAUST
by Joseph Abraham

The experiences of the Jews in the Far East at the time of the Holo- caust cannot be compared with the experiences of the Jews in Europe since the conditions prevailing in the Far East were so very different. The Holocaust was basically a European happening but there is a story to be told of the attempt of its perpetrators to extend it to the Far East.

Since they had a common enemy, it was natural that there was an al- liance between Nazi Germany and Japan during World War II. It was an alliance where Japan was an equal partner rather than a junior partner who might be willing to take orders. This was demonstrated in the case of the Jewish refugees who came to Shanghai from Germany and Austria prior to Pearl Harbor. How did this alliance affect the Jews residing in the Far East? The Japanese did have preconceived notions about the Jewish people and their influence on the countries in which they lived, particularly the United States. This went back to the days of the Russo-Japanese War of 1904. However, they were interested only in the Jews who were influential, the very wealthy, the industrialists and those involved in Wall Street and not with, for example, the employed individual and his family, who the Nazis, in their case, pursued with the same diligence as they did the rich and the intellectuals.

The immediate effect of the war on the Jews residing in Singapore and Hong Kong after the capture of these two cities by the Japanese, late in 1941, was that all those of British nationality were treated by the Japanese as enemy subjects, with no discrimination being made because of religion. This meant that the resident Jews, practically all of Iraqi origin but at the same time naturalized British subjects, were also considered enemy subjects by the Japanese. Prior to this, when it was realized that war was imminent, most of the British women and children in Singapore were evacuated to India, while those in Hong Kong were evacuated to Australia. Those men and women who remained, were interned for the duration, and the hardships they underwent have been documented in the many works covering the fate of the prisoners of war in those cities. However, the case of Shanghai was very different.

Shanghai was a city under three jurisdictions. The International Settlement, the French Concession and the area surrounding which was, of course, China. Each area had its own government, each had its own electric generating facility, with different voltages, each issued its own automobile licenses and so on. The make up of the police force of the International Settlement consisted of Chinese and turbaned Sikhs under British officers, while the French officers in their Concession wore the traditional "kepi" with the constabulary drawn from their Southeast Asian colonies. This is just to give an idea of the jurisdiction prevailing at that period. The French kept their concession to themselves, while the International Settlement was the result of a merger of the British and American Concessions. The International Settlement represented other nationalities too. But for the present it would suffice to say that it also included the Japanese. Within the International Settlement on its northern boundary was the area known as Hongkew and it extended east to the Whangpoo River.

Even though Hongkew was part of the International Settlement and Japan was a partner in its jurisdiction, the Japanese had built huge naval barracks there and let it be known that Hongkew was under their control only and no one else's, but, not so, when it came to maintaining it.

From 1933 to 1939 eighteen thousand Jewish refugees came from Europe to Shanghai mostly by ship, while some came by the Trans-Siberian Railway. This latter route was used only by a small minority. It was at a time when there was still the possibility to leave Germany but on very short notice, and getting a visa to any country in the world was an impossibility, except to Shanghai, where this requirement did not exist. The refugees arrived penniless but with some personal belongings, but in most cases, without any knowledge of English, the language used by all the non-Chinese in the foreign Settlements of Shanghai. They were received by the Jewish communities who aided them to the best of their abilities, until it reached the point where these communities were unable to cope with the situation alone. Then aid was asked for and received from Jewish organizations abroad.

In the beginning housing was provided by Sir Victor Sassoon, in his Embankment Building. The Chinese YMCA was also made available. Before long an epidemic of scarlet fever broke out. When a group of new arrivals came they had to be segregated in order to prevent them from catching the infection. Not having any place at all to go, the Sephardim made the Beth Aharon Synagogue available for temporary living quarters, literally in the Synagogue proper, where mattresses were spread on the floor.

In the meantime, little by little, these immigrants started to become self-supporting. The majority resided in the Hongkew district where affordable space was available. The availability of space was due to the fact that the Japanese had expelled most of the Chinese from that area when they declared war, in 1937, on Chiang Kai-Shek's Nationalist armies around Shanghai. The refugees were settled there in the camps or "homes" as they were called. The choice of location was actually voluntary, but in reality it was the only space available. Subsequently many were able either to find employment, or to start small businesses enabling them move to the preferred sections of the International Settlement or the French Concession.

Another group came to Shanghai as refugees under totally different circumstances. These were the Rabbis and students of the Mir Yeshiva, so named after the town in Poland where it was located. In the autumn of 1939 the Soviet army occupied the area of northeastern Poland which included both the town of Mir and the city of Vilna. At that time it was believed that the Soviet authorities would cede Vilna to Lithuania, which was still an independent, neutral state. Assuming that this would be the case, it would then provide those who had only recently left Mir, with the safety they sought. The entire Yeshiva moved to Vilna. In 1940, Russia invaded Lithuania and the Yeshiva group was in trouble again. The next move was to Kovno where there were foreign consulates and, hopefully, the possibility of visas to a haven of safety. But which nation would issue a visa? Russia would issue an exit visa provided that the applicant had an entry visa for a specific destination. Before long it was discovered that the Dutch government required no visa for Curacao. This was needed to leave Russia, but, because the United States was their intended destination, they asked for and received transit visas through Japan from the Japanese consul in Kovno. The visa written in Japanese had an English translation saying "seen for the journey through Japan (to Surinam, Curacao and other Netherlands countries.)" Needless to say, when it was found out, this Japanese consul was reprimanded and transferred back to Japan. It must be said here parenthetically that eventually the government of Israel did recognize the consul's action which saved so many Jewish lives. The Mir Yeshiva group of about 250 did reach Japan, traveling by train to Vladivostok and then by ship to Japan, with Kobe their next stopping place. Here another Japanese came to the aid of the travelers. He was professor Setsuzo Kotsuji who had converted to Christianity in his younger days. Later on in life, he studied religion in various Protestant universities in the United States. After returning to Japan, he taught Old Testament and Hebrew in a theological seminary. He managed to help the Yeshiva group in Kobe, aiding them in getting extensions for their stay there. Professor Kotsuji was really an "Oheb Yisrael." In 1959 he traveled to Israel and converted to Judaism and became Abraham ben Abraham Kotsuji, after which he returned to Japan. He died there and was finally brought back to Jerusalem after his death, for burial there according to his wishes.

In August 1941, the Japanese authorities in Kobe realized that there was little chance for the members of the Yeshiva to continue their travels and so they transferred them to Shanghai where they became a part of the Jewish refugee community already there.

This was the situation up to December 8, 1941, when Pearl Harbor was bombed and World War II reached the banks of the Whangpoo River, with Japanese cannon blasting at the British and American gunboats tied up there. On that day all sections of Shanghai were occupied by His Imperial Japanese Majesty's armed forces.

In Shanghai, under the Japanese occupation, if a non-Chinese suffered for one reason or another from the Japanese military, it would be because of nationality or allegiance, but not because of religion. Jews of British, American, Dutch or Belgian nationality were interned for the duration, while those with Iraqi passports were classified as non-belligerent enemies. Iraq had declared war against

Japan but did not actually participate, so the Iraqi Jews, numbering some where between four and five hundred, were not interned but were required to wear a red arm band when on the street. Jews of Russian origin and others were not restricted. Anyone caught in an act, or suspected of doing anything against the interests of Japan was treated accordingly.

The only place in the Far East where Germany had any interest in a Jewish community was Shanghai, where the Jews fleeing Europe had taken refuge.(1) Some German Gestapo officers had arrived in Shaghai by submarine in the Spring of 1942. (2) They were Robert Meisinger, the "Executioner of Warsaw," Adolf Puttkammer and Hans Neumann, who had experimented on Jews in Auschwitz and Bergen-Belsen. They had come to give guidance to the Jewish Affairs Bureau set up by the Japanese military. This bureau consisted of representatives from the Japanese consulate, the much dreaded Gendarmerie (Kempetai), the Army and the Navy. When the formation of a new Jewish Affairs Bureau took place, rumors started to circulate that, under the guidance of the German Gestapo, severe measures would be taken against all Jews regardless of their origin and length of residence in Shanghai. Only then, born of dire fear, was a joint committee formed by the Jewish residents consisting of two Sephardim, Messers. Ellis Hayim and Michael Speelman; two Russians, their chairman Topas and Joseph Bitker; and three central Europeans, the chairman Dr. Kardegg and Fritz Kauffmann as well as the Secretary Perutz. Late in July 1942 an emergency session of the committee was called. Present was Japanese Vice Consul Shibata who had been consular representative on the old Naval Jewish Affairs Bureau and was now in the same capacity on the new Bureau. He was well known to the members of the committee. They had found him sympathetic to the cause of the refugees and their problems. He had formerly worked in he United States in the Consular Service and had married a Nisei [a Japanese girl born in the United States]. He was definitely pro-American and belonged to the anti-war party if there was such thing in Japan. He related a gruesome story. The Jewish Affairs Bureau had met the day before and decided under Gestapo prodding to take steps to "liquidate" the Shanghai Jewish community. They hadn't as yet decided on the method to be used to achieve this. Some had suggested putting all the 25,000 Jews in Shanghai on some old ships lying idly there and sink them in the open sea; others had proposed to dump the Jews on the sparsely inhabited Tsungming Island in the mouth of the Yangtze River. In Shibata's opinion the only way to stop them was to get access to the General in Command of the Central China district, the Admiral in charge of the Navy in Shanghai, the top commander of the Gendarmerie in Shanghai and somebody high up in the Foreign Office in Tokyo. The Russian members of the committee had contact with the General in Command and also members of the Foreign Office, knowing them from Harbin at the time of the takeover of Manchuria. The secretary, Perutz, had contact with naval officers in Shanghai from before the outbreak of war. Then the question came up, as how to approach the Kempetai (Gendarmerie) who were undoubtedly the nasti- est and most difficult of the lot. They could not decide. Shibata pointed out that there was an old Shanghai Jewish resident by the name of Brahn who was known to have a Japanese girl friend related to the Imperial family. This girl, he was sure, could arrange an interview with the commanding officer of the Kempetai. Kauffmann was selected to approach Brahn as he was the only one who knew him. In Kauffmann's words his story continues "The next day I saw Brahn, told him the story and warned him expressly not to disclose the source of his information, as our friend Shibata would surely get into trouble and be court martialled if it was found out that he passed on to us the secrets of the Bureau meetings. I told Brahn. We all had agreed to state, if asked for the reasons of our action, it was the sudden flurry of anti-Semitic propaganda in the press, and that we were afraid that its launching presaged serious anti-Jewish measures." Brahn got his interview with a senior member of the Kempetai and was immediately disbelieved. He was threatened with punishment and, then losing his courage, told all. All those present at the meeting were arrested by the Kempetai, taken to Bridge House, their prison for interrogation of suspected spies and saboteurs, and detained in cells. Shibata was among those detained. He was dismissed from the consular service and sent back to Japan. Kauffmann described seeing him in Bridge House through a space in the cell's partitions.

Anyone suspected by the Japanese for any reason, was picked up and taken to Bridge House for interrogation. Among them were my aunt Mimi Hayim, also George Leonoff and Ossi Lewin both Jewish newspapermen. They became cell mates of the members of the Jewish committee who had been meeting with the Japanese consul Shibata and who were already under arrest. My aunt was released after sixteen days but my uncle, Ellis Hayim was held for many weeks before being released, and then it was to a Japanese hospital to be treated for Beri-beri which was the result of malnutrition. He was arrested once again some weeks later. The prisoners in Bridge House were in groups, who spent their days and nights on the concrete floor. Ossi Lewin in the Shanghai Echo Almanac of 1945, describes the conditions. "Many are suffering even today from frost bite contracted during their detention, since the detainees had to leave their shoes outside their cells. Inside the cell, one had to sit in the proscribed Japanese way, squatting on the floor with legs crossed, day in and day out, without being permitted to lean against the wall, to stretch atrophied limbs or to talk. You were only permitted to leave this painful position when you were taken out for your cross-examination to quarters above, where exhausting exercises were imposed on one, for no means were disregarded by the torturers to make their prisoners talk.

Everyone was apprehensive lest his name be called by passing sentries, for that meant the dreaded cross-examination.

"Nine o'clock was bed time, that meant it was permitted to stretch out on the floor from the squatting position, and to sleep if one's nerves, hunger, thirst and the cold permitted. But unfortunately there was no place on which to stretch yourself out. There were thirty-five in one cell, of smaller dimension than an average living room.

"A hole in a corner somewhere replaced to toilet, which was, despite its use by thirty-five prisoners, cleaned only once daily and which spread its terrible odor through the length and breadth of the cell. Despite the severe cold one was forced daily to undress completely in order to cleanse his clothes of a multitude of lice. These insects alone made life unbearable. Every prisoner without exception found an average sixty to seventy lice on his body daily. The writer of this, later contracted typhus". (3)

There was nothing but rice with some vegetables to eat. Permission was granted to have sandwiches, a thermos of coffee and a change of underwear brought in. To make delivery, one had to enter the building, always giving deep bows to the sentries. The items, in a wicker basket, would be placed on a shelf in a room adjoining the detention area. The next day this basket would be replaced by another, the former, sometimes still full and untouched, sometimes with the thermos broker, and the underwear was always filthy and ridden with lice. Among those mentioned earlier, Mr. Topas was kept the longest and when released, he was ill and never regained his health, eventually suffering a stroke.

In Shanghai on February 18, 1943, a proclamation was issued by the Japanese military, concerning the refugees who had arrived there after December 31, 1936. Stateless refugees in the Shanghai area, due to military necessity, had to be restricted to a designated area, namely, Hongkew, by May 18, 1943. Itself a frightening situation but more so because there was the constant speculation as to what would be the next step after being relocated to this "designated area." What actually did happen from this time until the war was over in August 1945 was that movement was severely restricted with extreme shortages of food and living quarters. Many tried to obtain permission for entry to the International Settlement, where there was still a chance to earn some money, but it was not at all easy. Appli- cants were subjected to a lot of harassment, particularly from the Japanese officer in charge, by the name of Ghoya, who gave himself the title "King of the Jews." An employment certificate from a possible employer had to be shown when applying for a pass and, if obtained, subject to a monthly renewal dependent on the whims of Ghoya. One of Ghoya's whims was the possibility of the applicant being slapped by him, while, Ghoya, being short in stature would be standing on his desk. The Mir Yeshiva students had a special imprint on their passes stating "Special Pass for Rabbi Student." A pass was needed in order to enter the International Settlement from Hongkew so as to enable the student to attend classes held in the Beth Aharon Synagogue.

The German Consul-General in Tientsin, at the period when the fate of the Jews in Shanghai was in the balance, was Fritz Wiedemann. He stated "This is to state that I have been Consul-General for Germany in Tientsin from 1941 to 1945. I hereby declare that I was thoroughly acquainted with the situation in the part of China occupied by Japan and that I followed the directives of the German government in all my activities there. I therefore confirm that the internment of Central European emigrants, as a rule primarily Jews who had emigrated from Germany and Austria to China, had taken place upon the instigation of the German government then in power. The Japanese themselves were not anti-Semitic, and we were

Jews who had emigrated from Germany and Austria to China, had taken place upon the instigation of the German government then in power. The Japanese themselves were not anti-Semitic, and we were under orders to instruct the Japanese authorities about the racial policies of Germany and to suggest appropriate measures. There is no doubt in my mind that the internment of Jews in the Shanghai ghetto had been instigated by the German authorities."(3)

While the Jews of enemy status were interned, and the European Jewish refugees were in the Hongkew ghetto, the Jews who remained "free" were having a very hard time. Two post-war reports were made by Maurice Dangoor (the son of the late Chief Rabbi Dangoor of Iraq) who was the president of the Sephardi community for the duration of the war and continuing in that post until he left Shanghai for good in 1946. Before the end of the war the two Sephardi Synagogues were taken over by the Japanese for the storage of ammunition and they placed anti-aircraft guns in the Jewish cemetery. All through the war monthly statements of income and expenditure had to be given to the Japanese authorities and from time to time Mr. Dangoor was called by various departments and subjected to searching questions about the community. The Shanghai Ashkenazi Jewish Community, when the Japanese Military Authorities took the premises of the Jewish school, Beth Aharon Synagogue and the Ohel Rachel Synagogue, were kind enough to put at the disposal of the Sephardim a room in their Synagogue for our daily prayers. In their hospital quarters they housed all the teakwood benches and chairs of the Ohel Rachel Synagogue. These chairs were back in their places ready for Rosh Hashanah services in September 1945.

This is basically the story of the effect of the Holocaust on the Jews residing in the Far East and the influence the Nazis used on the Japanese in order to continue their pursuit of those Jews who had so far escaped with their lives from Germany to Shanghai. They included those Jews already resident there. By the time the war ended the Nazi influence had not succeeded in anything further than sending the refugees to the Hongkew ghetto. It could be surmised that once it was known that the Germans had tried to influence the Japanese in how to handle the Jews, the Japanese showed their independence by being unwilling to annihilate the Jews in Shanghai as suggested by the Germans.

Something of a different nature took place at the immediate end of the war. The home we lived in, which was built by my grandfather in 1908, was a mansion with a large front lawn and was, in fact, a very desirable residence. It was taken over by the Japanese military when they finally interned every person of enemy nationality. We had British nationality derived from our grandparents and father being born in Bombay, India. India was a British possession at that time. The Japanese had allocated our house to the German consulate for their use. It was occupied by Consul-General Martin Fischer, who held that post long before Hitler and continued to hold it even though he was not a member of the Nazi party. The rest of my family were interned in the Lincoln Avenue Camp. My father and I were in the Shanghai General Hospital, a long established hospital run by French nuns. I had been there for a while but my father had come for some tests shortly before the war's end. The day the war was over, word was gotten to us in the hospital, that the German consul suggested that we come and reside in our house before the Chinese Nationalist government arrived to take over this enemy property. If that had been the case it would have taken ages for us to establish ownership in order to reside there once again, and surely it would no longer be in the same immaculate condition that the Consulate maintained. The Shanghai foreign community was one where most knew of each other, if they did not actually know each other. We moved into our home and for a few days we resided with the Germans under the same roof. It was to our advantage to do this, as others who did not have this opportunity had to continue to live in a former internment camp waiting to repossess their own homes. At this time, when the German consul was still in the house, a school friend of mine, Mickey Moore, who was Chinese and worked with the underground during the war, came to ask my help. General Wedemeyer, commander of the 14th Army Air Force, more familiarly known as the "Flying Tigers," had arrived by plane the day before from Chungking with some members of his staff and with a jeep for which gasoline was needed—could I help? I tried and I succeeded in getting some through a friend, Luiz Marcal, who was Portuguese and therefore not interned. A fifty gallon drum of gasoline was delivered to our home and then the jeep came to pick it up—the jeep was manned by local Jewish boys from the Betar group who had volunteered to help the arriving members of the United States Armed Forces.

Rabbi Marvin Tokayer, who was the rabbi of Tokyo's Jewish Community and the author of the book "The Fugu Plan," tells in the Epilogue of finding Mitsugi Shibata after the war. He was the Japanese consul who informed the Jewish community of the plan to rid Shanghai of all Jews in early 1942. "Mitsugi Shibata having been expelled from Shanghai, returned to Japan. Believing that he had done the Shanghai Jews a great disservice by mentioning the impending pogrom and causing their imprisonment, Shibata was too ashamed to contact any of the Jews in the Orient after the war. It was not until the research was being done that Rabbi Tokayer found Shibata and informed him that, in fact, he had saved the lives of thousands of Jews. Shibata was honored at a Passover Seder at the Jewish Community Center in Tokyo in 1976. He died in 1977.(4)

There is not a Jewish community in any part of China today except for Hong Kong. No Jew from pre-World-War II days still lives in China and less than twenty old timers relocated from Shanghai in the 1950's can still be found in Hong Kong. One must realize that this is a result of the Communist Revolution and not the after-effect of World War II.

Shanghai was a haven for 25,000 Jews, who were interned, relocated to a ghetto and restricted in many other ways but nevertheless survived while their brothers and sisters in other parts of the world perished.

BIBLIOGRAPHY

Dicker, Herman, *Wanderers and Settlers in the Far East.*

Hertzman, Rabbi E.Y., *Escape to Shanghai* (from his *Ness Hahatsala*).

Kauffman, Fritz, *Experiences of the Shanghai Jewish Community Under the Japanese in World War II.*

KOUNTRASS (Jan-Fev, 1987). L'Aventure de Changhai (1939-46).

From Rabbi E.Y. Hertzman's *Ness Hahatsala.*

Kranzler, David, *Japanese, Nazis and Jews.*

Leitner, Yecheskel, *Operation: Torah Rescue.*

SHANGHAI ECHO ALMANAC, 1946. Bridge House Memories by Ossi Lewin.

Tokayer, Marvin, *The Fugu Plan.*

NOTES:

1. Fritz Kauffman, a German Jewish businessman resident in Shanghai since 1931, delivered a paper before the Shanghai Tiffin Club, in New York on February 10, 1963. (Tiffin was the colloquial word in Shanghai for lunch, a word of Anglo-Indian derivation and not pidgin English). What follows is an abridgement of his paper. Some German Gestapo officers have arrived in Shanghai by submarine in the Spring of 1942.

2. According to Herman Dicker in his *Wanderers and Settlers in the Far East.*

3. *Shanghai Echo Almanac, 1946.* Bridge House Memories by Ossi Lewin.

4. In David Kranzler's *Japanese, Nazis and Jews* a post-war statement by Wiedemann is recorded.

5. Tokayer, Marvin. *The Fugu Plan.*

THE RESCUE OF THE BOUKHARAN
AND GRUZIAN JEWS IN FRANCE
by Dr. M. MITCHELL SERELS

On May 16, 1918, Gruzia (Georgia) became an independent country. In order to prevent the new Soviet Russia from disman tling the new republic, the Premier, Akaki Chkhenkeli, a social democrat, signed an accord with General Otto von Losson of Germa ny on May 28, 1918. At that time, a small German force landed of 3,000 men. Then a treaty was signed with Turkey ceding the ports of Artvin and Ardaban. Germany became the protector of independ ent Gruzia.

On December 27, 1918 the British landed a force at Batom which remained there until June 4, 1920. A free election was held in February 1919 and Zhordania was elected president. Evgheni Gheghechkori, the foreign minister went to Paris to gain Allied recognition. It was not until January 15, 1920 that the recognition was granted. On May 7, 1920 Soviet Russia signed a peace with Georgia. However on February 11, 1921 the Russians invaded Gruzia and the government fled on March 18, 1921, establishing itself in Paris as a government-in-exile. On August 27, 1924, another revolt broke out led by Kaikhosro Cholekashvili. Consequently, there was a history of Gruzian anti-Soviet activity, something the Germans could well appreciate. When the Germans invaded France, they found their old Gruzian friends and the government in exile. The Nazis hoped to use these anti-Soviets to establish a puppet government in Gruzia when they would cap ture it. Therefore the Nazis were extremely friendly to the Gruzian government-in-exile. However, Jews were another case. The anti-Jewish regulations were to be applied to all Jews, even to those from Georgia.

Particularly active were Misha Kedia and Sasha Korkia in urging the Gruzian government-in-exile to intervene on behalf of Jews. This activity was partially out of feeling of comradeship with Jewish Gruzians and partially because the intervention gave recognition and activity to the government in protecting its citizens. The members of the government-in-exile felt that regardless of the outcome of war, Stalin, the fellow Georgian who had smashed the independent Georgian republic, would lose and they would return to power—either by a German victory which would support them or by upheavals in the USSR against the Hitler-Stalin pact, and an independent Georgia would emerge. Many felt that the West would prevail and the Allies would install an independent government, free from Moscow.

In 1920, Marquet along with Ramsey MacDonald, Snowden and Vandemelde had visited the independent Georgian Republic and he had maintained contact with the members of the government in exile. Under the Vichy government, it was Marquet who became the Minister of Interior. It was Marquet in July of 1940 who alerted his friends that all Jews living in France would have to register with the police.

When the registration order was promulgated, the gentile Georgians forbade the Jews from Gruzia to register. Zhordania, the president-in-exile and Evgheni Gheghechkori, Premier and the foreign minister-in-exile told a meeting of ten Jews including Joseph Eligulashvili not to register, that they would protect them. The Jews listened and did not register although this was illegal. Kedia who had close connections with the Germans felt that he could obtain official exemptions for the Gruzian Jews and take official responsibility on behalf of his government for this failure to do so. Since the Germans felt that they would soon occupy Georgia and need this government in exile to put in place for it was staunchly anti-Stalinist, they would let the Georgians have all their citizens. All Jews with Gruzi sounding names were included in the protection by their government and the officials of the exile government did not denounce the Jews. The Germans on their own could not make easy distinctions based upon surnames.

Gheghechkori told the Jews that he had learned through Kedia that the German military authorities in Paris had received in structions from Berlin to treat Georgian Jews as if they were non-Jews. The Jews felt uneasy about this order, 1) because it relied on rumor, for no document was produced; 2) because it indicated that the Germans could now distinguish between gentile and Jewish Georgian.

De Brinon, the French delegue-general or equivalent to an ambassador to the German occupation was approached by Marquet at the request of the Georgians and, apparently, the Jews were, at least temporarily, exempted from the anti-Jewish regulations. The police had a committee formed of gentile Georgians who would determine who was a Georgian Jew and to issue identity cards exempting the bearer from anti-Jewish regulations. The chairman of the committee was an active social democrat member of the government-in-exile, who originally had been concerned about the Jews, Sasha Korkia. The committee compiled a list of 243 Jewish families which represented nearly 1,000 individuals. Many, if not most, of these Jews were not Gruzian but other Jews; some had their names changed simply by adding "shvili" to the end or replacing Slavic endings -

"witz" or "off" with "shvili". Levi Eligulashvili was active in adding names thus to the lists. The Germans overlooked this list because of their hope for a quick victory in Russia and the installation of this government-in-exile which they now controlled. Some of the Jews were given phony positions in the government-in-exile to insure their security. The identity cards helped to prevent arrests or to secure quick release.

The Nazi army never made it to Gruzia and their defeats and retreats meant threats for the Georgian population in France. The contact with the government-in-exile no longer had any value and their Jews were of less value. Unknown to the Georgians, Rosenberg, the Nazi theoretician had tried to classify Georgians as non-Aryans. However, on 12 September 1941 a directive from Heydrich not to treat Georgians or Moslems from USSR as if they were Jews was issued based on a meeting relating to POWs held in the summer of 1941 under Reineche. One family was arrested by the Vichy military and sent to Drancy after a Talith and Tefilin were found in their home in Lyon in 1943. They were released only when Misha Kedia intervened. The release took three weeks and meanwhile the entire community went into hiding. In 1944, another sweep in Nice meant the arrest of several families who were sent to Drancy and then on to Auschwitz. Liberation came shortly thereafter preventing the murder of the rest of the population.

The effective action of the social democratic government in exile rescued hundreds of Jews, Georgians and pseudo-Georgians because they acted to make the list inclusionary rather exclusionary.

This advice Joseph Eligulashvili, Sosipathra Assatiani and Premier-in-exile Evgheni Gheghechkori gave to Dr. Asaf Atchildi who obtained similar advice for Misha Kedia and Sosha Korkia. Dr. Atchildi was born in Samarkand, a town in Russian Asia. Atchildi`s family was unique in that his parents were open to western knowledge and he studied in a Russian gymnasium. He later became a physician but was forced to leave Russia as a political exile and to reestablish himself as a physician in France. In August 1939 he was drafted into the French military medicine but released to Paris. On August 16, 1940, only those whose fathers were French were allowed to practice medicine and Atchildi was removed from his position.

In October 1940, all Jews were called upon to register. The Vichy government defined Jews as either belonging to the Jewish religion or as having two Jewish grandparents. On October 4, 1940 Vichy ordered the internment of all foreign Jews at Gars. The Germans had on September 27, 1940 defined Jews racially. At the insistence of his wife, Atchildi refused to register. She wanted to flee with their two daughters to Spain. It was she who went to her friend, a counselor at the Afghan embassy. He offered the protection of his embassy if she would say she was Afghani and destroy her birth certificate which clearly marked them as Yahud (Jew).

This ruse began the so-called Juguti Affair. The Jugutis were Boukharan Jews who had at one point been compelled to become Moslem but who returned to Judaism. This would make Jugutis non-Jews according to the Germans and Jews according to the French. Mr. Kachurine and Mr. Nathanel had begun to use the complicated history of Boukharan Jews with the aid of a lawyer Kraehling from Malhouse. This first group who claimed to be Juguti had already been marked on their identity cards as "Juif." These 38 had already met with the custodian of Jewish property on October 18, 1940 as there was a law for the organization of Jewish owned property. Some had been detained in Drancy. In June 1941, Nathanel was about to be arrested and went into hiding. The two went surreptitiously to the attorney Kraehling who demanded 15,000f which was paid by Nathanel.

This event led Atchildi to the meeting with the Georgians. Atchildi had been the family physician to Misha Kedia, who was placed in charge of the Georgian Jews. Atchildi was naturally selected as the leader of the Boukharan Jews because he had not registered and was not on the list of 38. He was charged with saving their lives and other Boukharan Jews. On Saturday, June 21, 1941, Kedia asked Atchildi to prepare a memo on the Juguti for the Germans were now occupied with the invasion of Russia.

By August 1941, several Boukharans who now called themselves Juguti were arrested and held in Drancy. This was part of the first round-up of foreign born Jews living in France. On October 5, 1941, Kedia having already spoken to Dr. Weber at 19 Avenue Foch, Atchildi was told to draw up a list of all Juguti for whom he will be responsible. The police would then remove those people from the restrictions. Atchildi prepared his list of 38 and met instead of Dr. Weber, a M. Adam who told Atchildi to see Lt. Bandorf. Bandorf looked at the list and laughed— they all had Hebrew first names. But Bandorf was under orders to pass the list through Schultze to the police and therefore obeyed orders. On November 9, 1941, the list was accepted albeit reluctantly. Afghanistan was neutral but anti-Russian and Iran was pro-German so the Nazis did not want to offend potential allies. M. Tulard an anti-Jewish bureaucrat who was in charge of the Jewish Identity File Cards wanted to appeal to Xavier Vallat, the General Commissar of Jewish Affairs because although these people claimed to be Tadjik, their religion was Jewish and therefore by definition Jews. Vallat called Atchildi to his office at Place des Petit Peres. Already six Jugutis were under arrest. M. Adam revealed an important factor when Atchildi visited him—that neither Afghans nor Iranians will be shot. The word "Iranian" stood out because until now Atchildi had the help of the Afghans and advice from the Georgians—not Iranians.

On October 29, 1940, the Iranian consul had written the following:

"After an ethnographic and historic study relative to the Mosaic religious community of the non-Jewish race in Russia which has been placed in this consulate and which has been legalized for the Ministry of Foreign Affairs in Paris on 28 October 1940 by the Minister and for the delegation, the indigenous Jews (Juguti) of the territories of the former Khanate of Boukhara, Khina and Khoban (which are now part of the Soviet Republic of Uzbekistan and Tadjikistan) are considered as originating from Persia.

After this study, the Juguti of Central Asia are not part of the Judaic community but by their adherence to the Mosaic faith of which they observe the principle rituals. But by their blood, language and features form an integral part of the native race amongst whom they lived, the Parsis and the Sartis. Dated Paris October 29, 1940." This was three weeks after the enactment of the Vichy anti-Jewish legislation defining Jews.

When Amon signed the order exempting the Juguti community of Paris from the restrictions, the order compared the group to the Georgians.(1) However, the exemption was "for the moment" on August 23, 1941. On December 2, 1941, the president of the Juguti Group was advised in writing that the trustees of Jewish property were removed from the Jugutis. (2) On January 19, 1942, official notification was given of the consideration of Juguti as non- racial Jews which exempted the Juguti under German definition. (3) These two documents secured the Jugutis` future as long as they were on the list.

Esther Bakchieff, age 54, was able to gain her release from Drancy because she was able to prove she was on the Juguti list. The three Abramoff brothers, Arcadi, Albert, and Daniel were released when Atchildi went to Drancy on February 6, 1941 with his list. The camp commandant, after conferring with the German authorities released the three Abramoff brothers as Jugutis. However David Abramoff, age 20, was held as a suspect and transfered to another camp which held "suspects" rather than Jews per se.

On February 11, 1942, the Iranian Consul, Sardari, called in Atchildi and asked him to explain why he had excluded the Iranians from his list. Atchildi pointed out that there were already many Iranians on the list—Ilial, Hakimi, Davidad to name some. However, since there was no access to police files, Atchildi could not add others to this list. Sardani said he would prepare a list of Iranians to be included.

David Abramoff was still in the suspects' camp and Atchildi did not know how to gain his release. The doctor turned to the Gruzians, Kedia and Korkia. Korkia said he could not intervene directly because this Abramoff was not Gruzi. However, Atchildi was advised to go directly to those holding Abramoff with Korkia's calling card—the address to see: Obersturmfuhrer Christian, 86 Avenue Foch—Gestapo Headquarters. Atchildi reported to the Gestapo that Abramoff was illegally seized at his father's apple shop by a man seeking revenge. The German politely stated that he would check into the facts of the case. The next day Abramoff was released.

Atchildi continued to add names to his list. Twice Atchildi was arrested as a Jew because his own name did not appear on the list—a nearly fatal oversight. However, the police chief had had contacts with him and he was recognized as a Juguti. Atchildi had learned two things—never reveal yourself, and try to include others. By then, the French were tired of all these lists and addendum and asked for a final list. That was done in June 1943. At the last moment, Mara and his brother Jacob Zadeh were added to the list based on an oath of five Jugutis.

In February 1944, the Germans rejected the lists and the Community was once again in jeopardy. But on March 24, 1944 the regulation was amended to accept this list as is but no one new could be added to the list except by the police. The lists were now finished. No one new could be included. At least those on the list seemed safe. In June 1944, Professor Montandon visited Atchildi to state that he was certain that the Juguti are really Asian Jews. Montandon said he had developed a blood test to determine race and would charge 2,000f to test each member of the Juguti, which were now 150 people. Although Atchildi did not respond to the blackmail, it was apparent that the situation had become critical. Jugutis were now suspect and much less safe. Some were arrested. Mrs. Nazli Dorras` freedom was harder to obtain. But as the war went poorly, the Germans waged a greater war against the Jews. As of late July 1944 the Jugutis also went into hiding lest they be killed in the last days of the war. 15 days later, in August 1944 the country was liberated but it was too late for others. Some of those who died were:

Penina Slama, age 36, born in Boukhara, was arrested and sent to Drancy and put on convoy 67 on February 3, 1944 to die in Auschwitz.

Nissim Semoff, age 60, born in Bazardjik was sent in convoy 68 from Drancy to Auschwitz, February 10, 1944.

Sael Davidoff, born in Boukhara died at age 62 in the Drancy Camp on February 16, 1944.

Moise Rubin, born in Tashkent, age 43, was sent on convoy 72 on April 29, 1944 along with his wife Rachel, age 36, and daughter Eva, age 17. They had been interned in Vitel and died in Auschwitz.

Nessim Levy born in Abadazov, age 42 was sent on convoy 77 on July 31, 1944 to Auschwitz.

Marcelle Swibac, born in Teheran, age 36, was sent on convoy 71 to Auschwitz.

Some never made it to the death camps but were executed as hostages or where they were found, hiding or fleeing.

Jeanne Benjaminoff, age 63, died in Campeigne Camp.

Athanase Chabsky, born in Tashkent, died in Recebedou Camp on December 6, 1941, age 62.

Barouk Emir, born in Teheran, age 36, was executed on July 16, in Azergues along with his brothers Mario, age 30, and Joseph, age 17.

Abramoff was executed on August 13, 1944 at Riouperoux, with the war almost over, on his way to flee France to Spain.

The war ended in France and the Jugutis for the most part were saved, for the list was inclusionary and the advice and assistance of the non-Jews helped them avoid the German death net. It was a ruse, a risk that was boldly taken in a time when every decision meant life or death.

SEPHARDIM IN VIENNA AND HAMBURG
DURING THE HOLOCAUST
by Gertrude Hirschler

This presentation deals with a relatively little-discussed historical aspect of the Jewish communities of Hamburg and Vienna. These two German speaking cities (Hamburg between ca. 1600 and 1700 and Vienna between ca. 1700 and the early part of the twentieth century) had noteworthy entities of Sephardi Jews.

The Sephardi community of Hamburg first emerged during the early 1600 when the city was already acknowledged as the world's third-largest seaport and was carrying on extensive trade with lands in the Old World and the New. Most of the earliest Sephardim to appear in Hamburg at the time were Marranos who (or whose ancestors) had fled from the Iberian peninsula, had concealed their Judaism in their lands of earlier refuge and now, in addition to availing themselves of Hamburg's commercial opportunities, hoped to be able to return to their ancestral faith in what they perceived to be the city's tolerant Protestant climate.

Vienna first became the home of a Sephardi nucleus about 100 years after Hamburg. By that time, Vienna was already the polyglot capital of a far-flung empire and considered the political center of the Roman Catholic Church. The early Sephardi settlers in Vienna had been attracted by Vienna's commercial ties with the Balkan countries. They regarded themselves not as refugees but as colonists. Having come, for the most part, from Ottoman territory, they largely saw themselves as a "Turkish colony" in Austria. In fact, the Sephardim in Vienna celebrated the sultan's birthday each year until the collapse of the Ottoman Empire in 1918 and, as will be noted later on, Vienna's impressive Sephardi synagogue was known as the "Turkentempel."

In the framework of this lecture series, I was asked to discuss the part played by the Sephardim of Hamburg and Vienna in rescue and resistance activities during the Hitler era. Much to my sorrow, I was unable to find documented evidence of such collective Sephardi heroism either in Hamburg or in Vienna, because, as we will see, the Sephardi communities of both cities had become dwindling minorities even among their fellow Jews long before the introduction of Hitler's "Final Solution."

We will begin with a survey of Sephardi Jewry in Hamburg, because, as we have already noted, Sephardim settled there at least a century earlier than they did in Vienna and began their decline long before their brethren in the Austrian capital.

HAMBURG

The first Sephardim to settle in Hamburg in the late 1500s were Marranos from Portugal who were accepted by the city not as refugees from religious oppression but as "merchants of the Portuguese nation" who, supposedly, were Catholics. When these "Catholic merchants from Portugal" turned out to be Jews who had been forcibly baptized by the Inquisition, the good burghers of the city, led by storekeepers and artisans, wanted to have them expelled. The Senate of the city, a little more far-sighted, saw the Jews as an economic asset and a source of good tax revenue. Thus, despite the grumblings of the Catholic Emperor Ferdinand II that the Jews were being given better treatment in Hamburg than the Catholics, and the Lutheran clergy's thunder against the "blasphemers of Jesus," the Jews were permitted to remain in Hamburg and, under certain conditions, to hold Jewish religious services.(1) The newcomers from Portugal proved to be shrewd, resourceful and creative businessmen. They carried on a flourishing trade in sugar cane, tobacco, spices and Indian cottons and developed new business connections with Portugal, Spain and the new world. When the Bank of Hamburg was founded in 1619, the list of charter subscribers included 30 Jews from Portugal.(2)

By the 1620's Hamburg had three Sephardi centers for worship and a burial ground, all maintained jointly with the suburb of Altona. These early "centers for worship" were not synagogue buildings but private homes of merchants. One such center, named Talmud Torah, was at the home of the philanthropist Elijah Aboab Cardoso, who was of Spanish descent and had been one of the first Jewish settlers in Hamburg.

The first Sephardi Jewish spiritual leader in Hamburg was Isaac Athias (3) of Venice, who, before coming to Hamburg in 1672 had made a name for himself with an anthology of Jewish laws he had written in Spanish. The second spiritual leader of the Sephardim in Hamburg was Abraham Hayyim de Fonseca; he came of a family from Portugal that eventually spread to southern France, Amsterdam and the United States.(4)

The Sephardim of Hamburg were proud people. They considered themselves, and truly were, culturally and socially equal to their gentile neighbors. For two centuries, until the early 1800s, they clung to the Portuguese and Spanish languages. When Ashkenazim began to come to Hamburg in larger numbers during the mid-1600s, (some came from other German cities, attracted by Hamburg's business opportunities, others from Poland and the Ukraine in flight from the Chmielnicki massacres), the Sephardim permitted them to stay at their homes even though the Hamburg Senate had moved to expel the refugees. However, the Sephardim clearly looked down on the Ashkenazi newcomers, calling them *tedescos,* or "Germans."

By the year 1652 the three Sephardi centers for worship in Hamburg had united under the name Beth Israel and had chosen as their overall spiritual leader David Cohen ben Isaac de Lara, philologist and lexicographer who had written a monumental work comparing Hebrew words with words in Semitic and other languages and explaining words of Greek origin in the Talmud and of Latin origin in the Midrash.

However, what de Lara still lacked was a synagogue building in which to worship. He had to lead services at a private home rented from a Portuguese merchant. That building still survived some 200 years later, in 1847, but by that time it was used by German Jews because the Sephardim had long ceased to be in the majority.(5)

In addition to not having a proper synagogue, de Lara had other troubles with which to contend. The Sephardi community had brought to Hamburg as overall chief *hakham* R. Isaac Jessurun of Venice, the author of a guide to *halakhoth.* Apparently offended by the action of the community in calling another rabbi, de Lara went to live in Amsterdam, not returning to Hamburg until after Jessurun's death.(6)

In 1659, about seven years after the formation of Beth Israel, the community found that the house in which they worshiped was too small. A more spacious building was bought. To this end the entire community was taxed and certain silver ceremonial objects not considered essential to the service were pawned. In order to avoid overcrowding, the community enacted a statute limiting the number of people who could be called to participate in the procession with the Torah Scrolls on the festival of Simhath Torah.(7)

Since, alas, the new facilities still had insufficient space for everyone, the community enacted a statue in 1665 that no *tedescos* (lit., "Germans; i.e., Ashkenazim) could ever attend the synagogue on a regular basis unless they were servants in the employ of members, meaning of course, Sephardim. Members were told in no uncertain terms that they would have to accept whatever seats were assigned to them; anyone protesting was liable to penalties at the discretion of the community board.(8)

By the early 1660 the Sephardim of Hamburg were respected as an acknowledged social entity in Hamburg. They numbered about 120 families (9), including some individuals who served as representatives of the rulers of Poland and Sweden. At the time, a gentile nobleman, writing a history of the city of Hamburg, described the local Sephardim and Ashkenazim as follows:

> The Portuguese live mostly in the Old City and are actively engaged in maritime commerce. The German Jews, on the other hand, live mostly in the New City and do retail business with any merchandise they can lay their hands upon.(10)

Among the important Sephardi families in Hamburg were the Teixeiras. Abraham Teixeira (1581-1666) was originally a Marrano, son of a lady in waiting to the queen of Portugal. Shortly after being appointed representative of the Spanish crown to The Netherlands, he and his second wife "came out" openly as Jews and moved to Hamburg, where he had himself and his adult son circumcised. Together with a group of Sephardim in Amsterdam and London, he founded an international bank that created some order in the currency of the Free City of Hamburg. He served for a time as president of the city's Jewish community. On one occasion, Queen Christina of Sweden stayed at his home in Hamburg despite disapproval from the clergy.

Numerous Sephardim in Hamburg became well known as physicians. Perhaps the most prominent among these was Rodrigo de Castro (1550-1627), a Marrano who, before settling in Hamburg, had practiced in Lisbon, treating sailors of the Spanish Armada before they set out against England in 1588. In Hamburg he distinguished himself in his treatment of pestilence patients there.(11) Also in Hamburg, at the urging of another marrano physician, he converted to Judaism. He was the author of a textbook which even today is considered the scientific basis for the study of gynecology and another which is regarded as the groundwork for modern legal medicine. His son, Benedeto de Castro, set up a practice in Hamburg, where Queen Christina of Sweden was one of his patients.

Another Sephardi physician who lived in Hamburg was Benjamin ben Immanuel Mussafia (1601-72), whose textbook, Mei Zahav (Waters of Gold), discusses the curative properties of gold.

For a few years, Hamburg was home also to one of the most tragic figures in recent centuries of Jewish history: Uriel da Costa spent several years in Hamburg after he had been excommunicated in Amsterdam for his heretical views on Judaism. A former Marrano, he wanted to reembrace Judaism but found he could not accept Judaism as it was taught. The story of his tragic suicide is well known.

Hamburg's Sephardi community did not remain unaffected by the dispute around the figure of Shabbetai Tzvi in 1666. It seems that particularly the young Sephardim in Hamburg were taken in by the false Messiah. At the synagogue young men wore trimmings and sashes of green silk, which was considered the color of Shabbetai Tzvi.(12) Indeed, at one point even the adults became so caught up in the pseudo-Messianic enthusiasm that the governing board of the community put up community buildings including the newly built synagogue, for sale because they would not be needed any more if the Jews would go with the Messiah to the Promised Land.(13)

Among the Hamburg scholars who did not believe that Shabbetai Tzvi was the Messiah was R. Jacob ben Aaron Sasportas (c.1610-1698). His book, *Tzitzath Novel Tzvi,* summarizes his reasons for rejecting this false Messiah. What makes this book particularly important as a documentary source is the fact that it also quotes the letters and pamphlets of those who believed in Shabbetai Tzvi.

Some 30 years after the Shabbetai Tzvi debacle, the decline of the Sephardi community of Hamburg began. The Senate raised taxes for all Jews living in the city. The Sephardim were insulted that they were not exempted but treated like the lowly *tedescos*. Consequently, most of the more affluent Sephardim left Hamburg, moving either to Amsterdam or the suburb of Altona, which was then under Danish rule.

Eventually, in 1710, the Hamburg Senate repealed the tax but this action came too late to appease the Sephardim who still felt they should have been treated differently from the *tedescos*. Sephardim who were still in the city isolated themselves increasingly from the *tedescos*. Sephardim went to the New World and to London in preference to Hamburg. By the mid eighteenth century only about 200 souls were left in the city's Sephardi community.(14)

The ties of Hamburg's Sephardim to what was, for most of them, the "old country," i.e., Portugal, were still strong. When Lisbon suffered an earthquake in 1755, Hamburg's Sephardi community proclaimed a day of fasting and the *hakham* of Hamburg, Jacob de Abraham Basan,(15) composed a special order of prayers to be recited on that fast.

But while the Sephardim of Hamburg still produced outstanding Jewish individuals, the Ashkenazim forged steadily ahead of them in developing an organizational structure. By the late 1660's *shehitah* (the ritual slaughter of kosher meat) in Hamburg had come totally under Ashkenazi supervision.

Following the upheavals set off by the Napoleonic Wars, Hamburg's Sephardi synagogue (which had been built sometime during the early half of the eighteenth century) retained its congregational independence, but for all official purposes was regarded as part of the community set up by the Ashkenazi "establishment." Irmgard Stein (16) quotes the following passage from a memorial book written by Alfonso Cassuto, a member of the Sephardi community:

> According to the financial statement drawn up in 1827, the Sephardi congregation had no more assets left. In fact, there was a deficit of 1,300 marks which the congregation intended to wipe out by assuming a mortgage in the amount of 2,400 marks. But the financial condition of the congregation went from bad to worse, so that it should come as no surprise to note that the buildings owned by the congregation, along with the synagogue ...had to be disposed of in a forced sale because of inability to repay a mortgage on these buildings in the amount of 8,000 marks. On December 13, 1832, the buildings were offered for sale for a price of 40,000 marks. Since no purchasers appeared, the building were sold on January 30, 1933 to a broker for a total

of 30,550 marks. It later turned out that this broker had been sent by the German [i.e. Ashkenazi] community.

The proceeds from the sale, plus money raised in emergency fund raising campaigns launched by the Portuguese Jewish congregations of Amsterdam and London, enabled the Hamburg congregation to build a smaller house of worship adjoining the previous synagogue. The new synagogue was consecrated in 1834 but burned down only eight years later, in the great fire that razed Hamburg in 1842.(17)

Following the fire, the Sephardi congregation moved into a building formerly used by the Ashkenazim, who had moved into a newly built synagogue. Before long, the Sephardim formed a committee for the erection of a new synagogue building, which was indeed put up and consecrated in 1855, partly thanks to financial help from Portuguese congregations in France. After the closing of the Portuguese synagogue in neighboring Altona, the Portuguese synagogue in Hamburg was the only Sephardi synagogue left in Germany.(18) The building was praised for its architectural beauty in the writings of at least one student architect and one art historian as late as the 1920's.(19)

The last *hakham* of Hamburg's Sephardi community was Judah Cassuto, whose tenure extended from 1827 to 1893. Since he could not subsist on his income as *hakham,* he made his living as a translator and teacher of foreign languages, and officially-appointed interpreter and translator for the city of Hamburg.(20)

In 1920, the Sephardi population of Hamburg was 200 individuals out of a total Jewish population of 20,000. By the middle 1920's Hamburg's Sephardi community was so poor that, in 1927, when the question was raised how to celebrate the 275th anniversary of the organization of Congregation Beth Israel (1652), it was decided, according to the minutes, that "in view of the expenses involved, the difficulty of securing a Portuguese choir and a suitable hazzan (ours is a very honorable man but lacks an imposing appearance and has only modest vocal abilities) we would suggest that no celebration be held." Instead, a letter was sent to members appealing for funds to keep the synagogue going.(21) By 1931 there were no more weekday services at the Sephardi synagogue and the salaries of the hazzan and shammash had been cut. Eventually, the synagogue was taken over by the main community as an Ashkenazi house of worship, and was destroyed during the Kristallnacht pogroms of November, 1938.

After the Sephardi community had relinquished its synagogue to the Ashkenazim, those still anxious to worship in the Portuguese tradition took over (1935) an elegant villa on Innocentia Street, rebuilding the interior as a synagogue that seated about 90 persons. Visitors commented on the colorful interior decoration which they described as cheerful and typically Oriental. Since there was no more *hakham,* pious Sephardim in Hamburg addressed their religious questions to the Ashkenazi chief rabbi. During the final days before the start of mass deportations of Jews from Hamburg, the villa on Innocentia street was the place of worship also for the city's last chief rabbi Dr. Joseph Carlebach, who was later deported to Riga and killed together with his wife and most of his family. In 1942 the house was rebuilt by the Germans and later used as a private home.(22)

Some 7,800 Hamburg Jews lost their lives in the Holocaust.(23) There, as in other localities, Adolf Hitler made no distinctions between Sephardim and Ashkenazim.

What memories are left to us of Hamburg's Sephardi community? One physical memento is a Torah scroll from a small

Sephardi synagogue that once existed in the suburb of Altona. The scroll was brought to Israel by an Ashkenazi immigrant.(24)

Another immigrant to Israel, David Shealtiel, a member of a prominent Hamburg Sephardi family (1903-1969) was military commander of Jerusalem during the Israeli War of Independence. He came to what was then known as Palestine in the year 1923, when many German Jews still smiled patronizingly at idealism. Shealtiel became intelligence chief of Haganah, the semi official Jewish army of pre-Israel Palestine. After the establishment of the State of Israel, Shealtiel served as Israel's diplomatic representative to Mexico and, most probably by coincidence, to two countries well known in Sephardi history: Brazil and The Netherlands.(25)

During the nineteenth century Sephardi learning, custom and culture seem to have had a marked effect on one chief rabbi of Hamburg, an Ashkenazi by the name of Isaac Bernays (1792-1849). When he assumed Hamburg's chief rabbinate, he took the title of *Hakham* rather than *Oberrabbiner*. He translated Judah HaLevi's *Kuzari* into German with the assistance of his favorite student, Samson Raphael Hirsch (1808-1888). Hirsch, the giant of neo-Orthodoxy, frequently stressed that he acquired his love of Hebrew grammar, etymology and poetry from Bernays (probably under Sephardi influence), to whom he usually refers as *mein unvergesslicher Lehrer* (my unforgettable teacher).

VIENNA

In Hamburg the Sephardim had been the first Jews ever to settle in that city. In Vienna, they were relative latecomers. Jews had been living in Vienna on and off ever since the twelfth century but theirs was a history of constant expulsions and readmissions. By the time the Sephardim first arrived, however, Jews were already tacitly permitted to settle in Vienna: this applied particularly to the wealthy court Jews.

One of these court Jews was the founder of Vienna's Sephardi community,(26) Moses Lopez Pereira, also known as Diego de Aguilar (1699-1759), a member of a Portuguese Marrano family. Various legends have been told about the circumstances of Pereira's return to Judaism: For instance, a story to the effect that he had been a bishop in the Roman Catholic Church before reverting to the Jewish faith of his ancestors. But his life story (the German for the surname Pereira is simply Birnbaum, not exactly a rare name among Jews) is interesting enough even without the benefit of legend. He was born in Portugal, where his father, a Marrano, had held the tobacco monopoly. In 1722, when he was only 23, Moses moved to Vienna, where he openly avowed his Judaism and proceeded to reorganize Vienna's tobacco industry which was then (and I think still is today) a state monopoly. By 1726, when Moses was only 27, he was a baron and privy councillor. It was he who raised funds that enabled the Empress Maria Theresa to build her country home, the palace at Schonbrunn.

By his quiet but effective diplomacy (probably helped by his money and his tobacco interests) he was able to prevent the expulsion of the Jews from Moravia and Prague. Eventually, however, the Spanish Inquisition, discovering that he was a "renegade," requested the Austrian government, which was Roman Catholic, to extradite him. Moses thereupon gathered his family of 14 children and left for London, where the family became active in Sephardi communal life. Before leaving Vienna, he founded the first Sephardi synagogue there.

Until the Kristallnacht pogroms of November 1938, the great Sephardi synagogue of Vienna, the "Turkentempel," had a silver Torah crown and Torah ornaments marked with the name Moshe

Lopez Pereira and the date, 5498 (1737-38), the year in which Pereira founded Vienna's first Sephardi Congregation. Special memorial prayers were recited for Pereira at the "Turkentempel" on Yom Kippur eve each year.

It should be noted, however, that the house of worship set up by Lopez was not the first place where Sephardi services were held in Vienna. The first regular services of this ritual were held by a *minyan* consisting of three families from Spain—the families of Abraham Kammondo, Aaron Nisan and Naphtali Eskenazy, who worshiped together at a private home. The congregation founded by Pereira in 1737 was only Vienna's first Sephardi synagogue.

In 1750 large numbers of Turkish Jews settled in Vienna. It was they who placed their stamp on Vienna's Sephardi community. As already indicated earlier, these newcomers did not call themselves Spanish or Portuguese but Turks. They remained Turkish subjects and enjoyed the protection of the sultan in Constantinople because they were considered invaluable in trade relations between Austria, the Balkans and Turkey. The Austrian authorities regarded these Jews, and their synagogue, as part of a special Turkish "colony."

In 1778, about 40 years after the founding of their first congregation, the Sephardim of Vienna first set down a detailed constitution which was officially approved by the Turkish diplomatic representative in Vienna. This document included a provision that the congregation should not elect a president who was unable to read and write and that if, "contrary to all expectations, such a man should be elected," the congregation must appoint an assistant who would be literate so he could keep the books of the congregation in good order.

The first synagogue building of Vienna's Sephardic community was on the Obere Donaustrasse, a street that runs along the Danube

Canal and was part of a predominantly Jewish neighborhood before the Holocaust. Unfortunately, in 1824 the building burned down, along with many documents relating to the early history of Vienna's Sephardi community. The congregation, which had not yet obtained official approval from the Austrian authorities, moved into temporary quarters.

In 1843, Emperor Franz Ferdinand, uncle and predecessor of Franz Josef I, gave the Sephardi Jews permission to build a government-sanctioned synagogue because of the high respect in which they were held by that time.

It seems, however, that the Sephardim dragged their feet a little in this matter because it was not until almost 25 years later, in 1867, that they began construction of a synagogue, which was consecrated the following year. The new synagogue was located in the Fuhrmangasse, which, like the Obere Donaustrasse, was in the Leopoldstadt, Vienna's Jewish neighborhood.

Before too long, the young people of the synagogue expressed dissatisfaction with the services. Theirs was the only synagogue in Vienna with quaint Oriental chants and no choir. Other synagogues in the city enjoyed the music of the famous cantorial composer Salomon Sulzer. Vienna was a city of music, and the young people wanted religious music that would be in character with the spirit of Johann Strauss and other Viennese composers.

As a result, in the year 1880 the Sephardi synagogue of Vienna engaged a new cantorial staff: Jacob Bauer as chief cantor and Isidor Loewit as director of a choir to be organized by him. Though Loewit did have a Sephardi wife, neither he himself nor Bauer were Sephardim. Bauer was a native of Hungary who had come to Vienna as a teenager to obtain vocal training. Bauer was 28 years old when, after serving at various small communities in Hungary, he came to the "Turkentempel" in Vienna. He was to live to the age of 74; he died in 1926. Bauer transposed the old Turkish Sephardi chants into a more western mode and published the tunes, thus recast, in a book entitled *Shir haKavod* (Hymn of Glory). Bauer became famous throughout Vienna and taught many Ashkenazi cantors.

Loewit organized a choir of 10-15 boys and men. Most of the men engaged by Loweit were also members of the chorus of the Imperial and Royal Court Opera in Vienna. There never was any conflict between their work at the opera and their singing at the synagogue because Austrian law permitted singers of the Court Opera to be excused from opera duty if it conflicted with rehearsing or performing religious music, no matter of what faith. The choir soon became famous and people from all parts of the city attended services at the "Turkentempel" to hear Cantor Bauer and his choir.

When Bauer retired, he was succeeded by a Sephardi, Isaac Altaras, a native of Sarajevo (later Yugoslavia), who had studied music at the Vienna conservatory. The new cantor's music provided a blending of Sephardic background and Austrian musical modes. After World War I, Altaras left Vienna to become chief cantor of the Great Synagogue of Sarajevo. Eventually he was deported by the Nazis.

Meanwhile, all was not well with the synagogue building. By 1885, when the building had been in use for only 17 years, numerous structural defects were discovered. Since renovation was too costly, it was decided to tear down the whole building and erect a new one on its site. The cornerstone was laid in 1885 and the synagogue was dedicated two years later. The Sephardim not only got a new synagogue building on the same site as the old but also a new address because, at about the same time, the city fathers of Vienna had changed the name of the street from Fuhrmangasse (lit., "Coachman's Street," though the word is spelled with two "n"s, not merely one) to Zirkusgasse ("Circus Street").

The "Turkentempel" was the only beautiful building in a poor and ugly neighborhood. The cost of its construction were met by the sale of shares of 100 florins per person. It seemed that it would be possible to clear the debt within a reasonable time, but due to the outbreak of World War I and the runaway inflation that followed Austria's defeat, the synagogue was not debt-free until 1925, forty years after its cornerstone had been laid.

A gentile architect had been commissioned to design the synagogue. With its ornate style, it was regarded as one of the most resplendent and stylistically perfected synagogues in Vienna at the time. Most Jewish encyclopedias have photographs of the "Turkentempel." The actual building was set back somewhat from the street so that only little of the synagogue could be seen from the street, except for a wall with the Hebrew inscription, "In honor of the glorious and awe-inspiring Name of G-d."

Inside, the synagogue offered a variety of communal facilities. There was a reception room for brides and grooms and for the reception of digni taries. Before World War I the reception room boasted life-size paintings of the Austrian Emperor Franz Joseph I and of the Turkish Sultan Abdul Hamid II side by side. The sultan's birthday was the occasion for special religious services each year with Austrian and Turkish dignitaries in attendance. After World War I, when both Austria and Turkey became republics, the sultan's birthday celebrations naturally ceased and the portraits of the two rulers were replaced by huge mirrors.

Each seat in the synagogue had a spacious locker for *tallethot* and prayer books. The seating capacity in the main synagogue (men's section) was only a little over 300, but this could be expanded to almost 600, with standing room for another 500. The ladies' gallery, with seats upholstered in green, had a total of 100 seats and sufficient standing room to accommodate another 250 women. Behind the ladies' gallery was the "winter synagogue," with about 120 seats, for use during the winter season or during daily services because the heating of the main sanctuary proved to be very costly.

On the second floor there was an office for the secretary of the congregation and a two-bedroom apartment for the caretaker.

The acoustics of the synagogue were perfect; every note could be clearly heard throughout the hall.

In the courtyard there was an open well for *tashlikh* [i.e, the symbolic casting of one's sins into the water on Rosh HaShanah] and space for a collapsible *sukkah*.

Soon the congregation was embroiled in a controversy. An organ was installed, to be played at weddings and public celebrations. However, the assistant rabbi, Michael Nessim Papo, opposed this innovation because he feared that, before long, the organ would be played also on Sabbaths and festivals, when instrumental music was forbidden. The dispute was settled when a very devout (and wealthy) member, Abraham M. Elias, promised to donate the organ and to pay for its installation provided that the congregation signed a written, legally notarized contract specifying that the organ would be played only at weddings and on other occasions on which Jewish law did not prohibit instrumental music.

The synagogue also had auxiliary institutions; a burial brotherhood, a *bikkur holim* group for visiting the sick and a *hakhnassath orhim* society to accommodate needy Sephardim traveling through Vienna. An additional building was purchased to accommodate these facilities, which for a short time included a day school for children. That auxiliary building was some distance away from the synagogue and, as a result, escaped destruction during Kristallnacht. However, it received a direct hit in an Allied air raid in 1942. Only one corner was left standing. The site was returned to the Jewish community after the war.

The synagogue was well attended on Sabbaths but on weekdays a paid *minyan* [prayer quorum of ten adult males] had to be engaged so that daily services could be held.

High Holiday services were attended mostly by Sephardim because of the great differences in the Sephardi and Ashkenazi High Holiday liturgies. The Simhath Torah service, on the other hand, was considered one of the notable attractions everyone wanted to see. By three o'clock in the afternoon on the eve of Simhath Torah the doors of the synagogue were closed and all those wishing to attend had to form a line outside. At 4:30 the police appeared and the doors were opened, but only persons with membership cards were admitted to the synagogue, one by one. Three quarters of an hour before service, the doors opened again, but once the hall was filled to capacity, everyone else was turned away.

The *hakkafoth* procession was headed by the shammash dressed in full regalia, complete with a Turkish-style fez. He was followed by 20 choir boys in caps and gowns, marching in pairs. These were followed by the adult members of the choir, the choirmaster, the rabbi, the cantor, and male adults carrying all 15 of the synagogue's scrolls. Then came the *hatan Torah* and the *hatan Bereshith* [the men honored with the reading of the final portion of Deuteronomy, and the opening portion of Genesis, respectively]. The procession ended with schoolboys under bar mitzvah age bearing small Torah scrolls made especially for them.

The congregation offered four classes of weddings and funerals, depending on the family's willingness or ability to pay. A first-class wedding included a beautiful gold-ornamented *huppah* which took an experienced carpenter or upholsterer three hours to set up. There was an augmented choir, and organ music accompanied by a harp with melodies composed especially for the occasion.

In a second-class wedding the *huppah* was a little less ornate; indeed, it was simple enough to be set up by the synagogue's caretaker. There were no harps, only the organ and the normal choir.

The third-class wedding had the same *huppah* as the second-class ceremony; however, there was no instrumental music only a quartet from the adult choir, and no speech from the rabbi.

Fourth-class weddings were held in the "winter synagogue" without music, singing or speeches. There were only the rabbi and the cantor performing the essential marriage service.

A first-class funeral included singing by a full choir, in addition to a eulogy by the rabbi. In a second-class funeral, the rabbi also delivered a eulogy but only the adult members of the choir sang. The third-class funeral included the adult choir, but the rabbi only recited the service, without a eulogy. The fourth-class funeral service was conducted by the second cantor, without the rabbi and without a choir.

The last rabbis of the "Turkentempel" were Michael Papo, who served as *hazzan*-minister of Vienna's Sephardic congregation from 1873 to 1888, and as rabbi from 1888 until his death in 1918; his son, M. Papo (b.1898) and, in between the father and son, Nissim Ovadia, a Jerusalemite. The elder Papo was honored with the title of *haham bashi,* which the sultan could bestow upon chief rabbis within the Ottoman empire, but which, according to his son, was conferred upon him by the congregation in Vienna. He died early in 1918. His son held the position of assistant minister until 1925, when he assumed an Ashkenazi pulpit in Salzburg. In 1928 the younger Papo returned to Vienna and kept in close touch with his father's congregation but apparently did not assume on a full-time basis the position once held by his father.

The rabbi who succeeded the elder Papo directly, Rabbi Nissim Ovadia, was, as already noted, a Jerusalemite. A graduate of a Jerusalemite yeshiva, he was fluent in Ladino and, once he was in Europe, picked up German very quickly. Elected to the rabbinate of the "Turkentempel" after the elder Papo's death, Ovadia during the 1920s matriculated at the University of Vienna, receiving his Ph.D. in 1927. In 1929 he left Vienna to become rabbi of the Sephardi congregation of Paris.

Ovadia'a departure from Vienna was not caused by any clashes of personalities. In fact, he had become quite popular in his congregation and successfully mediated the dispute between the "old-timers" who enjoyed the western transposition of time-honored Sephardi melodies and the newcomers from the Balkans who sought a return to the traditional Oriental tunes. Rather, his decision to take the offer from Paris was influenced by Austria's economic instability. Immediately following World War I, a brief business boom brought numerous Balkan Jews to what had formerly been the capital of a world empire but which now, with the breakup of the Habsburg monarchy, had been characterized as a head too big for the body that had to support it. The mid-1920's brought a depression, causing many Balkan Jews to leave Vienna again, mostly for Paris.

Vienna's Sephardi community suffered from steady attrition.

During the 1920s the "Turkentempel" had a membership of about 500 out of a total of 172,000 Jews (or 10 percent of the total population) carried on the rolls of the *Kultusgemeinde*. The *Kultusgemeinde,* the government-sanctioned "establishment" community to which all Austrian Jews had to belong and pay taxes, was firmly in control of the Sephardim also. Only Sephardim were permitted to join the "Turkentempel," and the "Turkentempel" could not hire a rabbi or cantor without *Kultusgemeinde* approval of the candidate.

The last outstanding public event arranged in the "Turkentempel," according to the younger Papo, was the celebration, in 1935, of the eight hundredth anniversary of the birth of Moses Maimonides. The ceremony was attended by a large group of Austrian Jewish war veterans in full uniform and by numerous Austrian government dignitaries.

The "Turkentempel" was destroyed in the Kristallnacht pogroms of 1938, along with the compositions of choir director Isidor Loewit. Most of Loewit's music has not survived. Loewit himself died in 1938, of natural causes. Rabbi Nissim Ovadia helped found the World Sephardi Federation, eventually becoming its president. When Hitler invaded France, Ovadia escaped via Spain and Portugal to New York City, where he arrived in 1941. He was elected chief rabbi of the Central Sephardic Jewish Community but died of a heart attack only one year later, at the age of only 52. The younger Rabbi Papo escaped to the United States, as did Isaac Asseo, the last chief cantor of the "Turkentempel." The last president of the congregation, Sigmund Heskia, went to London.

We know of two physical relics of the "Turkentempel" of Vienna and its congregation: several graves in the Jewish section of the *Zentralfriedhof* with Sephardi names, and the beautiful Ark curtain of the "Turkentempel." Mended with painstaking and loving expertise, the curtain was somehow spirited out of Nazi-occupied Vienna and was on display at the Yeshiva University Museum, giving the visitor a sad inkling of how beautiful that curtain once must have been.

NOTES

1. Ismar Elbogen, Florence Sterling. *Die Geschichte der Juden in Deutschland.* Wiesbaden: 1982. p 131.
2. Ibid.
3. Herbert Gonsierowski. *Die Berufe der Juden von der Einwanderung bis zur Emanzipation.* Hamburg: 1927. p 12.
4. *The Jewish Encyclopedia.* Vol.6, New York: 1964. p 161.
5. Irmgard Stein. *Judische Baudenkmaler in Hamburg.* Hamburg: 1984. p 29.
6. *The Jewish Encyclopedia.* op. cit.
7. Irmgard Stein. op. cit. pp 30-31.
8. Ibid. p 34. By that time, the *Tedescos* already had worship facilities of their own, set up in 1650.
9. *The Jewish Encyclopedia.* p 191.
10. Irmgard Stein. op.cit. p 27.
11. Ibid.
12. *The Jewish Encyclopedia.* op. cit. p 192.
13. *Encyclopedia Judaica.* Vol III. p 1226.
14. Irmgard Stein. op.cit. p 40.
15 *The Jewish Encyclopedia.* op. cit. p 192.
16. Irmgard Stein. op.cit. p 40.
17. Ibid. p 41.
18. Ibid. pp 41-44.
19. Ibid. p 43.
20. William Aron. *The Jews of Hamburg.* New York: 1967. p 64.

21. Quoted in Ina Susaane Lorenz. *Die Juden in Hamburg zur zeit der Weimarer Republik, eine Dokumentation.* Teil 2. Hamburg: 1987.

22. Irmgard Stein. op.cit. pp 43-44.

23. *Encyclopedia Judaica.* Vol. VII. P 1228.

24. I am indebted for this and other information cancerning the last days of Hamburg Jewry to Mr. Manfred H. Meyer of New York City.

25. William Aron. op.cit. p 29.

26. Lacking access to original and archival sources, I have drawn heavily on the following two excellent sources for the present lecture on Vienna's Sephardi Community: A. Adolf von Zemlinsky. *Geschichte der Turkisch-Israelitischen Gemeinde zu Wien von Ihrer Grundung bis heute nach historischen Daten.* Vienna: 1888. B. Rabbi Dr. M. Papo. *The Sephardic Community of Vienna.* in Josef Fraenkel, ed. *The Jews of Austria.* Philadelphia: 1967. pp 327-46. These are, in part, the personal reminiscences of the assistant minister of the Turkentempel, whose father was the rabbi of the synagogue.

ALBANIAN JEWS DURING THE HOLOCAUST
By Dr. Anna Kohen

I come from Albania. It is a small country in Europe, located between Yugoslavia and Greece. There where three periods of migration of Jews to Albania. The first was in the 14th Century. They came from Spain by boat and settled in a port of Durres, the largest port of Albania.

The second time was in the year 1650. It is not known exactly where they came from but it was assumed that maybe they came from Janina, a small town in the Northern Greece. This is where most Albanian Jews came from. These people settled in Vlora, Gjirokaster, Berat and Elbasan . Albania was under the Ottoman Turkish Empire for almost four hundred years. At that time a Jew from Turkey, Shabbetai Tzvi, was trying to influence Jews to leave their countries and return to the Holy Land. He visited Albania for the same purpose. At the time, the Sultan imprisoned him. When he finally converted, he took the name, Shabbetai Mohammed Tzvi. He died in Berat. About 250 people eventually went to the Holy Land.

The third period was in 1850. Again, they came from Janina and settled in Vlora (where I was born after the Second World War). The language they spoke was Greek. These Jews kept their tradition and celebrated the holidays the same way they celebrated in Greece. They were not Jews from Spain.They had settled in Janina in Byzantine times and never spoke Ladino. In Greece there were two major Jewish communities before the war, Janina and Salonica. The Salonica Jews spoke Ladino and had Spanish surnames. After the Greek Jews settled in Vlora, they moved to different cities like Gjirokaster, Tiran, Fier and Kavaja. There was a synagogue in Vlora until 1915. The synagogue was burned during the first World War. The only reason, I believe, there were so many Jews in Vlora was because of the synagogue. Later a new synagogue was opened on the second floor of a private house. When the Second World War broke out, more Jews fled to Albania. They came from Janina, Yugoslavia, Bulgaria and Vienna. At that time there were about 600 people. Not one Jew was killed although Italy occupied the country. Only 5 people out of the 600, were caught in the city of Shkoder. They were not betrayed by the Albanians, who saved the Jews. There is evidence that clearly shows that these Jews were saved by the Albanian Moslems who took them into their own home. They took a risk, for if the Germans found out they would be killed. Secondly, the partisans in the mountains hid all the Jews they found locally. The Jews from Vlora hid in the mountains of Vlora; the Jews from Tirana in the mountains of Tirana. They were hidden in Moslem villages. They changed their names to Moslem names and lived there as Moslems until the war was over. Then they returned to their cities and to their lives. The Yugoslavian Jews were able to go back to Yugoslavia and later on to Israel. The Albanian Jews remained in Albania. In 1946 Albania became a communist country and there was no way for them to leave.

The Jews of Janina were taken to Auschwitz. There are two people who I want to mention, a man and a woman who were taken to Auschwitz with their families, which were murdered there. When they were liberated, they went to Janina and found no one there. They found out, though, that some of their relatives had fled to Albania and were saved. They decided to go to Albania. These two people met, married and had their own children. These three children married and had their own children. They were 12 out of the 37 Albanian Jews whom I sponsored to come to the USA. Their parents are both deceased.

Now I'll talk about an incident from my personal experience. I was born in Vlora after the War. My brother, the oldest of the four of us, was one year old during the war. My parents went to a Moslem village near Vlora and changed their names to Moslem names, as did everyone else, to save their lives. My father's name was Muhammad; my mother's was Bule; my brother's name was Ali; my grandmother's name was Fatime; my grandfather's name was Daut. When I was 8 years old, I was walking with my mother in the street. A lady yelled "Bule, Bule!," my mother's Moslem name. When I turned my head, I saw this lady running and I said to my mother, "Mom, this lady is yelling for you and she's calling you Bule. Why? She must have mistaken you for someone else." At that time, my mother, whose name is Nina Kohen, told me the story. We both cried.

Where are the Albanian Jews today? With the changes in Eastern Europe, Albania changed also. As of May 1990, everyone can travel with a passport which has not been allowed since 1946 when Albania became a communist country. Our closest relatives, a family of 10 out of a total of 37 people, are coming to be reunited with us. The David Kohen family left Albania in 1966, as Greek citizens, to Greece and later to the USA. David Kohen is my father. The remaining Jews received passports and visas for Israel with no problems. The total number of Albanian Jews is about 400. They left in groups of 20 through Greece and Italy. Only 15 families are left. We don't know whether they are going to stay or leave. We shall find out. The Albanian Jews were the first to leave Albania after the borders were opened. The Albanian Jews were never discriminated because of their nationality or religion. It is true that they couldn't practice their religion. No one could, whether Jew, Catholic, Moslem or Greek Orthodox. In 1967, Albania became an atheist country. In 1990, religion was permitted again. The best oncologist in Tirana was Jewish. His brother was working at the Atomic Research Institute. Today they are both in Israel with their mother and their families, enjoying a new Jewish life. There was a Jewish family that had come from Vienna to Albania during the war, named Schwartz. They settled in Tirana. Doctor Renata Schwartz today is in Israel. There was a Jew working in a government position. Today retired, he joined his relatives in Israel.

The Jews were not discriminated against and held high positions. The Albanians felt very close to the people of Israel because of their geographical position. They both feel that they are surrounded by enemies. About two months ago, I got a phone call from Albania and I was told that they formed an Albanian Israeli Friendship Society. My family and I are honorary members. The Inauguration was Sunday, April 21, 1991. Many Jews from Europe and Israel attended. A delegation of 25 people or more were there. My husband and I attended.

In July of 1990, an Albanian Moslem, Refik Veseli, was honored with the title Righteous Gentile. Refik's father saved many Jews in Yugoslavia. Among them was an Israeli photographer, Gavra Mandel. He tried for many years to visit Albania but did not succeed. He never forgot the Veselis who saved his life. He wrote a letter directly to the president of Albania, Ramiz Alia. When they actually visited, they were impressed with Israel as a country and the Israeli people. One thing that he objected to was the lack of mention of the Albanian Jews at the Holocaust Museum. There were no pictures of Albanian Jews.However, there were really no Albanian Jews who had come out of Albania recently to provide material. The only recent family had been my family which emigrated in 1966.

Now the majority of Albanian Jews are in Israel. This year's seder was the last seder for Albanian Jewry. Next year in Jerusalem has come true.

THE AMERICAN LADINO PRESS AND THE HOLOCAUST
by Dr. M. Mitchell Serels

"La Vara" (The Staff) was the most popular Judeo-Spanish newspaper in the United States. The weekly was published by the Sephardic Publishing Company, 7 Rivington St., on New York City's Lower East Side. The managing editor was Albert J. Torres and the editor Albert Levy. During the World War II period, the annual subscription rate was $2.(1)

At that time, "La Vara" was eight pages, seven of which were in Judeo- Spanish and the last in English. The Judeo-Spanish pages were consistently assigned specific coverage: Page one—war news and world events; Page two—editorial page and serial column; Page three—various communal news or rabbinically authored articles; Page four—"Novidades Judias de la Semana" (Jewish News of the Week); Page five—poems, serial romances, articles; Page six—general American Jewish news; and Page seven—"En La Colonia" (News of the Sephardic Union).

For a small journal, the periodical gave a great deal of coverage to world Jewish events, continually warning of the Hitlerian peril. In 1934, attacks on Jews in Munich, savage anti-Semitic attacks and even a statement by the former Greek Prime Minister that "Hitler is a menace to peace" were carried on its pages.

The response to German anti-Semitism favored by "La Vara" was settlement in Israel, then called Palestine.(2) By August, 1935, "La Vara" utilized a German-subtitled Judeo-Spanish article "Denk Ich an Deutschland in dem Nacht (I think of Germany at Night)," subtitled "Cuando yo penso de la almania en la noche." The author called the Nazis modern assassins who attack not only the Jewish body, but also the Jewish soul. The article reported that Hitler, Goebbels, Streicher and others planned to destroy Jews living in this inferno: Por destruir alla dgudiria beviendo en este inferno.

The author concluded that the League of Nations should resettle Jews just as it was doing with the Armenians and Greek expatriates of Turkey. Albert Levy wrote an editorial about Nazi Germany noting, "The Jewish world is not intimidated."

On the English page, Leonard Wacker called on American Jews to rally in support of the Catholic seamen who tore down the Nazi flag from the ship Bremen.(3)

Anti-Semitic acts in Germany and an attempt to analyze the origins of German anti-Semitism, written by Dr. Leon Abrevaya, were reported.(4)

When war broke out on September 1, 1939, Hitler was called Las Ambiziyones de ombre ke perdio toda razon. However, the paper believed France and Britain would quickly defeat the Germans. Polish Jews were encouraged to join the Polish Army. Negative events within the German-occupied areas were readily reported—the lack of bread, ghettoization of Prague before transport abroad and Jewish suicides. Joseph S. Crespi, a frequent writer, called on the U.S. to enter the war. Maurice del Bourgo, a letter writer, supported neutrality. This conflict appeared frequently in the pages of "La Vara."(5)

As early as September 8, 1939 details of concentration camps were outlined. Reports of the terror affecting the 2,000 Jews of Danzig were intermingled with reports of U.S. anti-Semitism, German-American Bund activities and the pro-pacifist speeches of Jewish leaders such as Rabbi Samuel Goldstein of Temple Emanuel. Calls for Judeo-Spanish readers to become citizens were frequently made.(6)

Reports about the treatment of German Jews were mixed with calls for neutrality by the Ashkenazi rabbinate. Most Jews under Hitler had no say in their fate. Palestine was the refuge demanded by the paper.

Rabbi Isaac Asseo,(7) the leading rabbi with a regular column in "La Vara," continued to write about holy days and communal bickering, particularly with Albert Matarasso, until the beginning of the deportation of Vienna's Sephardic community.

Each organization trying to help Jews in Europe was given support: the United Jewish Appeal, Hebrew Immigrant Aid Society, Jewish Agency, Salvation Army and Red Cross.

"La Vara" reported that Jews had good cause to despair when the Nazis openly stated Jews were not only responsible for the War, but the answer to the "Jewish problem" was extermination. The clear clarion call of the Nazi annihilation threat was sounded in "La Vara."(8)

To bolster that call, Z. Tygel was given free reign on the English page of "La Vara." Tygel wrote the 1939 book, *Lets Talk it Over—Present-day Jewish Problems,* before the opening of the death camps.(9) The book began, "Nazi Germany has declared war against us... he pursues a ruthless inhuman policy of complete extermination of Jews."

Tygel was born in 1870 in Poland. At age 20, he was a newspaperman for *"Unzer Leben"* in Warsaw and wrote a history of Warsaw's Jews during the last century. Tygel was imprisoned in 1910 by the Czarist authorities for organizing workers. Arriving in the U.S. in 1919, he became active in the community and served on the boards of the American Jewish Congress and ORT. Tygel also wrote about Hayim Salomon.

While the U.S. was neutral, pictures of Hitler and other officials appeared in "La Vara." However, the paper believed Hitler would be defeated quickly because: the allies would win quickly; German morale was waning; there would be a coup d'etat; and moral people everywhere would protect Jews. But, nothing could be done once the Germans took over an area.(10)

Even as the war dragged on, Allied propaganda proclaiming imminent victory constantly appeared. Until the U.S. entered the war, Jewish leaders—particularly Reform rabbis such as Samuel Goldstein, Jonah B. Wise and Abba Hillel Silver—preached a policy of American neutrality.(11)

The columns of the "La Vara" reflected other concerns as well. These included: encouraging citizenship for the heavily immigrant population; the belief that European Jews had to be benefiting from the many donations of Jewish organizations; concern about the spread of Nazism to the U.S.; American anti-Semites, such as Father Coughlin and the German-American Bund; conflicts in the Sephardic community; the public statements of national Jewish leaders; and concern about Communism in Russia and America.(12)

These concerns overshadowed Tygel's warnings that a bloody war of physical extermination against the Jews had been in progress since 1932.

The tragedy of Vienna's Sephardic community aroused a sense of urgency among "La Vara" readers, even more than the reports of the Dachau concentration camp.(13)

Moise Bensignor wrote poignantly of the need to help "our Viennese cousins," while the need for immigration affidavits was stressed by Dr. David deSola Pool.(14)

Both Sephardic and Ashkenazi Jews were involved in aiding non-Jews. Funds were raised in the general Jewish community to help Finland defend itself against the Soviet invasion.(15)

The earthquake in Turkey at the end of 1939 brought several weeks of appeals for help.(16) Rabbi Salomon Mizrahi of Los Angeles in particular reacted to the call to assist the Turkish victims.(17) However, reports of the formation of ghettos in Warsaw and Lublin continued to be detailed. Crespi moved from reports on Germany to attacks on Joseph Stalin.(18) Robert Fresco wrote in support of free speech and against Communism.

The seventh anniversary of Hitler's chancellorship inspired an editorial calling Jewry "the child who would not see the truth." It stated, only a miracle would destroy Hitlerism. Jews needed to fight this destruction by settling in Palestine, according to the editorial.(19)

By the time the U.S. entered World War II, Tygel's articles were replaced by others focusing on economic highlights, general health and how to buy bonds.(20)

Reports on the situation of Jews continued to filter into the pages of "La Vara." Although not mentioned by name, the "Einsatzgruppen" were described, as were deportations from the Warsaw Ghetto, Italian attacks on Falashas and Jewish resistance, including the "Nun" incident in Hungarian Transylvania.(21)

Petain's collaboration was condemned.

The two rabbis, Asseo and Mizrahi, rarely mentioned the Nazis and the fight against them in their columns. Even during holidays such as Purim and Hanukkah, which lent themselves to dramatization about European Jewry's plight, the rabbis showed that they had failed to grasp the situation and historical precedents.(22) The editorial pages also either seemed to avoid reporting the gravity of the situation or voiced a sense of helplessness about Jews in Nazi hands.

Throughout the war, "La Vara" provided significant coverage about Europe's Jews for a small paper. The Judeo-Spanish reader read weekly dispatches from Stockholm and Geneva on conditions in Europe as well as the stance of Turkey on the war and its refugees.

But space was also given to local social events and pages of humor, romance and poetry. There were very few letters to the editor so that reaction to the restrictions, killings and deportations can't be measured. In particular, the words of Tygel on the English page ring out. For it was Tygel in writing, "The German and Italian governments whose chief aim is the complete and ruthless extermination of the Jews," who sounded the warning before any death camps were opened.(23)

Tygel's writings were often translated into Judeo-Spanish the following week in "La Vara." However, other writers ignored the information and wrote as if nothing was happening. But, the thorough reader knew of the deaths and deprivation and clearly saw that in Europe there was a war against the Jews.

NOTES
1   La Vara tried to reach communities in New York City, Washington, Rochester (NY), Atlanta, Chicago, Indianapolis and Los Angeles;

2.   La Vara, Aug. 8, 1935, Vol. XIII No. 676 (old numbering).

3. La Vara, Aug, 16, 1935, Vol. XIII No. 677 (o.n.).
4. La Vara, May 24, 1935, Vol. XIII, No. 665 (o.n.).
5. La Vara, Sept. 1, 1939, Vol. XVIII, No. 1.
6. La Vara, Sept. 8, 1939, Vol. XVIII, No. 2.
7. Rabbi Isaac Asseo is listed either as the Chief Rabbi of the Se- phardic Union or Rabbi of the Sephardic Jewish Center of New Lots, Brooklyn.
8. La Vara, Sept. 22, 1939, Vol XVIII, No. 4. The warning was quite clear as to the German attempt to annihilate Polish Jewry: A manzura ke los almanes penetran en polonia miyones de dgudiyos son victimizados lideres de las comunidades arestados i en muchos lugares familias enteras fueron asasinados. (The Germans penetrated into Poland, millions of Jews were victimized, leaders of the communities were arrested and, in many places, entire families were killed).
9. Tygel, Z. *Lets talk it over.* Present-day Jewish Problems. New York: Defense Publishing Co., 1939. Tygel's plan for Jewish salvation included five major points;
a. Fund-raising and self-taxation on kosher meat;
b. Mission of cheer and help to Poland and Sudetenland to bring comfort, provide medical supplies to the Jews and report firsthand to the free press;
c. A $1 million project of defense against anti-Semitic propaganda;
d. Unity of American Jewry through a great Council of American Jewry. Tygel wrote to 50 leading American Jews to join in a show of unity. He reports only 35 percent answered.
e. The development of a committee to coordinate political action and relief work consisting of the A.J. Congress, A.J. Committee, B'nai B'rith and the Jewish Labor Committee.
10. Letter to the editor by Ralph Crespi, La Vara, Oct. 6, 1933, Vol. XVIII No. 6.
11. La Vara, Sept. 15, 1939, Vol. XVIII. No. 21.
12. La Vara, Citizenship, Jan. 19, 1940, Vol. XVIII. No. 2, Particularly, Joseph S. Crespi reiterates the call for citizenship.
13. The details of life in Dachau appeared in both English and Ladino texts in La Vara, Nov. 3, 1939, Vol. XVIII No. 10; in an editorial called El Teror Alman

(The German Terror) which cited a Jewish Telegraphic Agency report that destruction of Polish Jewry was only a matter of time.

14. La Vara, Nov. 17, 1939, Vol XVIII No. 12; Carried parts of a letter by Moises Bensignor calling on Jews to save their brothers from death by speaking out, donating and marching; Dr. David deSola Pool minister of Congregation Shearith Israel, the Spanish and Portuguese Synagogue of New York, called on Ladino Jews to sign immigration affidavits for the Sephardim of Vienna and Italian Jews and to help in resettling refugees; No mention of how to obtain affidavits was made.

15. La Vara, Dec. 22, 1939, Vol. XVIII No. 17 reports a donation of $1,000.00 by B'nai B'rith for Finnish relief.

16. La Vara, December 29, 1939, Vol. XVIII No. 18 reports 8,000 deaths in Turkey due to the earthquake. In the editorial of January 5, 1940, the periodical calls for aid to Turkey by all the Sephardic societies.

17. Ibid.

18. La Vara, January 5, 1940, Vol. XVIII No. 19. Reports of the Yellow Magen David, pogroms, ransoms, depravation of jobs, ghettoization, confiscation of property, desecration of religious sites and killings are readily found. Crespi in sympathy with the American mood against Stalin writes an article on freedom under Stalin.

19. February 2, 1940, Vol. XVIII. No. 23.

20. March 7, 1941, Vol. XIX. No. 27.

21. August 15, 1941, Vol. XIX. No. 50.

22. Salomon Mizrahi. Fiesta de Purim. La Vara, March 7, 1941. Vol. XIX. No. 27.

23. Tygel, Z. *Lets Talk it Over.* op. cit., pp 54.

THE JEWS OF SALONICA AND THE HOLOCAUST:
A PERSONAL MEMOIR
By Henry Levy

Most people today are aware of the heinous Nazi annihilation of the Jewish communities of Europe. However, comparatively little has been said or written about the 100,000 Ladino-speaking Greek Jews tortured and murdered by the Nazis.

As a survivor who can give personal testimony to its hor rors, I have always felt a responsibility to call attention to this little-known segment of the Holocaust. Indeed, not recalling would have meant completely abandoning the memories of the Holo caust's Martyrs (Kedoshim) and of those responsible for these crimes against the Jewish people.

My children often insist I tell them what happened to the Jews during the destruction of Greece's Jewish communities. I feel an obligation to them and my grandchildren, to tell the story of the forgotten Sephardim.

Since 1370, Thessaloniki (Salonica) had become a haven for Jews fleeing persecution in Western and Central Europe.

In 1430, Sephardic Jews began emigrating from Spain to Turkish-occupied Salonica. In 1470, Bavarian Jews arrived as refugees and formed an Ashkenazi community next to the Romaniot community.

THE 1492 EXPULSION

The largest mass migration of Sephardim came in 1492, during the expulsion ordered by Spain's King Ferdinand and Queen Isabella. They were welcomed by the Ottoman Empire under Sultan Bayasit II, who ordered his governors not to interfere with the new settlers and to treat them with respect and kindness. More than 75 percent of Sephardim found safe refuge in the Ottoman Empire.

The Sephardim made Salonica an important center for Torah study, commerce and industry and put Salonica on the international trade map. By 1680, Salonica had 32 synagogues, serving a very wealthy, powerful and well-organized Sephardic community.

In 1856, the Sultan visited Salonica and met with the Grand Rabbi (Haham Bashi) and other Jewish leaders, resulting in full equality and citizenship for Jews and other non-Moslems. In 1870, complete independence and full rights were granted to Judaism as a major religion.

On Oct. 10, 1912, Salonica was wrested from the Turks by the Greek Army. On November 19, King George I received Chief Rabbi Jacob Meir and Salonica's Jewish leaders to express his gratitude for the valuable contributions Jews had made to Salonica and all of Greece.

WORLD WAR II

Dr. Tzvi Koretz served as chief rabbi of Salonica from 1933 to 1943. An Ashkenazi native of Warsaw, Poland, he earned a master's degree in classical Greek and a doctorate in ancient Greek philosophy from the University of Vienna.

When the Italian Army under Mussolini attacked Greece on Oct. 28, 1940, 13,000 Jews were drafted into the Greek military to fight side by side with their countrymen against the Italians and Nazis. Approximately 1,000 Jewish soldiers died and more than 4,500 Jews were wounded. A street named after Col. Mordechai Frizis is a lasting testimonial to one of the many Jewish war heroes. Both my brothers, Edgard and Jack, were drafted into the army and fought the Italians at Ipeiros on the Greek-Albanian border.

The destruction of Greek Jewry began when the German Army attacked Greece on April 9, 1941. Salonica fell the next day.

ANTI-JEWISH PROPAGANDA

In April 1941 the Greek newspaper, "New Europe," carried a front page editorial in its Sunday edition. I remember the capital letters stating "DEATH TO THE JEWS!" The editorial blamed Jews for all wars, including the German defeat during World War I, and held Jews responsible for Germany's current economic problems.

It asserted that wars would cease if the Jewish race was exterminated, especially in Poland, Lithuania, Ukraine, Germany and Austria and other parts of Europe.

The editorial also urged that Jews be destroyed in Greece, even if doing so meant uniting with the Third Reich. The paper openly accused Jews of lying and of resorting to unthinkable acts to control the world.

The Jewish community pleaded in vain with the Greek authorities to force "New Europe"'s editors to stop the hateful rhetoric. Actually, the newspaper was receiving articles from the Minister of Propaganda in Berlin.

On the same editorial page, a call was made for the destruction of the capitalism and communism created by profiteering Jews to bring misery and destruction to the rest of the world. They asked that every Jewish store hang a sign in large black capital letters stating: "THIS IS A JEWISH STORE." Jews would be barred from conducting business with Greeks and from riding public transportation. Throughout Salonica signs "JUDEN UNERWUNSCHT" (Jews Undesirable) began to be posted. There were daily articles accusing Jews of atrocities.

THE BEGINNING OF THE FINAL SOLUTION

The Final Solution began expeditiously, without interference or complaint from the Greek authorities, Greek Orthodox Church, academicians or others. Two days after the Germans entered Salonica, "El Messagero," the only surviving Judeo-Spanish daily newspaper, was suspended and its editor, Elli Veissy, arrested.

The military confiscated many Jewish homes and businesses, including ours at Alexandrias 33, as well as all public Jewish buildings and the Jewish Hospital Hirsch, founded by Baron de Hirsch.

On April 15, 1941, members of the Jewish Community Council were arrested by the German Army and the council's offices ran sacked as typewriters, telephones and Persian rugs were taken away. Most possessions were sent to Germany. My father's factory and warehouses were given to a Greek, Stavros Antoniadis.

Jews were ordered to give up their radios on April 16. A new Jewish community president, Saby Saltiel, was nominated by the Germans. The Gestapo nominated Albala, a German-Jewish attorney who arrived in Salonica in 1937 as a refugee, as vice president. Austrian and Czech Jews comprised the rest of the community council. All except Saltiel spoke German and worked to help the

Jewish community.

An appeal was made April 17 by Sinto Allalouf and Isaac Angel, directors of the Zionist movement, asking all Jews to defend the honor of their beloved Greece against the German invaders. The same day the French language Jewish newspapers, "L'Independant" and "Le Progress," were silenced. Koretz, the chief rabbi, spoke at the Parnassos in Athens.

With the help of Greek collaborators Adam Papanaum and Kirkor Bourbouriam, the Germans went to the Zionist Organization at 4 Cyprus St. on May 17, 1941. Pretending to be praying, they took two Sefer Torah (scrolls) and threw them to the floor stepping on them and tearing them into many pieces.

With the help of other collaborators, Bourbouriam and Papanaum showed the SS where all 40 synagogues were located. The Torah scrolls, books and silver ornaments, some dating from the 15th and 16th centuries, were taken away while rabbis and cantors were abused and humiliated by Greek collaborators.

On May 22, the SS and Greeks took the Spanish Sefer Torah scrolls from 15th Century Castille and Toledo to Germany and burned the books and the three other Sefer Torahs. The chief rabbi returned from his famous lecture in Athens to find the libraries and Jewish manuscripts destroyed.

The winter of 1941-42 was very cold. With most of the wealthy Jewish homes and large businesses confiscated, the Jews were hungry and cold. The *Matanot Laevionim* Society (gifts for the poor) building was sold for very little to help feed 20,000 Jews. The society assisted the sick with medical supplies and paid the 12 doctors of the *Bikur Holim* Society and Hospital Baron de Hirsch.

On May 27, 1941, Koretz was arrested and sent to Vienna for three months before being released and returned to Salonica. While in Vienna, he met an SS officer, Dehagg, whom he liked and who nominated him as chief rabbi and president of the Jewish community. Koretz now had complete control of the destiny of the Salonica's Jews.

The Rosenberg Commando and Sephardic expert Dr. Z. Paul of Frankfurt, who spoke fluent Sephardic Hebrew and Judeo-Espagnol, settled in the U.S. Consulate at 10 Kalary St. in mid-June 1942. He was accompanied by famous Nazi poet Hans Heindrich, a Ladino poetry and song scholar, who stole thousands of Jewish poetry books with the help of an Armenian Greek collaborator. Paul, who read and understood the Talmud, requested that the rare sacred books and manuscripts be brought to him.

These handwritten books had been carefully transferred by freight train to Frankfurt, and sealed in crates stamped "By order of the Feldcommandatur for the museum." Some books were later translated for use as anti-Semitic propaganda.

Some Greeks assisted the Gestapo in identifying hidden Jews or in finding wealthy Jewish businessmen and homes. They would throw out the Jews and appropriate their wealth, which had been passed down for almost 500 years from generation to generation. To this day, Greeks reside in properties once owned by Jews since very few of their former occupants returned from the concentration camps.

Saltiel, president of the Jewish community, resigned rather than oversee the destruction of the Jewish people. But the vice president, Albala, continued to work with German authorities. After the war, he returned to Salonica and was jailed for 10 years by the Greeks for his role in persecuting Jews. Attorneys for the Jewish community were his prosecutors.

On Saturday, July 11, 1942, all 7,000 male Jews between the ages of 18-45 were squeezed into Liberty Square and kept standing all day in temperatures of more than 100 degrees. They were surrounded by soldiers armed with machine guns who severely punished them if they lowered their eyes. Many were sent to work 10-hour days under the hot sun with little food. According to IN MEMORIAM, 12 percent of them died of malaria within a few weeks.

At the same time, Koretz was installed by the SS as president, replacing Saltiel. In this double capacity, it was easier for the rabbi, who spoke fluent German, to communicate with the Germans. He tried to convince the Jews not to run away in fear and to obey Nazi orders.

On Feb. 6, 1943, a delegation of SS arrived in Salonica under Dieter Wislicenny and Alois Brunner. Their headquarters was at 42 Vellisariou St., a beautiful mansion once owned by a wealthy Jewish family. Brunner and Wislicenny's offices were on the first floor and had the best furniture. The living quarters on the top floor had silk and linen, the best Persian rugs and rare paintings—all stolen from Jews. The basement was filled with stolen Jewish wealth—gold, diamonds, Persian rugs and other very expensive items. They used the best Jewish gardeners to care for the unusual flowers, plants and the lawn.

As a prelude to the Final Solution, the Germans ordered all Jews to wear a yellow star, each assigned a number from a list of names, addresses, ages and occupations, prepared by Koretz. The community had two weeks to comply, but the rabbi forced the Jewish workers to be ready in eight days. The number-one yellow star was for Koretz and number-two for Albala. A total of 60,000 were printed. Children under six were not obligated to wear the Star of David, according to the rabbi's list.

On March 14, 1943 the residents of the Hirsch Quarter were assembled in the local synagogue and informed by Koretz that they would be deported to Krakow, Poland, where they would find new homes with their own people. He said Krakow's Jewish community and its president assured him Salonica's Jews would be treated with respect.

Koretz lied. The Jewish community of Krakow was completely destroyed in March 1943. The Jews wanted to kill the rabbi, but with the help of the SS soldiers, he escaped from the synagogue through the rear door. The deportations began.

JULY 8, 1943

The last transport included Jewish community employees and their families—including Koretz and his wife and son, Albala and his daughter, Tippouz—to Bergen Belsen. Vital Hasson was helped to escape to Albania by Alois Brunner, carrying Jewish wealth with him in leather suitcases filled with $10 million of merchandise, including diamonds, gold and gold watches.

He also took the carbon copy of the Jewish list Koretz had given to the Feldcommandatur, which later surfaced in 1968 in Moscow. It was offered to me for $5,000, but the seller, Panagiotis, never showed up in Athens as agreed. I waited for him at the Cafe Floca for more than an hour. I believe the list is now in the U.S.

The Final Solution was a vast killing enterprise with the efficiency of a 20th-Century factory.

When the first transports took victims to Auschwitz-Birkenau, the "New Europe" wrote, "We are now beginning to breathe the pure Greek fresh air not polluted by the scams. The Jews are universal poisoners of all people: the destroyers of civilization. Our Greek civilization, which we inherited from our philosophers, was corrupted by the Jews. The Germans are the leaders of an apocalyptic fight between the Aryans and the Jewish race who are subhumans, who corrupted all nations for their own benefits. They destroyed millions of lives with and without wars to control the world, just for monetary profits. Anti-Semitism is a matter of cleanliness, and not ideology."

After the war, both editors of "New Europe" were sentenced to death by firing squad by the Greek courts.

The 40 synagogues and other institutions, including orphanages for boys and girls, an old age home, hospital, two medical clinics and daily Hebrew schools and the Jewish Republic in the heart of Europe—the glorious city of Salonica—are gone. The gas chambers and crematoriums of Poland claimed this Sephardic community and its beautiful Ladino language.

For the 1,950 who survived, regaining our businesses and homes was impossible. Under protection of Greek law, the local citizenry who took these properties have refused to return them to their rightful owners.

During the war, Macedonian authorities and the mayor of Salonica never intervened to help the Jews or to stop the transports. They simply gave the empty Jewish homes to refugees fleeing Bulgaria-occupied Thrakia.

DURING MY ESCAPE
Under pressure from the Jews of Athens, General Tsokaloglou came to Salonica in April, 1942 to assure the Jews they would be safe.

"We are all brothers and sisters; the children of our beloved *patrida* (country)," he said. "Many of you died and were wounded fighting the enemy."

His words were meaningless.

CEMETERY

Koretz and the Jewish community's engineer, Eli Modiano, were forced by Nazis Brunner and Wislicenny, as well as the governor of Macedonia, Civil Engineer Panagiotis Ladas, to sign over to the city the Jewish cemetery, which dated back to before the Spanish Inquisition.

On Dec. 6, 1942, the city of Salonica became the owner of 360,000 square meters of prime land. Even worse, the Jewish community was forced to pay 500 gentile workers to destroy the graveyard.

In exchange, Salonica's mayor provided two small parcels of land to bury the Jewish dead, one of which remains in use today. The other in Kalamaria was used to bury those who died before 1900. The Jews were forced to squeeze up to 100 bodies into each burial container. People searching for valuables thought to be interred with the "wealthy" Jews would often unearth these containers.

TO SAVE THE JEWS

In Feb. 1943, some Jewish lawyers and prominent gentile attorneys—Dimitrios Spiliakos, Petros Levy, Dimitrios Dingas and Vizoudakis—tried to convince the Metropolitan of Macedonia, Panagiotaton Gennadion, to intervene with the Germans. Although he responded immediately, the Metropolitan and the church acted too late. The orders from Eichmann were irrevocable.

After that failure, the lawyers unsuccessfully attempted to see

Brunner. They then undertook a very dangerous mission to Simonidis, the Governor of Macedonia, who tried to get Brunner to reconsider the deportations. Brunner told the governor that he should be "proud and happy that once and for all the Third Reich was destroying the roots of the poisonous cancer and the evil of all people, the Jews."

He told Simonidis that the Jewish deportation was the will of the Greek people. Attorney Petros Levy wanted to bribe Brunner, but was stopped by the others. Dr. Maximilian Merten took a lot of gold from the Jewish community in exchange for the release of laborers from the malaria-stricken camps.

When they returned to Salonica, the lawyers were deported to Birkenau. Merten kept the 5,000 English gold pounds. In response to Athenian Jewry's pleas, Prime Minister Logothetopoulos, came in March 1943 to Salonica. He suggested to the Germans that the Jews be sent to a Greek island instead of Poland. Again, this was too late.

MATERIAL DESTRUCTION OF THE JEWS OF SALONICA

When the Jews were deported in August 1943, approximately $1.5 million in drachmas and more than $3 million in stocks and bonds was turned over to the military administration. The Jewish homes, apartments, businesses, factories and warehouses were turned over to Simonidis, the puppet Greek leader of Macedonia.

The Greek State placed the Jewish banks and insurance companies under the "trusteeship" of the Agrarian Bank (Agrotiki Trapeza Ellados) of Salonica.

By Aug. 19, 1943, the transit Ghetto of Baron de Hirsch quarter was completely vacant. The hospital was sold for 250,000 drachmas, the equivalent of 500 English gold pounds. The doorknobs were worth more than that. Rarely had a major business transaction been carried out so smoothly and successfully at the expense of the Greek Jews.

THE ITALIAN AND SPANISH JEWS OF SALONICA

The Italian and Spanish governments tried to save the Jews of Salonica. The Italian Consul General in Salonica, a Mr. Castrucci, insisted the Italian Government had a special interest in protecting Greek Jews.

With the full knowledge of General Franco and the foreign minister, the Spanish Government assisted its charge d'affaires in Athens, Eduardo do Gassetto, in saving 600 Salonica Jews. In April 1943, Franco opened an office in Athens in an effort to rescue Spanish Jews. The Spaniards declared that all Sephardic Jews who fled to the Ottoman Empire during the Inquisition were Spanish citizens with full rights.

The Nazis tried unsuccessfully to convince the Italian authorities in Athens to give permission to deport Jews with Italian citizenship. Instead, the Italians decided to send the 16,000 Jews to Italy or to the Ionian Islands.

At the end of July 1943, Mussolini was succeeded by Marshal Badoglio. Italy surrendered Sept. 8, 1943 and ceased being in the Axis. The Germans took control of all of Greece and the islands of Dodecannese and Albania, leaving these 16,000 Jews at the mercy of the Nazis.

Only the courage of Athens' Grand Rabbi Barzilai saved many thousands of Jews.

THE JEWS OF ATHENS

Barzilai promised to comply with a Gestapo order to provide a list of all Jews in six days. Instead, he told the Jews to take refuge in the mountains or countryside. The rabbi was responsible for saving many Jewish lives with the help of the Metropolitan of the Greek Orthodox Church of Athens and the Chief of Police.

The Jews in the Greek capital, Athens, had more of a chance of survival, thanks to an advance warning by Dr. Shaul, a Sephardi who was the legal advisor to the city's Italian Consul. Many took the opportunity to hide or to join the partisan forces in the countryside fighting the Nazis.

MY ESCAPE

The Nazi confiscation of our home and business and the prohibitions and restrictions placed on my people convinced me that it was unsafe to remain in my beloved Salonica. With my parents' consent, on March 12, 1942, I began my escape with three friends—one Jew, Benjamin Saltiel; and two Greeks, Konstantinos Bitzis and George Papadopoulos.

Our plan was to go to Palestine via Turkey, although legal entrance was prohibited by the British "White Paper." However, on March 24, 1942, we were captured in Samothraki near the Turkish border. Ioannis Laskaris, a friend of my two gentile companions, was waiting with the Gestapo when we arrived.

After the war, Bitzis and Papadopoulos took Laskaris to court in Salonica. Laskaris was expelled, by court order, from Greece to Germany for ten years as punishment.

Betrayed by friends, our government and allies, we feared suffering, humiliation and death was our destiny. It was either escape or die.

Benjamin and I were arrested and sent to Belgrade, Yugoslavia, where we were incarcerated until Oct. 5, 1942. We were subjected (without benefit of an interpreter) to endless and brutal interrogations by the Germans, including fists to the head and kicks from heavy boots.

We were separated and kept isolated in a small windowless, unlit cell. Our twice daily meals of 200 grams of bread with tea each morning and watery soup in the evening were shoved through a small window in the cell's wooden door. Our bodies were crawling with lice from the blankets we were given.

Each night Benjamin and I were taken naked to jog in the darkness, followed by hot and cold showers. The only item we wore was a sign with the word "JUDE."

Accused of being British spies, we were court martialled on Sept. 21, 1942 and sentenced to die by firing squad. I was given a military defense lawyer who asked no questions nor provided me with an interpreter.

On October 7, Benjamin and I were taken with our hands chained to the back and iron bars on our feet to the railroad station and shoved onto a freight train. We were weak with hunger. Benjamin, who spoke some German, asked that we be given food. We were taken to a dining car packed with German officers, where we let it be known that we hadn't eaten for two days.

We were separated and placed at opposite corners of the car. An intoxicated soldier forced open my mouth and shoved in a very large onion, causing me to lose my breath. A huge piece of stale bread was pushed into Benjamin's mouth. Bound and chained, we were helpless against our tormentors. The car shook with their sadistic laughter as they spat and threw food and utensils at us.

Finally, we saw from the train window signs indicating we were approaching Salonica. Thinking we were going home, we were overcome with a false sense of relief. Instead, we were sent to another Gestapo jail located in the former home of Mentesh Bessantchi, an ex-senator and editor of the daily newspaper, "Le Progress." We were again isolated in a tiny dark room and subjected to countless interrogations and beatings.

The deportation of Jews from Salonica to Poland began in March 1943, resulting in more than 60,000 being killed in Auschwitz-Birkenau and other concentration camps.

My entire family shared this fate, including my sister-in law Margot—wife of Edgard—who died in Auschwitz. They were newlyweds. My parents were sent directly to the Birkenau gas chambers. Prior to my departure to Warsaw in August 1943, I had a chance meeting with my oldest brother, Edgard, in Birkenau, where he was to die a year later. My second brother, Jack, was killed in Salonica after he and four friends attempted to escape by fishing boat. They were executed at Liberty Place after the vessel's Greek captain, who was paid in gold, exposed their plot to the Gestapo.

We were sent to Eftapyrgio, a Greek jail, on March 20, 1943 and placed in a cell with nine others also sentenced to die. Three cellmates were criminals and the others underground fighters. One of them, a young priest from a small village near Polygyros, later apologized to us for his misconceptions about Jews. Explaining it was hard for him to believe that we were Jews because his religious teachings portrayed us as criminals and manipulators, he asked, "Where were our long noses?"

I asked a boy to bring his father, who sold cigarettes and snacks to other inmates. I assured this man that both Benjamin's and my father would compensate him for information about our whereabouts.

I replied affirmatively when he asked if I knew a Stavros Antoniadis, a man my father had lent money to help establish a business. Now, as administrator for all the Jewish paper goods warehouses and factories confiscated by the Nazis, Antoniadis had become a multimillionaire.

After being notified of my predicament, Antoniadis visited me several days later. He said there were few Jews left in Salonica and the Jewish community was in total disarray. Although a powerful figure within the occupation government, he could not get us released. However, the next day after celebrating the Greek Easter in church, he returned with food, which I shared with my prisonmates. This small offering was a feast for us all, especially Benjamin and me.

As the Greek Church joyfully celebrated Easter, Salonica's Jews were being sent to the gas chambers and crematoriums. Salonica, the "Jewish Republic," became the city of destruction and misery for Jews. The same man responsible for the Warsaw Ghetto's destruction, General Stroop, was also guilty of devastating Salonica's Jewish community.

BARON DE HIRSCH HOUSING

Benjamin and I were imprisoned on April 7, 1943 at the Baron de Hirsch Housing Project near the railroad station, where we were given food each day by Jewish community workers.

Upon arrival, we were taken to a basement room with one small window. We noticed the walls were spotted with both fresh and dried blood and knew there would be more beatings and whippings. Fortunately, nothing happened to us. But, day and night we heard screaming, crying and pleading for mercy.

We were told by a fellow Jew who delivered our meals about Vital Hasson and his bodyguard, Leon Tippouz (Barsion), who were torturing wealthy Jews to find out where they hid their gold, jewelry, cash and precious metals. They and another German Jew, David Amstel, who came to Salonica as a refugee in 1938 with his wife, had become wealthy.

Although Hasson and Tippouz came to us, they saw we were young and had little and immediately left.

DEPORTATION

At the railroad station, I saw a long line of cars ordinarily used for cattle. Behind securely locked doors, they were now jammed with human cargo—fellow Jews awaiting the journey to Krakow.

Before I was tossed in a car like so much baggage by an SS trooper, a Red Cross volunteer managed to hand me a small cloth packet containing a pair of underwear, two pairs of socks, toothpaste and toothbrush, two loaves of bread, a few cans of sardines, a hunk of cheese, salami and soap.

There was barely room for my bruised and aching body among the some 80 whimpering and screaming people of all ages. Pressed next to me in this crunch of human misery was a terrified and trembling young woman clutching her infant son. I happily shared my food and assisted in caring for the little one. Not surprisingly, she became unable to breastfeed her child. I tried to provide comfort and hope based on what she told me about the statements of Koretz. Time proved the rabbi wrong. Our shared fate and misery made Sylvia Abravanel and her son, Dino, my instant family and responsibility. I vowed never to abandon them.

AUSCHWITZ-BIRKENAU

After our terrible ten-day journey ended, those of us who survived stumbled out of the cars to be greeted by the shouts of gunslinging "monsters" urging us to hurry.

Amidst the whipping and shoving, I couldn't take Dino from Sylvia as planned. As we were separated, I heard her scream in Greek, "Errikos, don't leave us. We love you!" I choked, unable to answer. Then, they were lost to me forever.

Old people, mothers carrying babies and children were sent to the left. I was relieved that Sylvia and Dino would be taken by truck to camp. Those of us sent to the right walked. If we stumbled, we were whipped and urged to go faster. Birkenau with its ugly gas chamber and crematoria was our final destination. Some of the human cargo was gassed upon arrival. Others were housed in wooden barracks to await extermination. Any mentally or physically disabled Jew was sent immediately to the gas chambers.

When the Nazis ran out of money, they forced Salonica's Jewish community to pay the chemical company Gedusa in gold for the Zyklon B used to kill fellow Jews. As a young person struggling to understand why I suffered such horrors, tortures, whippings and hunger, I developed new instincts and insights, which helped me stay alive at any cost to communicate what I had witnessed to my children and grandchildren and to generations to come.

I, as a survivor, am a messenger from the dead who must assure that the Holocaust is documented with dignity and accuracy. As Sephardic victims of the Final Solution, we deserve the same recognition as Eastern and Western European Jewry. Although the Ten Commandments teach against such things, we learned to steal to survive, to kill or be killed. It was the only way.

At Birkenau, we were ordered to undress. The barbers were waiting, but the Gestapo had already made sure my head did not need much shaving. Still a teenager, I was no longer to be known by my given name, but rather by the number 120928 tattooed on my arm. I was hurled into a dark world of death and destruction where Jews burned constantly in the crematoria. Sylvia and Dino were surely gas chamber victims.

I was reminded of the Inquisition where 400,000 Sephardim were tortured and expelled from Spain. I now expected to be part of an even more terrible fate. Would no Jew be left alive? Could this be an additional chilling chapter in Jewish history?

We were seven inmates to a bunk, wearing identical striped pajama-like uniforms bearing our individual numbers, awaiting our destiny. Ironically, the Jewish community of Salonica bore the cost of transporting us to Birkenau.

As a *haftling* (German, for prisoner), I was assigned to cut squares of grass from a pond outside the camp to beautify the Lager Commandant's house. I was given wooden shoes, one a size 7 and the other a size 11 to prevent my escape. The kapo (foreman) was a common criminal who killed 20 people in Poland for personal pleasure.

Three hundred men took cold showers together in a room with 100 showerheads operated by the same *haftling*. Afterwards, we were not given towels and remained naked for more than three hours. Our belongings were taken away and our striped uniforms were disinfected. We were kept in quarantine without work for three days.

Dr. Josef Mengele—with his Commandant Shwartzhuber—was responsible for deciding who survived. Within the electrified barbed wire at Auschwitz-Birkenau, were 35,000 to 70,000 Jewish prisoners, 12,000 Nazi guards and 200 guard dogs trained to kill for their master's pleasure or to enforce work rules. We were always hungry and thirsty. We had Polish-Jewish kapos, who were worse than Nazis and stole our food for their lovers.

I lived in Block 25. Benjamin was an interpreter for the Block Elder. The *stube* (helper) woke us at 4:30 a.m. each day and chased us to the bathroom to wash with cold water. We then put on our gray and blue uniforms and went to role call for one hour. At 5:45 a.m., we got hot water with a few herbs in it for breakfast and were ready for work at 6 a.m.

We received less than a liter of watery soup with rotten skinned potatoes, which we ate with old, flat spoons, for our noon lunch. The Greek Jews were given soup from the top of the container while the Eastern Europeans mixed theirs from the bottom, which had the potatoes and skins. Complaints meant beatings and whippings from the same Eastern European Jews. So we kept silent about this injustice. If there was a little soup left at the bottom when the food distribution ended, the Polish-Jewish helper would call the Eastern European Jews for seconds. We, the Greeks, got nothing.

After work at 6 p.m., we returned to camp for an up to three-hour roll call. Afterwards, we received dinner—200 grams of bread with a thin slice of margarine. Prisoners had to take off their jackets, shirts, rags, socks and trousers each night so clothes and bodies could be checked for lice. Lights were turned off at 9 p.m.

The routine never varied, except on Sundays when we only had to work for six hours and spent the rest of the day doing physical exercises. We were always hungry. After returning from work one day at 6 p.m. with dead bodies, I asked for Benjamin and was told he had been shot because the Block Elder caught him trading with the Polish civilians on the black market.

Birkenau was the worst camp. Himmler was responsible for all sorts of torture. The camp's four crematoria, housing 12 small ovens, burned 144 Jews every fifteen minutes. I, myself, saw bodies being carried from Block 10. When the steel gates of the gas chamber opened, a mountain of naked bodies of all ages was exposed.

We were beaten to force us to work faster and to avoid the gas chamber. All bodies were cremated and the ashes thrown in the Vistula River.

We marched to and from work accompanied by music. Subject to constant beatings, a grueling workload, little food and plagued by diarrhea and exhaustion, we returned each day bearing the dead bodies of 10 to 12 from our group. The Birkenau commandant always insisted we return with twice the number of dead the following day.

One morning on the last week of May 1943, 24 Greek Jews were asked to step out of the work line-up. I thought this was my last moment on earth. Instead, we were sent to collect the camp's countless dead bodies.

After three days of collecting corpses, we were sent to Block 10, where Salonican women were being used for gynecological experiments determining gene differences between Mediterranean and Eastern European women. Once they served their purpose, the women were killed by an injection of phenol to the heart.

Physicians trained in the finest medical colleges to save lives, and supposedly instilled with the highest ethics, had become murderers instead of healers. Some victims' faces were familiar to me. Suddenly, I froze at the sight of my neighbor and schoolmate, Yvone Naar. I recalled our daily lunches in school and our shared awareness of the first attraction to the opposite sex known as "puppy love." I will never forget the expression in her eyes, which seemed to say, "What have I done to deserve this cruel and inhumane treatment?" Her only sin was in being born Jewish. I stopped to recite the "Shema Yisrael" and the first sentence from the Kaddish.

As I stood transfixed, the kapo began hitting my head and screaming *"shneller* (faster)." Calling me a "Greek bandit," he threatened to make Greeks the next victims. Since we were responsible for removing victims' corpses, I asked a fellow inmate to help me put Yvone's body at the top of the pile. At the risk of being caught, I closed her eyes, kissed her and told her "goodbye forever." The assignment picking up dead bodies lasted 14 days.

The Greek Jews in Auschwitz-Birkenau met Jews from Eastern and Western Europe for the first time and found they had little in common. With our olive complexions and darker hair, we even looked different. They spoke Yiddish, Polish, German and some spoke Hebrew. We spoke Ladino, Greek, French and Italian. Even our Hebrew was different. Because we were strangers, up to the very end they refused to accept that we were really Jews.

Our inability to speak German or acquire the guttural sound of the language brought us a lot of grief. It was impossible for us to understand the SS or the kapos without an interpreter. The Eastern European inmates called us *"Grekco bandito"* and we called them *"mashemecha"* (Hebrew for What is your name?) or *vouz-vouz* (what-what in Yiddish). The SS called us *dumbkopf* (stupid).

Without a common language with the Ashkenazim, the Sephardim in the camps quickly perished (see *Sephardic Experience* by Jacob Gladstein, vol. 3, #23, 1987). The Ashkenazim in both the camps and ghettos declared, "If the God of history has been involved in the Holocaust, then the Jews must sue for divorce from him."

But the Sephardim always hoped for a miracle and accepted the omnipotence of Hashem (God). We recognized that there is no life without Him. We knew our suffering, humiliation and brutal treatment would not be in vain. In fact, some us lived to see the establishment of the State of Israel. In time, we learned to understand and speak German, Polish and Yiddish.

There was one elderly man, whom we thought of as an adopted *nono* (grandfather), who asked that we recite the Kaddish (mourners' prayer) in silence every night and not lose hope in Hashem. His faith was rewarded because he survived to die in Israel.

Rumors circulated in June 1943 that the Nazis were preparing to kill the Greek Jews in Auschwitz-Birkenau. In one week, 600 healthy Greeks went to the gas chamber. Our *nono* insisted on saying a silent Kaddish for them and others.

"Where there is darkness, He will bring light," he told us in Ladino. "Where there is despair, He will always bring hope."

Our God helped us to live by our faith. All *kedoshim* (martyrs) have given their lives for *Kiddush Ashem* (sanctification of God's name). Many times we believed that our *nono* had lost his mind. Although he did not realize what he was saying to us, he proved to be right.

THE DEADLY GREEK REVOLT IN AUSCHWITZ-BIRKENAU
The transports of Hungarian Jews were arriving daily. Up to 11,000 were being gassed daily. The inmates decided to revolt. In the book and film *Genocide,* it was not mentioned that the SEPHARDIC-GREEK JEWS were the true heroes of the revolt. Some risked their lives to prevent the killing of the arriving Hungarians. There is documentation to show that the September 1944 revolt in Auschwitz was organized by Col. Joseph Baruch and Capts. Joseph Levy, Maurice Aharon, Isaac Baruch, all from Athens; and Sam Carasso and Yomtov Yakoel from Salonica.

A group of 135 Greek Jews, along with some Sephardic Jews

from France, managed to blow up and destroy Crematorium #3. At the last minute, the Eastern European Jewish prisoners lost their courage and abandoned their comrades. But not Rosa Robota, who along with Matilda Haguel and Allegra Uziel (both from Salonica), was secretly working with Col. Baruch to smuggle explosives.

I was later surprised to read that my brother, Edgard, was hung by the Germans for attempting to blow up the two crematoriums during the revolt. It gives me satisfaction to know that his life was not lost in vain. He and others sacrificed their lives to save others. At the time, 30,000 gassed bodies were piled up waiting to be cremated.

It is time to give credit to the Sephardic-Greek Jews at Yom Hashoah when commemorating the Warsaw Ghetto Uprising. After the destruction of the two crematoria, most of the remaining Greek and French Sephardim were killed. Only the boxer Salamo Arouch was left alive and isolated from the others. He is now living in Israel. [Please see the film TRIUMPH OF THE SPIRIT].

WARSAW GHETTO

In August 1943, 3,500 Greek Jews were taken from Birkenau by car to remove debris from the Warsaw Ghetto and to build Warsaw's concentration camp. Since there was no crematorium, this was a slight improvement over Birkenau. Our first assignment was to remove the bodies of SS officers and others who died during the ghetto's Jewish revolt. In the course of our duties, we discovered the corpses of a number of Jewish men, women and children killed while bravely fighting with only their bare hands as weapons.

While digging for bodies we found many handwritten letters, diaries and notes of forgiveness in Yiddish, Polish, French and Hebrew. I remember reading a diary written in French which noted that by mid-1942 the Germans had deported more than 300,000 Jews from the Warsaw Ghetto to Treblinka.

The writer, a woman named either Rivkah Solowicz or Slobowicz, had come to Poland to visit her mother and oldest brother and was not allowed to return to her family in Marseille. Writing sometimes in Yiddish about her husband, Moise, and children, Sarah and Jacob, she asked forgiveness for leaving and implored Moise to be both father and mother. She added that only 60,000 Jews remained in the ghetto and reported seeing numerous troops and tanks.

The Jewish underground believed that all Jews were being gassed. Realizing the Nazi plan for resettlement meant death, Jews decided to fight. Early in the morning of April 19, 1943, the ghetto was surrounded by storm troopers as the uprising began.

Although the attack failed, Rivkah mentioned the ghetto was set afire. Ending the page with a Yiddish poem about a little flower, which we did not understand, she signed her name as Rivkaleh.

When we arrived at the ghetto, all the buildings had been burned by order of General Jurgen Stroop. During the gory clean up, many prisoners died of typhus, diarrhea and malnutrition. In Warsaw, I met others from Salonica for the first time. Four of them (Danny Namias, David Pardo, Eli Mucher and Eli Montekio) remain my close and devoted friends to this day.

One afternoon an SS man took me and five other Greek Jews to the kitchen to get food for the horses. We were horrified to find the animals housed in the beautiful old Nozyk Synagogue, which the Nazis had converted into a stable.

The Polish civilians working beside us in the Ghetto let us know we were more acceptable than the Polish Jews, who were accused of killing Jesus and exploiting others for many years, and "got what they deserved." Without pity for the murdered Jews, they declared that Poland was gladly "free of the Jews and their smell." They did, however, regret the loss of the burned buildings.

The Greek Jews stuck together like brothers. We were supportive, did not steal from each other and aided those threatened by Poles or non-Greeks. Although the Eastern Europeans had no desire to befriend us, they respected this devotion and our ability to maintain our dignity as Jews and human beings under such terrible conditions. We never wept or begged an SS guard or kapo for mercy or exposed fellow inmates who transgressed.

Leon Yahiel, a kindly Greek Jew who served as elder of Block 4, where I was stationed, risked his life many times for us. Once he attempted to bribe an SS officer with gold, jewelry and other valuable articles—found by Sabetai Matarasso, Moshico Hazan and others in their diggings—in exchange for bread and potato soup.

The Nazi replied, "I have so much gold, jewels, diamonds, etc. from Lodz, I will never spend it if I live 100 lives."

For his "crime" and refusal to expose those in possession of these treasures, Yahiel received 25 lashes, preventing him from sitting for three weeks. Ironically, he survived and became an Israeli Army general before dying of cancer.

Shortly after Yahiel's beating, fellow inmate and mechanic Vital Dassa "repaired" the motorcycle of this officer, whom we nicknamed "Tiger," causing the Nazi's death. Dassa was shot for this offense.

Another inmate, Shaul Senior, ran off with a laundry truck to see his Polish girlfriend. He was hung and his body left for three days as an example to those who had thoughts of escaping. That day we were kept in roll-call for 10 hours in heavy rain without being permitted to eat or use the lavatories. Our pajamas were soaked and stuck to our skin.

Our one advantage over the kapo and SS was being able to communicate with each other in a foreign language. We could make plans to steal food and spoke during lighter moments late at night. Among us were two cantors and a guitarist from Salonica who led us in songs in Italian, Greek, Ladino and Hebrew. One night we would sing sentimental romantic songs in Italian and Spanish and another night we would sing the very slow parts of *"Selihoth,"* or Penitential prayers, and *"Avraham Avinou."*

We said the *Selihoth* not because we were sinners, but because we were victims. We kept our dignity as Jews. They were the criminals, persecutors and beasts. My prisoner number in Warsaw was 2421.

Although Yahiel attempted to protect us by seeing to it that all doors and windows were securely sealed, we were heard by the SS and kapos four nights later. Far from their homes and families, these brutes were touched by our romantic ballads and demanded we entertain them for which they rewarded us with more food. We wept with joy when they encouraged us to continue singing without fear. [See also Maidaneck Among Men & Beasts by Paul Trepman, Library of Congress #77-89648].

THE EVACUATION OF THE WARSAW GHETTO

As the Russian Army advanced, in November 1944, the entire ghetto was razed and we were ordered to prepare to move to another camp. We were told to clean and fill in the tell-tale holes. Polish civilians were demolishing all buildings with explosives. Many of these workers went home rich with hidden Jewish wealth. The park planned to disguise the concentration camp's existence was never completed.

When the evacuation began, 2,466 Greek Jews remained from the original 3,500. In his book, *Destruction of the European Jew,* Raul Hilberg never mentioned that only Salonica Jews worked in cleaning the ghetto.

We left by foot on a 27-day journey without adequate clothing, food and water. The SS men in charge were from a new regiment of mostly Poles, Lithuanians, and Ukrainians who were crueler and more sadistic than the Germans. They were always drunk on vodka and mercilessly stole what little food we had. When the young men forced to gratify them sexually became too weak, they were killed.

To compensate for the lack of food and as a form of amusement, many of us were shot to death. We collected the bodies onto trucks. Each time we had 100 corpses, we were forced to bury them in mass graves—a procedure repeated several times. Before the burials, we stripped our fallen comrades of clothing in better condition than our own.

Fourteen days into this terrible trek, we were assembled in the forest and told that the next day we would be allowed to wash and quench our thirst in a lake. When we saw the water we could barely control the urge to instantly plunge in. We were told only 300 could enter at a time and warned not to swim further than 1,000 meters from shore. Machine guns were placed in position on the trucks to thwart escapes.

However, the water soon turned red as they opened fire on the unsuspecting bathers. We were ordered to retrieve the corpses, but hesitated fearing the same fate awaited us. We were told to dig a mass grave for the victims, some of whom were buried alive. Their screams for help and mercy still haunt me today.

We were given a portion of bread and small piece of cheese to sustain us through the cold night in the forest. After a sleepless and terror-filled night, we continued our endless journey. Talk of revolt began, but weak from exposure and hunger, chained at night and with no weapons, we knew any attempt would be futile. Although we outnumbered them, we could not murder our captors or prevent them from murdering us.

The two cantors, Avram Modiano and David Esformes, were killed at the river. The singer Mordo Toledano—weak, hungry, dehydrated, with swollen feet and a fever—was shot in the head by a Ukrainian SS officer. He was thrown in the truck with the others.

Finally, on the 28th day we arrived in Dachau more dead than alive.

DACHAU

Along the march of death 1,481 lives were lost. Only 985 of us completed the journey, arriving weak, sick, hungry, dehydrated, bleeding, exhausted, clothes in tatters and without anything to protect our feet. The German General Commandant of Dachau was shocked at our physical condition and ordered an investigation. After we described our journey, all the SS officers, Eastern European kapos and block elders, with the exception of Leon Yahiel, were detained. I never learned what happened to them.

The Commandant ordered us to take showers, issued new striped uniforms and doubled our rations. Some were even sent to the hospital. For us, Dachau was heaven. Unfortunately, our stay there was to last only one week. We promised the Commandant we would work hard if he kept us there, but he had orders from Berlin. As Jews, we did not belong in Dachau. The day before our departure a young Sephardi rabbi from Belgium told us in Ladino not to lose hope and have faith in Him.

Our next journey was a continuation of the annihilation of the Sephardim of Salonica.

MULDORF-WALDLAGER

The General from Dachau came to say goodbye to us and apologized for our suffering. He arranged to have us travel by freight cars with new SS officers and kapos to a different concentration camp.

Based on past experience, we weren't deceived by the trucks and ambulances awaiting our arrival. Our SS guards were Ukrainians, Lithuanians and Poles with only a few Germans. Pointing their machine guns at us, they screamed that we would be killed like dogs if we did not move faster. We were confused and skeptical when they ordered us to undress. At that moment, Allied airplanes began bombing the area surrounding the camp. We were ordered not to move as our captors fled to shelters.

Following the bombings, we were assigned to barracks. I was with my four friends in Block 12. The Nazis were badly in need of workers to continue the war with the Red Army. We told the Commandant that we were so traumatized and shattered by our past experience, death would be more welcome than further torture but we were willing to work in any factory to assist the Third Reich. We knew the war would soon be over.

I worked in a cement factory manufacturing concrete blocks with steel wire. We made sure that 40 percent of the blocks produced were defective. My friends, Daniel and David, worked in an ammunition factory where they succeeded in producing defective machine gun bullets.

The Allies bombed the factories two or three times a week, but avoided bombing the camp. We did little work. We took any risk to steal food from the SS and kapos. By the end of February 1945, our cowardly captors knew they had lost the war and became kind to us hoping that we would give the Allied forces a favorable report about our treatment.

GOING TO THE ALPS

On March 27, 1945, we were told to prepare to evacuate camp. We spent 33 days in a train which was constantly changing direction to avoid the Allied bombing of the railroad tracks. Unfortunately, some of our trains were inadvertently bombed resulting in the death of 457 Greek Jews. Nissim Alhadech lost his younger brother in one such air raid.

We awoke one morning to find the freight car doors unlocked. There were no guards in sight, only uniforms, guns and boots strewn all over the ground. We knew the war was over and ran, screaming with joy. It was May 1, 1945. We were liberated outside of Munich by the 7th U.S. Army under General Patton and taken by Army trucks to Feldafing. American, Russian and British troops came to free us. But, for six million, 1.5 million of them children, it was too late.

ARRESTS AND PUNISHMENTS

DAVID AMSTEL, the German-Jewish refugee, asked to be sent to Athens to continue the "excellent" work he did in Salonica assisting the Nazis in destroying the Jewish community. He arrived in August 1943 with a letter from Dr. Merten and Brunner commending him for his devotion to completing the Final Solution.

While in Athens, Amstel notified the Feldcommandatur about the hiding place of five Jewish families. The following night the Germans arrested all five, together with Amstel. He pleaded with the

Nazis to leave him, but was sent to Auschwitz where he died. His non-Jewish wife went to Germany with Salonica's stolen wealth.

KOPEL was sent to Birkenau on April 23, 1943 bearing a letter of highest recommendation from Brunner and Merten for his role in deporting the Jews of Salonica to their deaths. The Salonicans recognized him on his third day there and forced him to electrocute himself by throwing himself on the barbed wire.

LEON TIPPUZ and ALBALA returned from Bergen Belsen after the war. With information provided by the Jewish community, they were sentenced to 10 years in jail by the Greek courts. Tippuz later converted to Christianity and is believed to be still living in Salonica.

KIRKOR BOURBOURIAN and ADAM PAPANAUM were sentenced to death by firing squad in absentia by the Greeks. But, they and their wealth left with the retreating German Army.

DIETER WISLICENNY was arrested and sent to Germany. The German courts sent him to Prague, Czechoslovakia, where he was executed for his role in the deportation and killing of Czech Jews.

DR. MAXIMILIAN MERTEN, responsible for the destruction and killing of Salonica's Jews, also left with the retreating Germans, but was arrested when he returned to Athens in April 1957, to testify for his friend Arthur Meisner. Although 200 witnesses were called during the 18-month trial, he was acquitted for lack of evidence. Attorneys from the Jewish community were told to get a retaining order, but while they were in court, he left aboard a waiting Lufthansa airplane. His suitcases were hidden and later shipped to Germany.

VITAL HASSON returned from Italy in 1956 to recover and take back items he was forced to leave behind in 1943 when he fled to Albania. Upon arriving illegally in Salonica, he attempted to bribe two policemen to assist him in digging in the 151 Suburb. Instead, the police told the community attorney, who notified authorities. Hasson was arrested and sentenced to die by firing squad. He was executed by six soldiers, two of them Holocaust survivors.

GRAND RABBI TZVI KORETZ died of typhus April 21, 1945 at the train station just outside Berlin. His wife and two children went to Israel in 1946.

As Sephardic survivors, we must hand down our legacy to future generations so they may continue to carry the torch of freedom and respect for the Jewish people. We must keep Israel strong to ensure the sufferings of the Holocaust and destruction of Jews will never be repeated.

The Holocaust occurred in the most civilized of Christian nations. Germans bear the burden for the genocide of the Jewish people, along with the burning of their synagogues, Torahs and other religious artifacts. My wife, Ida, was a victim of Kristallnacht and survived the horrors of the Bergen Belsen concentration camp. Born in Vienna, a jewel of European culture, she too was abandoned by the "civilized" society in which she was raised.

I returned to Greece in 1946 and was drafted on April 12, 1947 into the Greek Army. I fought the Communists in the mountains of Ipirus until December 31, 1950. By Greek law, Jews who lost one family member during the German occupation of Greece were not required to fight on the front line. Ironically, several Holocaust survivors died fighting for Greece.

Throughout Europe, both before and after the war, Jews served and sacrificed for the lands of their birth. Our commitment went unpaid, but must not be forgotten. Acknowledgement of our equality as citizens is the key to preventing the past from becoming the future.

We who lived to see our mothers, fathers, brothers, sisters, wives and children sacrificed on the altar of hate and destruction of the Jewish people also heard the cries of children who never got to enjoy life. Our survival in this world of darkness and madness was miraculous. Nonetheless, there is no cemetery plot for me to visit to say Kaddish for my family.

SALVATION IN VOLOS, GREECE

By Asher Matathias

I was born on Hanuka Dec. 3, 1943 during a fierce winter in a small cave embedded in the side of rugged Mt. Pelion in Ay Lavrentinos, a village of several hundred people several miles from Volos, Greece, where my parents were hiding from the Nazis.

My mother gave birth to me without medical attention. A midwife living in the same village took a long time to reach the cave because of a severe snowstorm. Fortunately, the delivery was without complications and we lived in this cave for the rest of the occupation, supported by a family of Righteous Gentiles until liberation in 1945.

My parents, who were distantly related, met and eventually fell in love in 1940 while attending Jewish holiday celebrations. My father, Jack, was a young Jewish businessman and itinerant peddler living in Volos; my mother, Nina, came from Salonica.

My father risked capture for violating military regulations to visit his love in Salonica. During the occupation they were faced with the choice of marrying or separating, with the understanding that they would meet again after the war. They decided to marry on Sept. 6, 1942.

Before they took over Volos, the Nazis occupied Salonica, which played an important role in Greek-Jewish history. Settled by Jews more than 2,000 years ago, it was home to 60,000 of Greece's 80,000 Jews before World War II.

Unwilling or unable to accept the extent of Hitler's plans, people rebelled at the thought of leaving the main city to seek refuge. Therefore, in many cases, entire families were taken by the Germans to concentration camps, never to be heard of again.

One such family was my mother's parents and brothers. My maternal grandparents owned a restaurant in Salonica. The desire of my grandfather, Daniel Atoun, to continue working may have prevented him from leaving. A younger sister, Mendi, chose to go with my parents to start a new life in Volos.

Life continued normally for awhile despite the occupation. When Hitler's soldiers and decrees came southward to Volos, my mother was already pregnant. No time to agonize about a family. The equation was as stark as it was simple: marriage = child(ren)!

My father's business associates came to him with news of the imminent round up of the Jewish population. A family named Stamos convinced my father of the seriousness of the Nazi plans for the Jews of Volos. The Stamos family encouraged him to leave his business and follow his friend to the mountains. This Righteous Gentile had the means to hide my family for as long as necessary.

Salonica's aforementioned importance grew when many Jews settled there following the Spanish Inquisition of 1492. Others arrived from Italy and Eastern Europe. They were welcomed by the Ottoman Turkish Empire, which controlled the city until it was given to Greece in 1912. This large thriving colony of Jews never learned Greek, preferring to speak Ladino (Judeo- Spanish) in secular as well as sacred matters.

During the Holocaust, Salonica's Jews were easily identified by their isolation from native Greek cultural currents and influences. The Nazis destroyed 90 percent of the country's Jewish population, and today, less than 1,500 Jews and two synagogues remain.

Because my father's family had a Romaniot (Greek-speaking) background, they were better able to seem assimilated. The acquisition of Christian- sounding names was a common subterfuge.

I have been told that several times we came close to being captured by the Nazis. When the Germans arrived in Volos, they possessed lists of resident Jews who were systematically rounded up and shipped to concentration camps for extermination—the final solution.

Because Volos' Jews had enough warning, based on the unfortunate experience of Salonikan Jews, many fled by any means possible to safety. As the dragnets failed to bring in registered Jews, the Nazis figured out that many were hiding on the outskirts of Volos. On a bright spring morning in 1944, they began to comb the Volos suburbs, villages and countryside, successfully augmenting their catch. My parents have spoken of close calls and of the heroism of a gentile family which faced summary execution if discovered harboring Jews.

No one can recall how many families were hiding in our place or in nearby villages. Many Jews who lived in Volos managed to survive absorbed in the fraternal bosom of Christian compatriots.

My father was a supporter of the underground, returning successfully to us each night. Families with babies ran the risk of being given away by crying children when the frequent patrols passed. Several tragic infant deaths were caused by parents who inadvertently suffocated their children with pillows. It is a sobering thought to think that also could have happened to me.

Deprivation was commonplace. My mother could not nurse me properly and I was fed goat milk. To overcome my aversion to its taste, coffee was added.

Our diet included cheese, olives, olive oil, and bread—plentiful and brought daily, very often hot—by the family that was protecting us. Food was prepared outside in clay ovens under coals. People brought their stuffed leaves, peppers and tomatoes to cook in this community oven. Although we did not appear to be extremely deprived of food, it was not the diet we were used to in the city.

Alas, one Nazi patrol was able to locate the mountain hideaway where we spent daylight hours. With guns poised, they knocked the door down and came upon a nativity scene—a mother and child. Of course, instant death could have followed. Instead, the German soldier, a man in his twenties, smiled broadly and said that he had someone just like that baby in Hamburg, Germany. He left them in G-d's hands.

With V-E Day, people returned to their homes in cities ready to resume their lives. For Greece, there followed several years of fierce civil war between government forces loyal to the King and leftists supporting a workers' socialist republic. The timely American intervention, through the Truman Doctrine, infused prostrate Greece with needed capital and military material to stave off the Communist challenge. The crisis forced my father's military tour to be extended until Sept. 9, 1948. Meanwhile, a sister, Miriam, was born.

The cataclysmic events during the 1930's and 40's partially culminated in the establishment of the State of Israel on May 14, 1948. My father's younger unattached brother, Moshe, was an early Palestinian settler, braving Britain's blockade to Jewish immigration.

He told my father it was a propitious time to come to the Promised Land, but it was not to be!

Instead, we continued our lives in Volos—father in business, mother a busy housewife and a third child, Rachel, arriving on Jan. 11, 1952. This was the calm that foreshadowed momentous natural disaster. In the early 1950's, Greece suffered a series of devastating earthquakes. Coming to the rescue was an organization specializing in disaster relief, the American Jewish Joint Distribution Committee, or as we called it, simply the JOINT!

However, my parents were made a tantalizing offer to emigrate to America. The American immigration quota system, based on the National Origins Act of 1924, allowed in a tiny number of Greek immigrants each year. However, because of the extreme suffering, the quota was waived. My parents, then in their thirties, decided to rebuild in America!

Trips ensued to Athens, the capital, to prepare papers for emigration, and get passports and medical examinations, as well as visits to friends and relatives. We also had to choose between a 32-hour airplane ride or a trip by sea. On Jan. 18, 1956, we set sail from Pireaus, Greece, on the local steamer *The Aegean* for Brindisi, the west coast of Italy, with stops in the Ionian Sea Isles, including Corfu.

Now, years later, my sister, Rachel, is a teacher living on the West Coast with her husband and four children.

In 1970, as a 26-year-old bachelor, I returned to my roots in Greece, where I met my wife Anna, who was in Volos to visit her parents for the summer.

I came to Volos to meet the family that had helped mine and to learn what transpired during those critical years. The Stamos family now had a place in the suburbs of Volos, just beyond Agria. As I entered the courtyard, an old man who must have been several hundred feet away, yelled to me, "Asher, you are Asher!" He instantly recognized me, although he had not seen me since 1945.

We embraced and kissed. He gathered his grandchildren from the fields and neighborhood and recounted the story of our survival. It was a wonderful experience for me, for his narrative confirmed many of the details of my early life. However, it was the last time I'd see him alive.

His heroism might have been prompted to demonstrate patriotism at a time when he was suspected of being a leftist. The Stamos family were personal friends who went out of their way to save us. There was never a monetary payment to these people.

It is becoming less and less likely that my grandparents, who did not hide, are still alive. We count them among the dead although we do not say *Kaddish* (the prayer for the dead) because we do not know when they died. However, we remember them on Yom HaShoah and other occasions of suffering for the Jewish people.

Some Greek Jewish survivors picked up where they left off before the war, returning to inherited businesses which they will, in turn, pass to their descendants. All have found that the world has changed. Many Jews have emigrated to Israel or America. The younger generation of Jews continues to forsake Greece and its legacy of anti-Semitism.

Others find themselves less willing to forsake old and comfortable ways—my in-laws being a case in point. They refuse to emigrate, settling for periodic visits to and from their children and grandchildren. Greek life with its siestas and slow tempo is very pleasant for middle aged and elderly couples. Israel will remain a haven for younger Jews because of its proximity to Greece and the Zionist ideal Jews everywhere hold, as will the United States.

BIBLIOGRAPHY

Angel, Marc D. *The Jews of Rhodes, The History of a Sephardic Community,* Sepher-Hermon Press, Inc.: New York, 1980.

Angel, Marc D. *La America, The Sephardic Experience in the U.S.,* The Jewish Publication Society of America: Philadelphia, 1982.

Angel, Marc D. editor. *Studies in Sephardic Culture,* The David N. Barocas Memorial Volume, Sepher-Hermon Press: New York, 1980.

Benardete , Mair Jose. *Hispanic Culture and the Character of the Sephardic Jews,* Sepher-Hermon Press, Inc.: New York, 1982.

Cavioli, Frank J. and Salvatore J. LaGumina. *The Peripheral Americans,* Robert E. Krieger Publishing Company: Malabar, Florida, 1984.

Dobrinsky, Herbert C. *A Treasury of Sephardic Laws and Customs,* Yeshiva University Press: New York, 1986.

Hansen, Marcus Lee. *The Immigrant in American History,* Harper Torchbook: New York 1964.

Handlin, Oscar. *Immigration as a Factor in American History,* Prentice- Hall, Inc.: Englewood Cliffs, New Jersey, 1959.

Jones, Malwyn Allen. *The Uprooted,* Little Brown: New York, 1973.

The Sephardic Home News, Published Monthly by Sephardic Home For The Aged, 2266 Cropsey Avenue, Brooklyn, New York 11214, Vols. 39 & 40 #'s 1-12.

Sevillias, Errikos. *Athens-Auschwitz,* Lycabettus Press: Port Jefferson, New York 1983.

Sitton, David. *Sephardi Communities Today,* Translated from the Hebrew, Published by the Council of Sephardi and Oriental Communities, Jerusalem, 1985.

Tape-recorded interviews conducted by The Center for Holocaust Studies, 1609 Avenue J. Brooklyn, New York 11230.

AMB. ANGEL SANZ-BRIZ,
AND THE SALVATION OF HUNGARIAN JEWS
By Dr. M. Mitchell Serels

Fifty years ago there were little humane sentiments in Nazi occupied Hungary. Spain was a non-belligerent member of the Axis. Its embassies were to be found in every country allied with Germany. The Spanish Embassy in Budapest was located in a 19th Century building acquired in 1920. It was to this embassy that Angel Sanz-Briz was posted in 1942 as Commercial Consul. This was his first assignment as such, a unique charge.(1)

Sanz-Briz arrived with his wife, Adela Quijano who gave birth to her daughter, Adela, there. He was previously posted in Alexandria, Egypt where he had met many Sephardic Jews.(2)

On April 20, 1942, Kallay, the president of the Council of Ministers announced the onset of anti-Semitic regulations, particularly in the economic areas. In early 1944, the government of the Regent went even further. Sanz-Briz was responsible to Spanish Ambassador Miguel Angel Mugiro who placed the young diplomat in contact with Hungarian Undersecretary for Foreign Trade Szentmiklosy. In March 1944, Mugiro informed Madrid that the Regent remained secluded in his palace while German troops marched into the country. Mugiro noted the deportation from Ungvar and Munkacs to their probable death in Poland.(3)

Most countries withdrew their diplomatic missions from Budapest. Only Spain and Sweden retained their embassy staff. The Hungarian Ambassador in Madrid resigned. Tension rose between Hungary and Spain. The new Hungarian Undersecretary for Foreign Trade, Jungerth-Arnothy raised protests because Spanish Radio transmitted the resignation of Hungarian Ambassador Ambro, although Ambro had left Spain.(4)

The Spanish Embassy also received 500 visas for children from The Spanish Red Cross in Tangier. The Spanish Embassy hurried to fill that number only to be stymied by the rapidity of the deportations.(5) The Jewish hospital was destroyed on June 25. The hospital was situated only 200 meters from the embassy.

Sanz-Briz was entrusted to find the estimated 50 Sephardim in the Capital. He was able to find only 45 people who had linguistic ties to Spain. He issued regular passports to them. Sanz-Briz wanted to do more and solicited the regent to act, through the Ministry Foreign Affairs.

On August 21 a united letter of protest was signed by The Papal Nuncio, The Swedish Ambassador and the Commercial Consuls of Spain, Portugal and Switzerland.(6)

Sanz-Briz petitioned his government and received permission to negotiate with the Hungarian authorities to protect individual Jews. The Hungarian government authorized Spanish protection to 200 individual "Sephardim." This was an important concession which granted Spain protection over all Sephardim, conditional to their evacuation to Spain. Sanz-Briz then converted these 200 passports into 200 family passports. Sanz-Briz then petitioned the Hungarian government to allow 100 protégé protection. Then 300 protected individuals. He turned the 300 individual protection documents into 300 family protection documents. In return the Hungarian government requested that the Spanish authorities take physical charge of these people. Tangier became the most likely destination with the help of Renee Reichmann.(7)

In the interim, Sanz-Briz needed housing for this ever growing Jewish population now shielded from death. With the help of some Jewish friends, the young diplomat rented several small building compounds. Posted over the door were placards in Hungarian and German, "Annex of the Legation of Spain. Extraterritorial Building." The signs were not accurate but the falsehood worked. When the International Red Cross finally visited, they were amazed. Additional buildings were marked in the same manner.(8)

By a verbal agreement of November 14-16, 1944 between the United States Embassy in Madrid and the Ministry of Foreign Affairs official recognition was given to the 300 Jews who held provisional passports as well as to the nearly 2,000 holders of letters of protection. However, the Hungarian government placed two conditions: 1) These Jews had to leave Hungary for Spain by November 15; 2) Spain must recognize the government in Hungary and aid the Hungarian representative in Madrid to take possession of its legation.

The Russian troops were advancing on Budapest. The Germans tried ever harder to export more Jews to death camps. Sanz-Briz was able to gain liberty and return of 30 Jews who were being transported to Germany.

The cost of housing and feeding the housed Jews escalated. The small building now housed 352 provisional passport holders, 1,898 protégés and the original 45 Sephardim who received regular passports for a total of 2,295 people.

By December 25, 1944, the city was encircled by Russian troops. Finally, the city was liberated. The Jews protected by Sanz-Briz had survived. Spain had completed its humanitarian mission. Spain's representatives were withdrawn to Bern, Switz erland.(10)

Additionally, the 500 children sent to Tangier and the 1,500 internees at Bergen-Belsen brought the total to nearly 4,300. Some, like F.D. Gross' parents had placed the placard of "Annex of the Spanish Legation" over their door. They too were saved.(11)

Angel Sanz-Briz was born in Zaragoza on September 28, 1910. He entered the Diplomatic School in 1933 after earning his degree in law at the University of Madrid. After Hungary, he was assigned to Bern, San Francisco, Washington D.C., Lima, Vatican and Bayonne.

In 1960 Sanz-Briz was appointed Ambassador to Guatemala and later Consul-General in New York. Later he was appointed Ambassador to Holland, Belgium, China (the first Spanish Ambassador there), and the Vatican, where he died in 1980.

After his death, Angel Sanz-Briz was recognized as a Righteous Gentile by Yad Vashem. (12)

NOTES

(1) Speech of Ambassador Pablo Benavedas Orgaz, Ambassador of the Kingdom of Spain to Hungary. Budapest, August 1994.

(2) Adela Quijano de Sanz-Briz. Santander, August 1994.

(3) Federico Ysart. *Espana Y Los Judios En La Segunda Guerra Mundial.* DOPESA: Barcelona, 1973. Pp. 134-137.

(4) Ibid. Pg. 138-140.

(5) M. Mitchell Serels. A *History of the Jews of Tangier.* Sepher-Hermon Press: New York, 1991. Pp. 155-160

- (6) Federico Ysart. Pg. 142.
- (7) Ibid. Pp. 143-148.
- (8) Haim Avni. *Sefarad Ve Ha Yehudim B'Yimei Hashoa Veha Emansipasia.* Hebrew University Press: Jerusalem. Pp. 194-201.
- (9) Federico Ysart. Pp. 149-150.
- (10) Mordecai Paldiel. *The Path of the Righteous Gentile.* Rescuers of Jews During the Holocaust. KTAV: Hoboken,1993. P. 304.
- (11) Federico Ysart. Pg. 203
- (12) Official Biography of Ambassador Angel Sanz-Briz. Ministry of Foreign Affairs. Madrid, 1994.